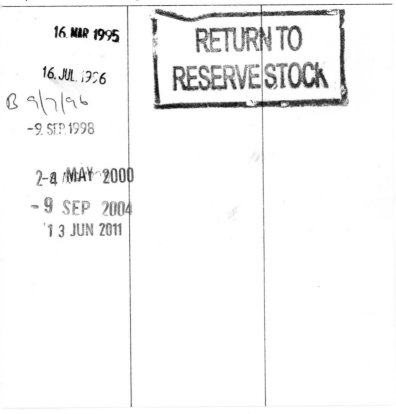

ORDNANCE SURVEY
GUIDE TO THE
WATERWAYS

3: NORTH

Series editor: David Perrott

Nicholson
An Imprint of Bartholomew
A Division of HarperCollinsPublishers

Also available in this series:

Nicholson/Ordnance Survey Guide to the Waterways 1. South
Nicholson/Ordnance Survey Guide to the Waterways 2. Central
Nicholson/Ordnance Survey Guide to the River Thames
Nicholson/Ordnance Survey Inland Waterways Map of Great Britain

*The indication of a towpath in this book does
not necessarily imply a public right of way. If you
are in any doubt, check before you proceed
with the latest published Ordnance Survey Map.*
Pathfinder Series (2½ in to 1 mile scale or
1:25 000). These OS walker and rambler maps
show the countryside in great detail, including
rights of way in England and Wales.
Landranger Series (1¼ in to 1 mile scale or
1:50 000). This OS series covers the country
in 204 sheets and is ideal for detailed
exploring by car or on foot.

First published in 1983 by
Nicholson
77-85 Fulham Palace Road
Hammersmith, London W6 8JB
and
Ordnance Survey
Romsey Road, Maybush
Southampton S09 4DH

6th edition 1993

© Text, Nicholson 1993

Nicholson
An Imprint of Bartholomew
A Division of HarperCollins*Publishers*

© The maps in this publication are reproduced from
Ordnance Survey maps with the permission of the
Controller of HMSO. Crown Copyright Reserved.

The series editor gratefully acknowledges the help
given by British Waterways and their staff. Thanks
is also due to CAMRA representatives and branch
members for their help in recommending real ale pubs.

Research: Jane and Jonathan Mosse;
also I.R. Harrison, Ray Butler, Chris Dodge.

Cover photograph: Derek Pratt

Great care has been taken throughout this book
to be accurate, but the publishers cannot accept
any responsibility for any errors which appear
or their consequences.

Keyed by Perrott CartoGraphics, Machynlleth
Typeset Output by Litho Link Ltd, Welshpool
Printed in Scotland by Bartholomew,
The Edinburgh Press Ltd.

Ordnance Survey ISBN 0319 00348 5
Nicholson ISBN 07028 2256 6

83/6/69

1188

INTRODUCTION

The canals and navigable rivers of Britain were built as a system of new trade routes at a time when roads were virtually non-existent. After their boom period in the late 18th and early 19th centuries, they gradually declined in the face of fierce competition from the new railway companies, and large-scale commercial carrying ended by the time of the Second World War, when many of the routes had slipped into decay and ruin. It is true that in a few areas goods continue to be carried profitably to this day, but for the majority of canals it was the new traffic of pleasure boats that provided the impetus for rescue and restoration.

The founding of the Inland Waterways Association by L. T. C. Rolt and Robert Aickman in 1946 brought together enthusiasts from all over the country who were to campaign to save and restore these 2000 miles of navigable waterways that are so much a part of our history. During the past few years an amazing transformation has taken place. British Waterways, local councils, and IWA volunteers working with various job creation schemes have tidied up great lengths of town and city canal, and much of the dereliction that was once commonplace has been replaced with gardens and parkland. The completion of the restoration of the Kennet & Avon Canal in 1990 is the most recent achievement, and one of the most remarkable.

There is something for everyone in the canals: engineering feats like aqueducts, tunnels and flights of locks (all of which amazed a world that had seen nothing like it since Roman times); the brightly decorated narrowboats which used to throng the waterways; the wealth of birds, animals and plants on canal banks; the mellow, unpretentious architecture of canalside buildings like pubs, stables, lock cottages and warehouses; and the sheer beauty and quiet isolation that is a feature of so many canals.

A special feature of this guide is the many new or expanded pub entries, giving details of real ales as recommended by CAMRA. So use this book to discover the waterways for yourself; it is one of four volumes covering the South, Centre and North of England and Wales; and the rivers Thames and Wey, and the Basingstoke Canal. A full-colour Nicholson/Ordnance Survey *Inland Waterways Map* is also available to help you plan your route.

CONTENTS

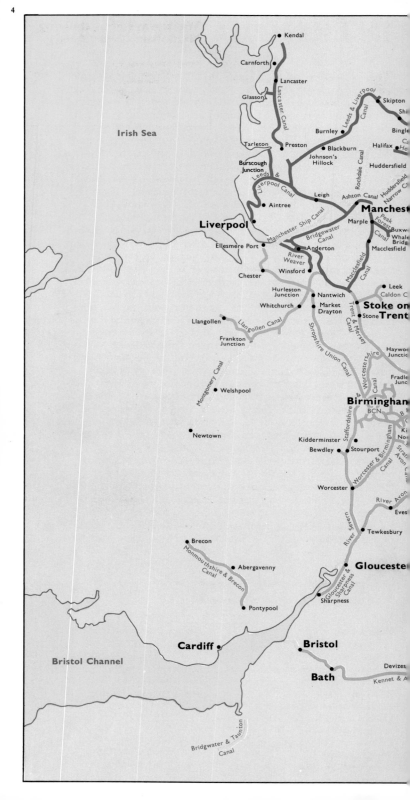

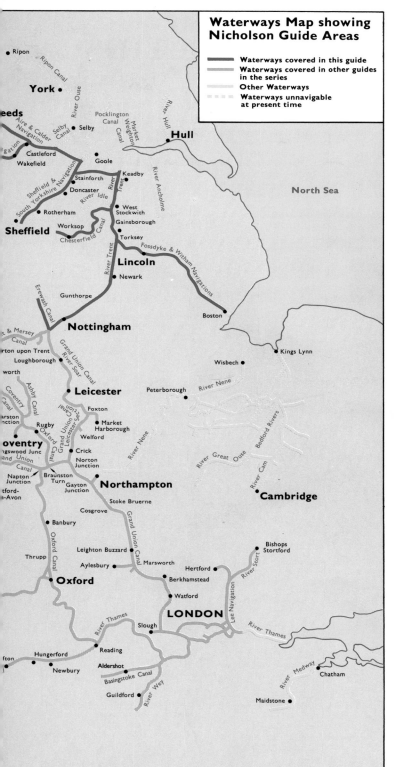

5

Waterways Map showing Nicholson Guide Areas

▬▬▬ Waterways covered in this guide
▬▬▬ Waterways covered in other guides in the series
▬▬▬ Other Waterways
▬ ▬ ▬ Waterways unnavigable at present time

Ripon

Ripon Canal

York

Leeds

Aire & Calder Navigation

River Ouse

Selby Canal

Selby

Pocklington Canal

Market Weighton Canal

Hull

River Hull

North Sea

Castleford
Wakefield

Goole

Sheffield & South Yorkshire Navigation

Stainforth
Doncaster

Keadby

River Trent

River Ancholme

Rotherham

River Idle

Sheffield

Worksop

West Stockwith

Gainsborough

Chesterfield Canal

Torksey

Fossdyke & Witham Navigations

River Trent

Lincoln

Newark

Boston

Erewash Canal

Gunthorpe

Nottingham

Kings Lynn

Wisbech

Trent & Mersey Canal

Burton upon Trent

Grand Union Canal

River Soar

Loughborough

Peterborough

River Nene

Tamworth

Leicester

Ashby Canal

Foxton

River Nene

Coventry Canal

Grand Union Leicester Section

Market Harborough

Rugby

Welford

Polesworth

Marston Junction

Oxford Canal

Crick
Norton Junction

River Great Ouse

River Cam

Bedford Rivers

Coventry

Kingswood Junc

Grand Union

Napton Junction

Braunston Turn

Gayton Junction

Northampton

Cambridge

Stratford-upon-Avon

Stoke Bruerne

Cosgrove

Banbury

Grand Union Canal

Oxford Canal

Leighton Buzzard

Bishops Stortford

Thrupp

Aylesbury

Marsworth

Hertford

River Stort

Oxford

Berkhamstead

Watford

Lee Navigation

LONDON

Slough

River Thames

River Thames

Lechlade

Hungerford

Reading

Newbury

Aldershot

Basingstoke Canal

River Wey

River Medway

Chatham

Guildford

Maidstone

HOW TO USE THIS GUIDE

The maps are drawn at a scale of 2 inches to 1 mile. Adjacent to each map section is a description of the countryside and places of interest together with a commentary on the course of the canal or river. Details of the boatyards and pubs marked are also given, adjacent to each map, and are arranged in order from the top of the page to the bottom.

Symbols and abbreviations used in the text:

Ⓑ	Boatyard or boatyard services
Ⓡ	Refuse disposal
Ⓢ	Sewage or 'Elsan' disposal
Ⓦ	Water
Ⓟ	Petrol
Ⓓ	Diesel
Ⓔ	Electric boat recharging
🍺	Public house
✕	Restaurant
❗	Licensed to sell alcohol
L	Open for lunch
D	Open for dinner
EC	Early closing
MD	Market day
BW	British Waterways
IWA	Inland Waterways Association
NT	National Trust

Symbols used on maps:

Ⓑ	Boats or boatyard services
🍺	Public houses
R	Refuse disposal
S	Sewage or 'Elsan' disposal point
W	Water point

28 8' 8"	Locks, with number and 'rise'. The symbol points uphill.
	Staircase locks.
197	Bridge and its number. Many are named.
	Pipe bridge.
	Tunnel - often described in the text.
	Aqueduct - often described in the text.
	Winding hole - turning point for boats longer than ordinary width of the canal (it's pronounced as in the wind that blows). Canal junctions are also good places to 'wind'.
	Weir

Towing Path

Scale and north point
The strip maps are drawn at 2 inches to 1 mile. North is indicated on each map.

Navigational notes
These appear where necessary to point out potential hazards, navigational limits or other vital information.

Boatyards
Services listed are those usually available; do not, however, expect a hire base to stop what they are doing on fleet 'turn around' day (usually Saturday) to help you - *they will be extremely busy*. Any other day you are sure to be made to feel welcome. Remember also that moorings get filled very quickly, so do not assume that there will be space for your boat. Always ask.

A feature of these guides is the 'milestone' which appears on every map thus:

This performs many useful functions. It reminds you of your direction of travel - in this example **up** the page is towards Napton, **down** the page is towards Oxford; it denotes distances and indicates the number of locks between the milestone and strategic points (usually junctions) along the waterway - in this example, Napton is 22¼ miles (M) with 22 locks (L) from the 'milestone', and Oxford is 27 miles and 17 locks from the milestone. By deducting the miles and locks on one milestone from those on the next, distances from page to page can be accurately estimated. Using the 'lock-miles' system (see **Planning a cruise,** page 12) the time your journey will take can be calculated, and with a little experience based on your speed of travel and lock operation, your own time formula can be arrived at.

Where this device occurs on a map it simply means that the actual route of the waterway would not fit neatly onto the page, so the cartographer has 'bent' the map, using two north points. The navigator on the water, or the walker on the bank, will notice nothing amiss. Distances in this book should be measured along the thick blue line only, not including these gaps.

LOCKS AND THEIR USE

The different locks and their attendant machinery are a source of endless fascination for all waterway users. Understanding why they are there and the principle upon which they work will help you in their use.

A lock is a device for transporting craft from a higher water level to a lower level, or vice versa, for example when a canal crosses a range of hills. It consists of a box with gates at each end, and a separate means of letting water in at the top (higher level) and out at the bottom (lower level). This is controlled by paddles. These paddles may simply open and shut holes in the gates (gate paddles), or they may open and shut underground culverts (ground paddles). A windlass (carried on the boat) is used to wind the paddles open and shut. Whilst locks differ in detail, the following instructions will apply in the case of the vast majority of *narrow* canal locks. Some extra points regarding wide locks are covered later.

A typical narrow lock

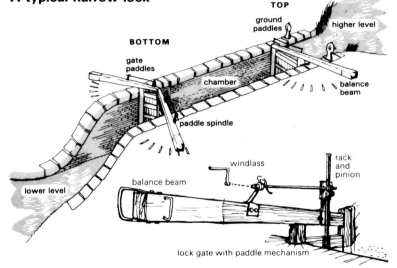

How to go through a lock

PRELIMINARIES

Stop the boat well outside the lock and secure it. If members of your crew can get off the boat before the lock (at the narrow point under a bridge for example) and run ahead to prepare the lock, this will save time.

GOING UP IN A LOCK (LOCKING UP)

Lock empty - ie water at lower level

Open bottom gates(s)
Drive boat in
Close gate(s)
Check bottom paddles closed
Keep boat near to the bottom of lock
Open top paddles to fill lock
Open top gate(s) when lock is full
Drive boat out
Close top gate(s)
Close up paddles

Lock full - ie water at higher level

Check top gate(s) and paddles closed
Open bottom paddles to drain lock
Open bottom gate(s)
Drive boat in
Close bottom gate(s) and paddles
Keep boat near to the bottom of lock
Open top paddles to fill lock
Open top gate(s) when lock is full
Drive boat out
Close top gate(s)
Close top paddles

GOING DOWN IN A LOCK (LOCKING DOWN)

Lock full – ie water at higher level

Open top gate(s)
Drive boat in
Close top gate(s)
Check top paddles closed
Keep boat near to the bottom of lock
Open bottom paddles to empty lock
Open bottom gate(s)
Drive boat out
Close bottom gates and paddles

Lock empty – ie water at lower level

Check bottom gate(s) and paddles closed
Open top paddles to fill lock
Open gate(s)
Drive boat in
Close top gate(s) and paddles
Keep boat near to the bottom of lock
Open bottom paddles to empty lock
Open bottom gate(s)
Drive boat out
Close bottom gate(s) and paddles

If you have to drain or fill a lock in order to enter it, make sure there is no boat approaching that could usefully use the lock before you. Always try to conserve water, which is being continually passed down the canal from its summit and thus requires constant replenishment at a higher level.

SOME GENERAL DO'S AND DON'TS AT LOCKS

Do not leave your windlass slotted onto the paddle spindle - if something slips it could be thrown off and cause injury.

Always leave all gates and paddles closed when you leave, but look out for notices which may give other instructions for the proper operation of a particular lock.

Always wind the paddles down - letting them drop is bad practice, and causes damage.

Beware of protrusions in the side walls of the lock chamber that may damage the boat, and don't use fenders in narrow locks - they may jam.

When opening and closing lock gates, keep to the landward side of the balance beam.

Don't rush around at locks, especially in wet weather, when the sides are slippery. Never jump across partly opened gates.

Always make the safety of the crew and boat your prime concern and remember that if things do start to go wrong, you can stop everything by closing the paddles.

There is no reason why your children, wearing buoyancy aids and properly supervised, should not help at locks - it is all part of the fun, after all - but impress upon them the potential dangers, and establish some common-sense rules. You have no authority over other people's children, and their participation should be discouraged. Great difficulties could ensue should they be injured in any way.

Beware of fierce top gate paddles, especially in wide locks.

Don't leave your windlass behind; hundreds are lost this way each year.

WIDE LOCKS

Taking a narrowboat (7ft beam) through a wide lock (14ft) can present special difficulties, especially when locking up. If all the top paddles were to be opened fully at the same time, the boat would be buffeted considerably. The diagram below illustrates one method of ensuring a smooth passage. The stern line held ashore will provide added security.

Locking up in a wide lock
(a suggested technique)

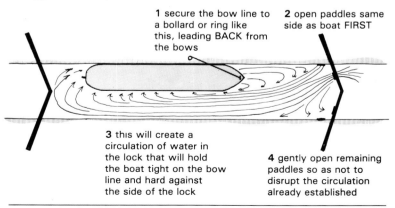

1 secure the bow line to a bollard or ring like this, leading BACK from the bows

2 open paddles same side as boat FIRST

3 this will create a circulation of water in the lock that will hold the boat tight on the bow line and hard against the side of the lock

4 gently open remaining paddles so as not to disrupt the circulation already established

---

STAIRCASE LOCKS

Where the top gates of one lock are the bottom gates of the next. Usually there is a board nearby giving operating instructions - read it carefully and make sure you understand it before you start. And remember: in a narrow staircase you can't pass a boat coming the other way.

GENERAL CRUISING INFORMATION

The majority of the waterways covered in this book are controlled by British Waterways. All craft using BW canals must be licensed and those using BW rivers must be registered. Charges are based on the length of the boat and a canal craft licence covers all the navigable waterways under BW's control. Permits for permanent mooring on the canals are also issued by BW. Apply in each case to the British Waterways Offices listed on page 12 or to:

Customer Services
British Waterways
Willow Grange
Church Road
Watford,
WD1 3QA
Telephone: 0923 226422

Other river navigation authorities relevant to this book are mentioned where appropriate.

Getting afloat

There is no better way of discovering the joys of canals than by getting afloat. The best thing is to hire a boat for a week or a fortnight from one of the boatyards on the canals (each boatyard has an entry in the text, and most of them offer craft for hire; brochures may be easily obtained from such boatyards). Or, go on one of the trip boats for a couple of hours, or longer. The notes on page 13 will help you plan a cruise.

General cruising

Most canals are saucer-shaped in section and so are deepest in the middle. Very few have more than 3-4ft of water and many have much less. Try to keep to the middle of the channel except on bends, where the deepest water is on the *outside* of the bend. When you meet another boat, the rule is to keep to the right, slow down, and aim to miss the approaching boat by a couple of yards: do not steer right over to the bank or you will most likely run aground. The deeper the draught of the boat, the more important it is to keep in the middle of the deep water, and so this must be considered when passing other boats. If you meet a loaded working boat, keep right out of the way. Working boats should always be given precedence, for their time is money. If you meet a boat being towed from the bank, pass it on the outside rather than intercept the towing line. When overtaking, keep the other boat on your starboard, or right, side.

Speed

There is a general speed limit of 4 mph on most British Waterways canals. This is not just an arbitrary limit: there is no need to go any faster,

and in many cases it is impossible to cruise even at this speed. Canals were not built for motor boats, and so the banks are easily damaged by excessive wash and turbulence. Erosion of the banks makes the canal more shallow, which in turn makes running aground a more frequent occurrence. So keep to the limits and try not to aggravate the situation. It is easy to see when a boat is creating excessive turbulence by looking at the wash - if it is 'breaking' or causing large waves, you are going too fast and should slow down.

Slow down also when passing moored craft, engineering works and anglers.

Slow down when there is a lot of floating rubbish on the water: old planks and plastic bags may mean underwater obstacles that can damage a boat or its propeller if hit hard. Try to drift over obvious obstructions in neutral.

Slow down when approaching blind corners, narrow bridges and junctions.

Running aground

Running aground is a not uncommon event, but is rarely serious, as the canal bed is usually soft. If you run aground, try first of all to pull the boat off by gently reversing the engine. If this fails, use the pole as a lever against the bank or some solid object, in combination with a tow rope being pulled from the bank. Do not keep revving the engine in reverse if it is obviously having no effect. Another way is to get your crew to rock the boat from side to side while using the pole or mooring lines. If all else fails, lighten your load; make all the crew leave the boat except the helmsman, and then it will often float off quite easily.

Remember that if you run aground once, it is likely to happen again as it indicates a particularly shallow stretch - or that you are out of the channel. If you are continually bumping the bottom in a shallow stretch, it may be that you are going too fast, causing the boat to 'dig in' at the back. Going slower may make things more comfortable.

In a town you may run aground on sunken rubbish; this is most likely to occur near bridges and housing estates. Use the same methods, but be very careful as these hard objects can easily damage your boat or propeller.

Remember that winding holes are often silted up - do not go further in than you have to.

Mooring

All boats carry metal stakes and a mallet. These are used for mooring when there are no rings or bollards in sight, which is usually the case. Generally speaking you may moor anywhere to BW property but there are certain basic rules. Avoid mooring anywhere that could cause an obstruction to other boats; do not moor on a bend, in a winding hole or a narrow stretch, do not moor abreast boats already moored. Never moor in a lock, and do not be tempted to tie up in a tunnel or under a bridge if it is raining. Pick a stretch where there is a reasonable depth of water at the bank, otherwise the boat may bump and scrape the canal bed - an unpleasant sensation if you are trying to sleep. For reasons of peace and quiet and privacy it is best to moor away from main roads and railway lines.

Never stretch your mooring lines across the towpath; you may trip someone up and face a claim for damages.

There is no need to show a riding light at night, except on major rivers and busy commercial canals.

Beware of mooring at unrecognised sites in cities - you may attract the unwelcome attention of vandals.

So long as you are sensible and keep to the rules, mooring can be a pleasant gesture of individuality.

Knots

A simple and easy way of securing a rope to a bollard or mooring stake is to use a couple of round turns and a half hitch or two made with a loop and pulled tight. This can be released quickly by pulling the loose end, which will have been left tidly coiled.

When leaving a mooring, coil all the ropes up again. They will then be out of the way, but ready if needed in a hurry. Many a sailor has fallen overboard after tripping on an uncoiled rope.

Fixed bridges

At most bridges the canal becomes very narrow, a means of saving building costs developed by the engineers. As a result, careful navigation is called for if you are to avoid hitting either the bridge sides with the hull, or the arch with the cabin top. As when entering a lock, the best way to tackle 'bridgeholes' is to slow down well in advance and aim to go straight through, keeping a steady course. Adjustments should be kept to a minimum for it is easy to start the boat zig-zagging, which will inevitably end in a collision. One technique is to gauge the width of the approaching bridgehole relative to the width of the boat, and then watch one side only, aiming to miss that side by a small margin - say 6in; the smaller you can make the margin, the less chance you have of hitting the other side of the bridge. If you do hit the bridge sides when going slowly it is not likely

to do much damage; it will merely strengthen your resolve to do better next time.

Moveable bridges

Swing and lift bridges are an attractive feature of some canals and cannot be ignored as they often rest only 2 or 3ft above the water. They are moved by being swivelled horizontally, or raised vertically. Operation is usually manual, although some have gearing to ease the movement. There are one or two mechanised versions; these have clear instructions at control points. Before operating any bridge make sure that approaching road traffic is aware of your intention to open the bridge. Use protective barriers if there are any and remember to close the bridge again after you.

Some lift bridges are *very unstable,* and could close while your boat is passing underneath, with disastrous consequences. For this reason it is prudent to have your strongest (or heaviest) crew member hold it open until the boat is clear. Many swing bridges are very heavy to operate, and require two strong people to move them. Keep your crew off the sides of the boat when you are negotiating narrow bridges - they could easily be knocked off and seriously injured.

Tunnels

Many people consider a canal incomplete without one or two tunnels, and certainly they are an exciting feature of any trip. Nearly all are easy to navigate, although there are a few basic rules:

Make sure you boat has a good headlight in working order and *always* use it.

If it is a narrow tunnel (ie 7ft) make sure there is no boat coming the other way *before* you enter. Craft of 7ft beam can pass in some wide tunnels - slow right down when you meet to lessen the almost inevitable bump.

In most tunnels the roof drips constantly, especially under ventilation shafts. Put on a raincoat and some form of hat before going in.

A notice on the tunnel portal will give its length, in yards, and will say whether unpowered craft are permitted to use it.

Where there are restrictions on time of entry, and one-way systems, these must be adhered to. To meet head on half way through a long narrow tunnel would create great difficulties.

Safety

Often the gap between a canal craft and tunnel walls or bridges is very narrow, and it is possible for crew members to get crushed while underway. Ensure that everyone is safely inboard when negotiating these hazards.

Care of the engine

Canal boats are generally powered by either diesel, petrol or two-stroke engines. If you have a hire craft, the boatyard will give you instructions for your daily maintenance, which will no doubt include some or all of the following:

Every day before starting off, you should:

Check the oil level in the engine.

Check the fuel level in the tank.

If your engine is water-cooled, check that the filter near the intake is clean and weedfree.

Otherwise the engine will over-heat, which could cause serious damage.

Check the level of distilled water in the battery, and ensure that it is charging correctly.

Lubricate any parts of the engine, gearbox or steering that need daily attention.

Check that the propeller is free of weeds, wire, plastic bags and any other rubbish. The propeller and the water filter should be checked whenever there is any suspicion of obstruction or overheating - which may mean several times a day.

Pump the bilges every day.

If there is a stern gland greaser, screw it down a turn at the end of each day's cruising.

When navigating in shallow water, keep in mind the exposed position of the propeller. If you hit any underwater obstruction put the engine into neutral immediately. When running over any large floating object put the engine into neutral and wait for the object to appear astern before re-engaging the drive.

Fuel

Petrol engines and petrol/oil outboards are catered for by some boatyards and all road-side fuel stations. Running out is inconvenient; remember you may have to walk several miles carrying a heavy can.

Diesel-powered craft, and narrowboats, in particular, can usually cruise for over two weeks before needing to be refilled. Those using diesel-powered hire craft rarely need to be concerned about fuel. Those with their own boats, however, should bear in mind that boatyards are few and far between on some parts of the network, and should a diesel-powered boat run out of fuel, the system will need to be bled before the engine can run again. Most boatyards sell marine diesel (indicated **D** in the text), which is cheaper than the road fuel.

Electrically powered boats

These are becoming increasingly popular on the inland waterways, in view of their quietness and lack of environmental pollution. Indicated **E** under the **BOATYARD** heading are those establishments known to offer recharging facilities - polite enquiry by electric boat users will certainly reveal more. If you are lucky enough to be using this form of power, please note the following:

All boats using this information are assumed to have a battery charger on board and 50 metres of cable fitted with standard 13 amp terminals.

It is essential for the safety of the boater, the owner of the supply and the general public that a proper residual current circuit breaker (RCD) be carried by the boat and fitted between the boat's cable and the supply unless the supply is already so protected. The RCD must be tested for correct operation before battery charging starts.

Water

Fresh water taps occur irregularly along the canals, usually at boatyards, BW depots, or by lock cottages. These are marked on the maps in the guide. Ensure that there is a long water hose on the boat (BW taps have a ½-inch slip-on hose connection). Fill up every day.

Lavatories

Some canal boats are fitted with chemical lavatories which must only be emptied at one of the sewage disposal points marked on the map **S** (for which you will need a BW key) or located at boatyards. Many boats now have pump-out toilets, which must be emptied with a special machine - usually at boatyards and indicated in the text. This symbol at the canalside indicates just such a 'pump-out station' (although not all boatyards with the facility display it). Expect to have to pay.

Some BW depots and boatyards have lavatories for the use of boat crews; again, you may need your BW key.

Litter

Keep all rubbish until you can dispose of it at a refuse disposal point, indicated **R** on the map, or at a boatyard equipped to deal with it. Do not throw anything over the side.

By-laws

Although no-one needs a 'driving licence' to navigate a boat, boat users should remember that they have certain responsibilities to others on the waterways and should abide by the Waterways Code (available from BW offices). Prospective navigators are advised to obtain a copy of the by-laws relevant to the waterways on which they are to travel.

FREEPHONE CANALS

Ring 100 and ask the operator for this service if you are confronted with an emergency out of office hours. Vodaphone and Cellnet users should ring 0384 240948.

Stoppages

Although BW and other navigation authorities plan their maintenance for the winter months, it often becomes necessary to carry out repairs during the cruising season. Many of the structures on the canal system are beginning to show their age (especially the tunnels) and repairs are a lengthy and costly affair, sometimes resulting in stoppages lasting many years. A long dry spell can lower water levels and restrict lock operation, and a canal embankment can, of course, breach at any time.

To avoid disappointment it is wise to check that your planned route is clear before you set off, and that there are no time restrictions on locks that may upset your schedule. Those using hire craft may be able to get this information from their boatyard, although some are surprisingly lax. It is best to check for yourself by ringing the BW Area Offices (listed at the end of this book) or the relevant navigation authority. News of any last minute stoppages is available on 'Canalphone', as a recorded message. Ring 0923 201401 for the North and Midlands, or 0923 201402 for the South and Midlands. Check before you go.

PLANNING A CRUISE

It is wise when planning a cruise to establish a means of calculating the time it takes to travel any given length of canal. This ensures that you can reliably work out whether you will reach a shop or pub before closing time. And of course for those who have hired their boat, it is vital to return to the starting point on time.

The time taken to navigate any canal depends, of course, on the average cruising speed of your boat and the amount of time it takes to negotiate the locks along the way. Remember that there is in any case an overall legal speed limit of 4 mph on all canals. In practice, 3 mph is a realistic canal cruising speed for most boats and this is the maximum which can be achieved on shallow canals, such as the Peak Forest.

To the uninitiated, 3 mph may sound an unbearably slow rate of progress through the countryside; but a few hours of gentle cruising on a fine day is usually enough to convert most people to this pace. For only by proceeding at walking pace can you appreciate the peace and beauty of the countryside, watch the bird life, and see the scurry of voles, rats and other creatures as they suddenly notice the slowly approaching boat.

The length of time taken to work through a lock depends on several things: whether the lock is full or empty, wide or narrow, deep or shallow. It depends on the number and size of the paddles that control the sluices, on the presence or otherwise of other boats near the lock, and of course on the number and competence of the boat crew. Most people take between 10-20 minutes on average to work through a typical lock – or, to put it another way, they may take as long to get through a lock

as they would have taken to travel another mile at 3 mph. Herein lies a basis for a simple method of estimating time required to travel along a given length of canal: take the number of miles to be travelled and add the number of locks to be negotiated on the way. This gives the number of 'lock-miles'. Divide this by three, and the result is the approximate length of time it will take, in hours. Thus if you intend to travel 30 miles, and there are 12 locks along the way, the calculation is as follows: 30 + 12 divided by 3 (mph) = 14 hours, assuming your average cruising speed to be 3 mph and assuming you take about 20 minutes to get through each lock (if they are all narrow locks in good condition then you may well better this time). The length of your journey and the number of locks can easily be calculated using the 'milestones' that appear on every map in this series of guides. To refine the system, simply tailor it more closely to the actual cruising speed of your boat and the efficiency of your lock-operating technique.

There are many circular cruising routes available – a glance at the planning map on pages 4 and 5 will reveal numerous options. Of course, there is also much to be said for a straight out and back cruise – it will all look different when you are coming the other way, and you can arrange to re-visit that favourite pub again. The whole secret is to *allow plenty of time,* for shopping, for exploring and for gentle cruising. Many a holiday has been spoilt by becoming a race against time. The most comprehensive source of information for planning a waterways cruise is Nicholson's *The Ordnance Survey Inland Waterways Map of Great Britain.*

See also 'Stoppages' in the **General Cruising Information** section.

BRITISH WATERWAYS OFFICES

CUSTOMER SERVICES
British Waterways, Willow Grange, Church Road, Watford, Hertfordshire WD1 3QA (0923 226422).

AREA OFFICES

Will deal with enquiries regarding stoppages, long-term moorings and specific problems on a particular canal. The canal manager's telephone number is given on the introductory page for each waterway.

North-East Area British Waterways, 1 Dock Street, Leeds LS1 1HH (0532 436741).
Aire & Calder Navigation
Calder & Hebble Navigation
Chesterfield Canal
Erewash Canal
Fossdyke & Witham Navigations
Huddersfield Broad Canal
Nottingham Canal

Sheffield & South Yorkshire Navigation
River Trent

North-West Area British Waterways, Navigation Road, Northwich, Cheshire CW8 1BH (0606 74321).
Lancaster Canal
Leeds & Liverpool Canal
Macclesfield Canal
Peak Forest & Ashton Canal
Trent & Mersey Canal
River Weaver

For assistance from operational staff outside normal office hours, and at weekends, dial 100 and ask for **FREEPHONE CANALS**. *Vodaphone* and *Cellnet* users should call 0384 240948.

Other navigation authorities are listed in the appropriate place in the text.

AIRE & CALDER CALDER & HEBBLE HUDDERSFIELD BROAD CANAL

Maximum dimensions

Aire & Calder
River Lock to Leeds Lock
Length: 143'
Beam: 17'
Headroom: 12'
Leeds Lock to Castleford
Length: 200'
Beam: 20'
Headroom: 12'
Castleford to Wakefield
Length: 140'
Beam: 17'
Headroom: 12'

Calder & Hebble
Wakefield to Broad Cut
Length: 120'
Beam: 17'
Headroom: 12'
Broad Cut to Sowerby Bridge
Length: 57' 6" (or 60' narrowboat)
Beam: 14'
Headroom: 9' 6"

Huddersfield Broad Canal
Length: 57' 6" (or 60' narrowboat)
Beam: 14'
Headroom: 9'6"

Manager

(0977) 554351

Mileage

LEEDS to:
Castleford: 10 miles, 6 locks
Wakefield: 17½ miles, 12 locks
Cooper Bridge: 30½ miles, 28 locks
Sowerby Bridge: 37 miles, 41 locks

Huddersfield Broad Canal: 3¼ miles, 9 locks

The River Aire was first made navigable to Leeds in 1700, and rapidly became a great commercial success, taking coal out of the Yorkshire coalfield and bringing back raw wool, corn and agricultural produce. Improvements were then made to the difficult lower reaches, with first Selby and later Goole becoming Yorkshire's principal inland port. The opening of the New Junction Canal in 1905 further secured its suitability for commercial traffic, which today still amounts to some 2½ million tonnes, mainly coal and petroleum.

The construction of the Aire & Calder resulted in pressure to improve the Calder above Wakefield. After much opposition, the Calder & Hebble was built, with boats finally reaching Sowerby Bridge in the 1770s. Never as successful as the Aire & Calder, it did, however, benefit from trade coming in from the Huddersfield Broad Canal and later, in 1811, from the Huddersfield Narrow. Commercial traffic ended in 1981, when the last coal barges unloaded at Thornhill Power Station. Becoming increasingly popular and yet still uncrowded, the waterways covered here have much to offer, with great industrial interest and, in many places, considerable charm.

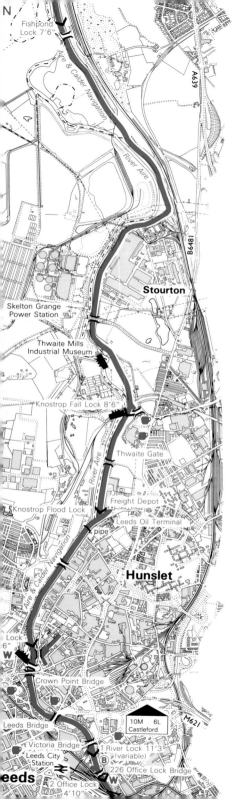

Leeds

The great Aire & Calder Navigation joins the Leeds & Liverpool Canal at River Lock, in the centre of Leeds by the City Railway Station. The area above the lock is now an attractive canal centre, with boatyards, canal warehouses and a crane; trees, moored craft and some handy shops, including an off-licence. Heading east, the waterway passes under three substantial bridges, generally hemmed in by tall buildings and warehouses with much new building and development, particularly housing. Industry predominates below Leeds Lock, although the lock itself is quite handsomely situated – overlooked by tall Victorian warehouses and accompanied by a houseboat. Keep right to avoid the weir at Leeds Lock. Boaters should take the centre channel at Knostrop Flood Lock, through the gates which are usually open (they are closed when the river level rises after prolonged heavy rain, effectively closing the navigation), avoiding the river and a weir to the left, and the basin of Leeds Oil Terminal to the right. Passing the Leggett Freightway Group Depot the navigation enters an artificial channel, with the River Aire to the north, which is to persist for a little over 7 miles until the river is rejoined below Kippax Lock. At Knostrop Fall Lock use the larger of the two locks, indicated by lights. Passing the Thwaite Mills Industrial Museum and Skelton Grange Power Station (the fuel for which is no longer delivered by boat), a no man's land of closed collieries and landscaped spoil heaps is entered. The towpath is diverted at Fishpond Lock, a lonely outpost, to avoid a small wooded area now maintained as a local nature reserve.

Navigational notes
1 All the locks on the Aire & Calder operate mechanically, and are controlled by lock keepers, so progress through them is quick. Obey the traffic light signals.
2 Remember that this is a river navigation. Many of the locks are accompanied by large weirs, so keep a sharp look-out for the signs which direct you safely into the locks.
3 When the river level rises after prolonged heavy rain, the flood gates will be closed. Pleasure craft should stay put until they are advised by a lock keeper that it is safe to proceed.
4 This is a commercial waterway, used by 600-tonne tanker barges and push-tow coal barges. Keep a look-out for them, and give them a clear passage. Moor carefully, using bollards or fixed rings rather than mooring stakes, since the wash from these craft can be substantial.

The towpath
The indication of a towpath alongside this waterway does not entail the existence of a public right of way. Indeed the towpath generally on the Aire & Calder to Castleford is often badly overgrown and incomplete. Where there is some evidence of a path it has been marked on the map – but many diversions may be necessary. It is hoped that this situation will improve in the not too distant future.

Leeds
W. Yorks. EC Wed. MD Tue, Fri, Sat. All services. A vast industrial city that was a wool centre in the Middle Ages and has continued to grow to prosperity under the textile and clothing trades; indeed Marks & Spencer started business here with a stall in the market. Montague Burton also became established here, building what was to become, by 1921, the largest clothing factory in the world. However the last few years have brought substantial changes, with old industries being replaced by new, and the atmosphere is one of growth and prosperity.

The great Town Hall in Victoria Square (walk north from Victoria Bridge and turn left at Great George Street) stands as a magnificent monument to Victorian civic pride. Recently cleaned, it was designed by Cuthbert Brodrick and opened in 1858. Looking at the Corinthian columns on all sides and the clock tower some 255ft high, it is hard to believe that Brodrick was only 29 years old when he submitted his plans. As a measure of this man's self-confidence, note that he also designed the organ, installed in 1859, which itself weighs almost 70 tonnes, has 6,500 pipes and stands 50ft high. The light and airy Corn Exchange (north of Leeds Bridge along Call Lane) built in 1861 is also Brodrick's work. Always the cultural centre of Yorkshire, the city hosts an international concert season and an international piano competition. It has several splendid theatres, including The Grand in Briggate, modelled on La Scala, Milan; the City Varieties, the oldest surviving music hall in the country; and the Leeds Playhouse repertory theatre. There are also splendid parks and rich museums, and excellent shopping facilities, including the ornate Victorian Queens and County arcades. Headingley, the home of Yorkshire cricket and a test match venue, attracts an enthusiastic following in the area, and of course the city's association football and rugby teams are known world-wide. Boaters should try to spend a day here if they possibly can – there are good moorings on the Leeds & Liverpool Canal by Office Lock, or above Leeds Lock.

See also page 114 for information on Armley Mills Industrial Museum and Abbey House Museum.
Tourist Information Centre 19 Wellington Street, Leeds (0532 462454). Walk west from the front of City Station – the usual mine of free information and the first place you should visit. You can obtain a free guide to all the museums and galleries in West Yorkshire, and for £1.00 the useful *Museum of Leeds Trail Guide* is a must.
Art Gallery and Henry Moore Sculpture Centre The Headrow, Leeds (0532 462495). Walk north from Victoria Bridge. A large collection of mainly 19thC paintings, drawings and prints. Sculpture by Henry Moore, Barbara Hepworth and Jacob Epstein. *Open all day Mon-Sat, & Sun afternoons.* Free.
City Museum Calverley Street, Leeds (0532 462465). Walk north from Victoria Bridge. Archaeology, natural history, ethnography, coins – exactly what you would expect in a large city museum. *Closed Sun & Mon.* Free.
Leeds-Settle-Carlisle Line From Leeds City Station. The 70 miles from Settle to Carlisle is said to be one of the most memorable rail journeys in the world, so this would make an excellent day trip away from the boat. *Every Sat & Sun from May-Oct* there are free guided walks from trains on the line. Coach tours around the Yorkshire Dales also connect. Details from leaflets at the station or Tourist Information Centre.
Middleton Railway Tunstall Road, Leeds (0532 645424, *evenings*). Built in 1758 to link Leeds with the Middleton Colliery, this is considered to be the world's oldest railway. It

operates at *weekends Easter-Sep* from the industrial suburb of Hunslet, where steam engines were once built.
Thwaite Mills Industrial Museum Thwaite Lane, Leeds (0532 496453). A canalside flint and china stone-grinding mill built in 1872 and powered by two waterwheels until 1975, when they were washed away, bringing closure a year later. Visitors are able to see the working conditions in the mill, as well as a Marshall engine and various artefacts. *Open 10.00-17.00 Tue-Sun.* Charge.

BOATYARDS

ⓑ**Yorkshire Hire Cruisers** 26 Canal Wharf, Leeds (0532 456195). Ⓡ Ⓢ Ⓦ Ⓓ Ⓔ Pump-out, gas, overnight mooring, dry dock, toilets, café (closed Mon).

BOAT TRIPS

Kirkstall Flyboat is a restaurant boat seating up to 52 persons. For details ring 0532 456195.

PUBS AND RESTAURANTS

A fine city such as Leeds has many pubs and restaurants. The following are a selection of those fairly close to the navigation.
✗ ❢**Bibi's Pizzeria** 7-8 Mill Hill, Leeds (0532 430905). Off Boar Lane, close to the station. A jolly Italian restaurant. *L & D. Closed Sun.*
✗ ❢**Star of Bengal** 68 New Briggate, Leeds (0532 451608). North of Leeds Bridge. An upstairs restaurant doing the usual range of curries very well. *L & D daily.*
✗ ❢**Whan Hai** 20 New Briggate, Leeds (0532 435019). Good value for money in a Pekingese restaurant. *L & D. Closed Mon.*
▰**Grove** Black Row, Leeds. South of Victoria Bridge. Small traditional pub with a choice of rooms. John Smith's real ale, *lunchtime* food (*Mon-Fri only*). Folk music some *evenings.*
▰**Adelphi** Hunslet Road, Leeds. South of Leeds Bridge. A superbly restored and very grand Edwardian pub, with lots of etched glass and mahogany. Tetley's real ale, food *lunchtime* (*Mon-Fri*). This is the closest pub to the Tetley's brewery.
▰**Whitelock's** Turk's Head Yard, Briggate, Leeds. North of Leeds Bridge. An unspoilt Edwardian pub, one of the first buildings to have electricity. Younger real ale, excellent fresh traditional food *lunchtime and evenings until 19.30* (*Sun snacks only*).
▰**Duck & Drake** Kirkgate, Leeds. North of Crown Point Bridge, near the church. Simply decorated pub with an open fire and a choice of 15 real ales. Food *lunchtime*, live music *Wed, Thur & Sun.*
▰**Old Red Lion** Thwaite Gate, Leeds. Down-to-earth Tetley's real ale pub, with a fish & chip shop opposite.
▰**Crooked Billet** Thwaite Gate, Leeds. Comfortable Tetley's real ale pub with beams and brasses. Food, garden.

Cruising on the Aire & Calder Navigation. *Derek Pratt.*

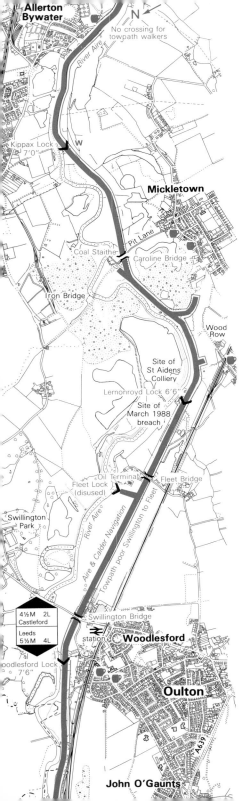

Woodlesford

The navigation continues along its straight
course with the River Aire just to the north, its
meanderings having endowed it with a series
of oxbow lakes. All around are the remains of
disused coal workings, some landscaped into
smooth grassy banks, others a gaunt pale grey.
At Woodlesford a path up from the lock leads
to two pubs, a post office, café and shops.
Further up the hill there is a useful
delicatessen and wine merchant. Just before
Fleet Bridge an arm branches off to the north.
A disused lock here once used to connect with
the river. Enclosed by the arm is an oil
terminal – notice how the storage tanks have
been colonised by house martins. The river by
Fleet Lock was the site of a disastrous breach
which occurred in March 1988, when the
ground separating it from the adjacent St
Aidens open-cast mine collapsed and the
water poured in. Apparently the river below
the breach flowed backwards for half a day,
such was the volume of water consumed, and
the workforce only just managed to rescue the
large cranes. At Caroline Bridge a modern
staithe loads regular trains of compartment
barges with coal for the huge Ferrybridge
Power Station downstream. Rejoining the
river at Kippax Lock (use the larger one with
lights and a gantry) the mining village of
Allerton Bywater appears. There is a welcome
waterside pub here, but make sure you moor
securely if you stop, since passing commercial
craft cause a considerable wash.

The towpath
From Fishpond Lock to Kippax the towpath is
generally good. Unfortunately there is no
means of crossing to The Boat pub.

Woodlesford
W. Yorks. PO, tel, stores, garage, station. Good
moorings above the lock, and nearby pubs
make this a popular stopping place for boaters.
Temple Newsam House (0532 647321).
Walk north from Swillington Bridge, fork left
after the river – 2 miles. A superb
Tudor/Jacobean house in 900 acres of
parkland. Magnificent Georgian and Regency
interiors. *Open 10.30-18.00 (20.30 Wed, May-
Sep; dusk in winter). Closed Mon.* Charge.
Mickletown
W. Yorks. PO, tel, stores. Claimed by the locals
to be the second largest village in England – it
is suggested that Wroxham in Norfolk is the
largest – Mickletown has clearly had its
problems since the neighbouring colliery
closed. The next-door village of Wood Row is
very close by, and the pub, store and post box
there can be easily reached via a path from
Lemonroyd Lock.
Allerton Bywater
W. Yorks. Stores, tel. A mining village, but the
pit is now closed. Coal was once loaded from
wagons onto barges from a small staithe here.

PUBS AND RESTAURANTS
🍺 **Two Pointers** Woodlesford. Up the hill
from the lock. A smart pub serving real ale.
Patio.
🍺 **White Hart** Woodlesford. Just past the
Two Pointers. A snug and comfy Tetley's real
ale pub. Food, family room, garden. Post
office, shops and Chinese take-away close by.
🍺 **United Kingdom** Wood Row. Up the
path from Lemonroyd Lock, just over the level
crossing. A Tetley's real ale local with a nice
garden. Food.
🍺 **Old Bay Horse** Mickletown. Turn right
out of Pit Lane, up from Caroline Bridge (do
not moor anywhere near the staithe). A lovely,
cosy, traditional Tetley's real ale pub with fine
lace curtains and a piano. Garden with swings.
🍺 **Boat** Riverside, Allerton Bywater. An
attractive Bass Yorkshire pub with a waterside
garden. Take care when mooring here, as
passing commercial craft can create a sizeable
wash.

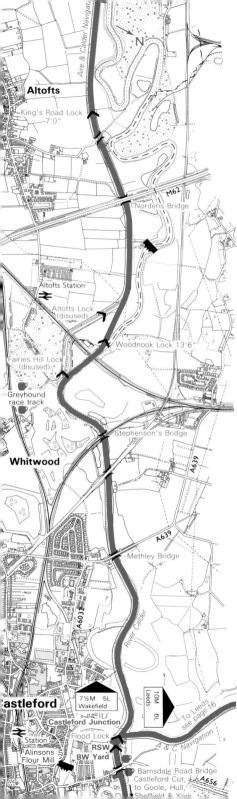

Castleford

There is a waterways 'crossroads' at
Castleford. Navigators heading towards
Sowerby Bridge should turn right here and
must on no account go straight across – since that
way leads to the huge Castleford Weir. To the
left, through the Flood Lock, are a sanitary
station and good moorings, beyond which lies
the route to Sheffield (see page 27), Goole,
Hull, York, the River Trent and ultimately the
North Sea. The large commercial craft which
trade to Leeds emerge from here, so take care.
Entering the River Calder, navigators will
notice that its course here has been
straightened, as the oxbow lakes either side
will testify. After ducking under a large road
bridge and two railway bridges a path which
gives access to two fine pubs at Whitwood can
be seen to the south. Your nose will also tell
you there is a large sewage works here.
Pressing on, the large, deep mechanised
Woodnook Lock is reached. This replaced the
earlier Fairies and Altofts locks (now disused)
to the south. By comparing the sizes of the
locks, an impression of the improvements
carried out on the navigation during the last
100 years can be gained. Beyond the large
motorway bridge is King's Road Lock (also
mechanised) and paths from here lead to
Altofts, although there is little reason to walk
the half mile or so, except for supplies.

Navigational notes
Boaters must on *no account* take the river
course towards the weir at Castleford
Junction. Make sure you are clear about where
to go *before* you get there.

The towpath
The path on this section is generally very poor
and overgrown.

Castleford
*W. Yorks. EC Wed. MD Mon, Fri, Sat. All
services.* Once the Roman settlement of
Lagentium, now a busy industrial town which
has grown up at this important waterways
junction. The British Waterways Area
Engineer's Office can be seen by the Flood
Lock, and Allinsons water mill is situated by
the huge weir – here they produce their
popular stoneground flour.
Castleford Museum Carlton Street,
Castleford (0977 559552). Changing
exhibitions of local interest, including recent
finds from the Roman town of Lagentium.
Open 14.00–17.00 Mon-Fri. Free.
Altofts
W. Yorks. PO, tel, stores, station. Originally a
mining village and now a suburb of Wakefield,
with a pick-your-own fruit farm at the western
end, but little else. There was once a pub by
the river, but it is now a private house. There
are still two pubs in the village.

PUBS AND RESTAURANTS
● **Old Mill** Just south of Castleford Junction,
at the Barnsdale Road Bridge. Superbly kept
Theakston bitter (real ale) in a friendly local.
Food, garden, children's playpark at the rear
and post office and stores close by.
● **Griffin** Opposite The Old Mill.
Comfortable pub offering food and John
Smith's real ale. Outside drinking area.
● **Bridge Inn** Whitwood. A most interesting
pub, newly built but with old bricks and
timbers. There is a lofty ceiling over the bar,
with more intimate drinking and eating areas
off to the sides. Good bar meals, friendly staff
and Theakston real ale. Patio.
●✕ **New Wheatsheaf** Whitwood (0977
553052). Large, brightly decorated traditional
pub, where someone clearly takes a great pride
in their flower arrangements. Tetley's real ale,
food, carvery restaurant, garden.
Between these two pubs is the Castleford &
Whitwood Greyhound Racing Stadium (0977
559940), where there are races *every Mon,
Wed & Fri at 19.30.*

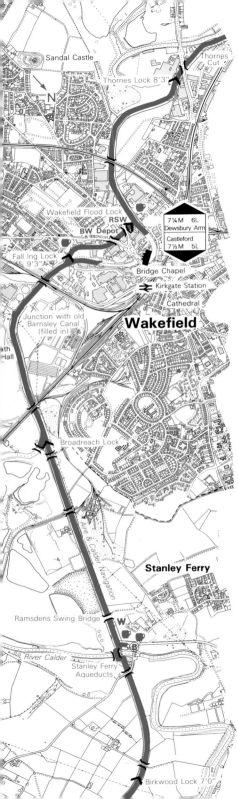

Wakefield

Birkwood Lock is the last mechanised lock when travelling upstream. At Stanley Ferry the canal is diverted over the new aqueduct, which stands alongside the original and was opened in 1981. The original aqueduct was thought to be at risk from the large craft which can now navigate here. There is a British Waterways repair yard immediately before the aqueduct, and a fine new marina, with a pub and a museum immediately after. This has been built in a defunct loading basin. After Ramsden's Swing Bridge (padlocked open – the key is at the Ferryboat Inn) the navigation continues in a dead straight line, passing Broadreach Flood Lock and Heath Old Hall before turning west to join the Calder & Hebble at Fall Ing Lock. There are craft moored here by an old loading chute, a picnic area and convenient pub. Below Wakefield Flood Lock the river is navigable for a short distance towards the boatyard, giving access to a boatyard. Leaving Wakefield you pass under a splendid curving brick railway viaduct known locally as 'the 99 arches'. A careful count will reveal only 95. At Thornes Lock only one of the two chambers is now in use – you will need a Calder & Hebble 'handspike' to operate this, and subsequent locks. Here the navigation enters a short cut.

Navigational notes
1 Take heed of the notices and flood indicator boards at the locks. Pleasure craft should only proceed if the water level is in the *green* sector.
2 Most locks on the Calder & Hebble have a unique type of paddle gear, consisting of a small perforated wheel which is turned using a 'handspike'. These are obtainable from boatyards on the navigation, and from Castleford Lock. Or a piece of 3" x 2" hardwood, 3ft long, will do just as well.
3 When coming downstream (from Sowerby Bridge direction) keep a sharp look out for the entrance to Wakefield Flood Lock. There is a large weir on the river, a short distance beyond the boatyard, by the bridge.

Stanley Ferry Aqueduct
It is a good idea to moor at Stanley Ferry Marina and walk to the road bridge for a full view of this fine structure – a trough suspended from a two-pin cast-iron arch – built on the same principle as the Sydney Harbour Bridge, which it predates by 100 years. Nearly 7000 tons of Bramley Fall stone and 1000 tons of cast iron were used in its construction. The first boat to pass across it was the *James*, a schooner of 160 tons drawn by three grey horses, on 8th August 1839. The 700 men who worked on it were fed at the nearby public houses, one of which, The Ship, still stands. Designed by George Leather, the strength of the structure was severely tested when, soon after opening, the largest flood for 20 years caused the river below to actually flow into the trough. The towpath is carried on a separate wooden breakwater designed to protect the aqueduct during such floods. The concrete aqueduct was built in 1981, and the original, by its side, is still in water.

Wakefield
W. Yorks. EC Wed. MD Mon, Tue, Thur, Fri, Sat. All services. The city centre is north of the navigation. The regional capital of West Yorkshire, it gained city status in 1888 when the cathedral was granted its charter. Mainly 15thC Perpendicular in style, the cathedral's 247ft spire is a landmark for miles around. On a much smaller scale, but perhaps of equal interest, is the Chantry Chapel of St Mary, a rare 14thC example of a bridge chapel, just a short walk north of Fall Ings, by the weir. The city itself is set on a hill, and still contains some quiet streets and dignified Georgian houses, notably those in St John's Square, with its delightful church and handsome council buildings. There has been a settlement at Wakefield since Saxon times, and the strategic importance of this site on the River Calder is confirmed by the remains of the 12thC Sandal Castle. The Battle of Wakefield,

a significant conflict in the Wars of the Roses, was fought near here in 1460, and resulted in the death of Richard, Duke of York. Wakefield's prosperity was founded on the textile and engineering industries, both of which have taken a battering in recent years. However, the city has been successful in attracting new industry, such as Coca Cola/Schweppes; and the vast and spectacular Ridings shopping complex has created many new jobs. The Theatre Royal & Opera House provides a lively programme of entertainment, and the Yorkshire Sculpture Park at Bretton Hall displays some important works by Barbara Hepworth and Henry Moore, both local artists.

Tourist Information Centre Town Hall, Wood Street, Wakefield (0924 370211). North west of the cathedral.

Wakefield Museum Wood Street, Wakefield (0924 370211). Local history and archaeology, excavations from Sandal Castle, and the Waterton collection of exotic birds and animals. The building, designed in 1820, was originally a music saloon. *Closed Sun morning.* Free.

Wakefield Art Gallery Wentworth Terrace, Wakefield (0924 370211). Sculpture by local artists Barbara Hepworth and Henry Moore, plus contemporary paintings, prints and drawings. *Closed Sun morning.* Free.

Heath Village 2 miles east of Wakefield. A beautifully preserved village with some 18thC merchants' houses amongst other substantial buildings. Heath Hall is a fine Georgian house by John Carr (1753) with carved woodwork and moulded plaster ceilings. The gas-lit pub is a gem (see below).

BOATYARDS

Ⓑ **Stanley Ferry Marina** Ferry Lane, Stanley, Wakefield (0924 290596). Ⓡ Ⓢ Ⓦ Ⓓ Ⓔ Pump-out, gas, overnight mooring, winter storage, slipway, dry dock, groceries, chandlery, books and maps, boat sales, museum, telephone, toilets, showers.

BOAT TRIPS

Restaurant boat with bar cruises between Stanley Ferry and Wakefield City Centre. Details from 0924 290596.

PUBS AND RESTAURANTS

➡✕ **Ferryboat Inn** Stanley Ferry Marina. (0924 290596). Theakston real ale in one of the old, well-converted buildings. Restaurant upstairs. Children's room and play area, patio.

➡ **Ship** Stanley Ferry, close to the marina. Comfortable pub with flocked wallpaper. There must have been much merriment here on the day in August 1839 when the new aqueduct opened. Wilson's real ale, children's room, garden with swings, food *lunchtime and evenings Tue-Sat.*

➡✕ **King's Arms** Overlooking the common, Heath Village (0924 377527). Tetley's real ale in an historic old pub with a gas-lit, wood-panelled bar; full of antiques. Open fire, food *lunchtime and evenings*, garden and restaurant.

➡ **Graziers** Just south of Fall Ing Lock. Tetley's real ale pub with some outside seating. *Take-away food shop opposite.*

➡ **Jolly Sailor** Thornes Wharf, opposite Wakefield Flood Lock.

➡ **Henry Boon's** Westgate, Wakefield. West of the cathedral. Fine traditional brewery tap for Clark's Brewery. A real ale enthusiasts' pub, with live jazz several times each week.

✕ **Val's Tea Shop** 61 Kirkgate, Wakefield (0924 378996). Traditional breakfasts, sandwiches and cakes, substantial lunches, all served by aproned waitresses. *Open 08.30-17.30. Closed Sun.*

The new Stanley Ferry Aqueduct, next to its more elegant predecessor. *Derek Pratt.*

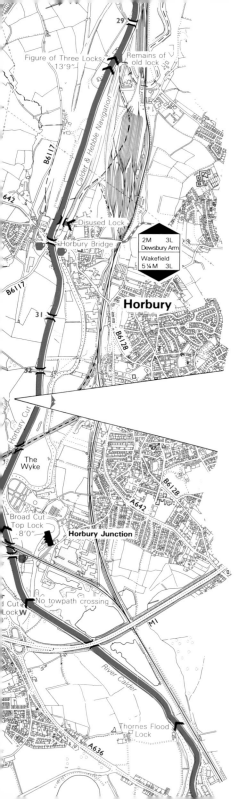

Horbury Bridge

The navigation rejoins the River Calder at
Thornes Flood Lock, and passes under the
M1 motorway. Ahead is the tall spike of
Elmley Moor television transmitter. The
beautifully kept Broad Cut Low Lock, with its
flowers and trees, marks the start of a 5-mile-
long canal section with 8 locks. There was
regular trade on this stretch until 1981, when
West Country barges took coal from the
British Oak Colliery to Thornhill Power
Station. Remains of loading staithes can be
seen opposite the Navigation Inn. The
navigation now becomes more intimate and
enclosed, and is indeed quite pretty at The
Wyke. There are good moorings at Horbury
Bridge, and a post office and farm shop are
close by. A short arm here used to connect
with the river – the remains of a lock can still
be seen. Beyond the bridge a tree-lined cutting
leads to Figure of Three Locks. There are two
locks on the navigation with another now
disused, behind the lock keeper's house,
which used to connect with the river. Is it this,
or the fact that the river here makes the shape
of a '3', which gives these locks their unusual
name? Experts seem unable to agree. The
towpath from Broad Cut to Dewsbury is good,
having been improved by the local authority,
the Manpower Services Commission and
British Waterways Board in 1986-7.

Horbury
W. Yorks. EC Wed. PO, tel, stores. A small
town up a steep hill from the bridge,
overlooking the Calder Valley. The most
attractive feature of Horbury is the delicate
spire of the parish church, designed, built and
paid for by the architect John Carr, a son of
the town. The hymn 'Onward Christian
Soldiers' was written and first sung here; it was
composed by the Reverend S. Baring-Gould
as a marching song for the children to sing on
their way to church.
Yorkshire Mining Museum Claphouse
Collier, New Road, Overton, Wakefield (0924
848806). On the A642, a little under 2 miles
south west of Horbury Bridge (bus service)
and also accessible by bus 263 from
Huddersfield and Wakefield. Go 450ft
underground to visit old- and new-style
coalfaces, examine machinery and visit the pit-
head baths, in the company of friendly ex-
miners. Audio visual show, café, shop, picnic
area. Wear warm practical clothes; not
suitable for very young children. *Open 10.00-
17.00 Mon-Sun.* Charge.

PUBS AND RESTAURANTS
◗ **Navigation** Broad Cut Top Lock, by the
railway viaduct. Handsome stone-built
canalside pub serving Tetley's real ale.
Garden, food, games area. Good moorings
here; *post office and fish & chips* just a short
distance to the south. Showers available for a
small charge.
◗ **Bingley Arms** Horbury Bridge. Tetley's
real ale in another fine looking pub.
◗✕ **Ship** Horbury Bridge (0924 272795).
Comfy local with a restaurant.

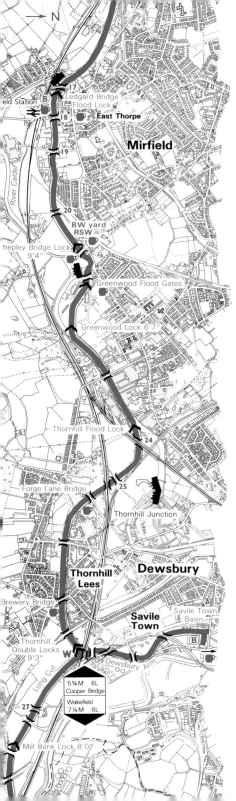

Dewsbury

After Mill Bank look out for a milestone marked 'from FALL INGS 7 miles' on the towpath side, by the next bridge. Thornhill Double Locks mark the junction with the Dewsbury Arm, which branches off to Savile Town Basin. This is a worthwhile diversion, although much of the original charm of the basin was lost when the wooden warehouses were demolished. There are still some attractive buildings left, however, and Robinson's Hire Cruisers maintain a small but very interesting museum in the old stables. Climbing Thornhill Double Locks (good moorings here) the navigation enters a deep secluded cutting spanned by tall bridges, which eventually gives way to an open industrial wasteland (for which there are large-scale redevelopment plans) around the site of Thornhill Power Station, where barges once used to unload coal. Between Thornhill Flood Lock and Greenwood Lock a short, wide, river section intervenes before the navigation enters another artificial channel to the south of Mirfield. There is plenty of interest around the pub and boatyard here, and landscaping and pretty waterside gardens make this a pleasant spot. At Shepley Bridge Flood Lock the river is rejoined. The towpath is generally good on the canal sections, less so, or indeed non-existent, on the river sections.

Navigational notes
1 When coming downstream, look out for the entrance to Ledgard Bridge Flood Lock. A large weir awaits those who miss it.
2 There are landing stages below the locks which you can use, as well as ladders in virtually all the locks.

Dewsbury
W. Yorks. EC Tue. MD Wed, Sat. All services, BR station. An industrial town that has long been the focus of the heavy woollen manufacturing area of Yorkshire. The compact and attractive town centre is a mile away from Savile Town Basin.
Dewsbury Arm Extending for ¼ mile to Savile Town Basin, this used to be the main line of the navigation, until the Thornhill Cut made it redundant in the 1790s.
Thornhill
W. Yorks. PO, tel, stores. This old stone-built mining village up on a hill above the canal offers fine views across the valley.
Mirfield
W. Yorks. EC Tue. MD Fri. All services.

BOATYARDS
British Waterways Shepley Bridge (0924 492151). R S W Overnight mooring, long-term mooring, toilets, dry dock. 'Handspikes' are made here.
Ⓑ **Robinson's Hire Cruisers** Savile Town Basin, Dewsbury (0924 467976). R S W D E Gas, pump-out, overnight mooring, long-term mooring, slipway, winter storage, boat building, boat and engine repairs, boat sales, crane, excellent museum, chandlery, books and maps, showers, toilets.
Ⓑ **Mirfield Boatyard** 10 Station Road, Mirfield (0924 492007). Below Shepley Bridge Flood Lock. W Long-term mooring, winter storage, dry dock, boat building.

BOAT TRIPS
Calder Lady Trips from Savile Town Basin to Horbury in this restaurant boat with a bar. Contact Robinson's Hire Cruisers (above).

PUBS AND TAKE-AWAYS
🍺 **Savile Hotel** Turn left out of Savile Town Basin and follow Mill Street East to the traffic lights (5-minute walk). Webster's real ale in a large hotel with some nice clocks and a *chaise longue* by the fire. Food, sheltered garden.
✕ **Agra** Warren Street, Savile Town, Dewsbury (0924 467365). Turn left out of the basin, left again, over the bridge and bear left. Superb inexpensive Indian take-away. *Open Mon-Thur & Sun, Fri & Sat to 24.30. PO and grocers close by.*

Nelson Scramble up the bank at Brewery Bridge. Food, games room.

Perseverance Inn Thornhill Junction. Canalside pub built in 1905.

Bull's Head Tetley's real ale pub near Greenwood Flood Gates.

Ship Inn East of Shepley Bridge Lock. Large, smart and comfortable pub serving food and Whitbread real ale.

Swan Above Shepley Bridge Lock. Smart Tetley's real ale pub with a roadside patio. Food *lunchtime and evenings*.

Navigation Canalside near Shepley Bridge Flood Lock. A fine Whitbread real ale pub dwarfed by the Bass Charrington building next door. Meals *lunchtime and evenings*, garden.

Black Bull North of bridge 18. Imposing Tetley's real ale hotel. Food *lunchtime and evenings* and occasional live music.

Kirklees Lock, Calder & Hebble Canal. *Derek Pratt.*

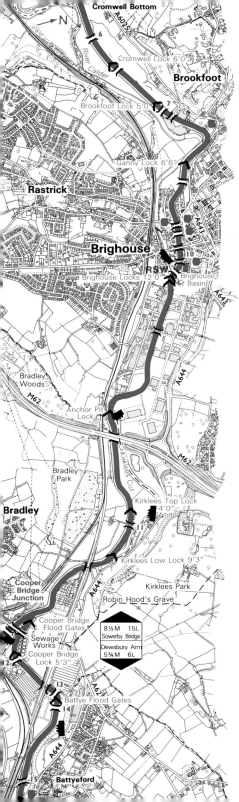

Cooper Bridge

At Battyeford there is a short canal section which rejoins the river opposite a large sewage works. A fine display of roses suggests they are not short of fertiliser! Cooper Bridge marks the junction of the Calder & Hebble with the Huddersfield Broad Canal (see page 26), which branches off to the south below the flood gates, overlooked by the tall chimney of Bottomley & Sons. Kirklees Park lies on a hillside to the north before the navigation passes under the M62 motorway and enters a cutting on its approach to Brighouse, completely enclosed by factories. There are good moorings between the two Brighouse Locks, and the passage through the town is pleasant, with gardens, seats and willow trees. Leaving the town the canal is now more reminiscent of the narrower Midlands canals; indeed there is a pleasant wooded mooring, ideal for a picnic, at Cromwell Bottom. Flooded gravel pits to the north are used for waterskiing. The towpath improves above Brighouse.

Kirklees Park In the grounds are the modest ruins of a priory founded in the 12thC for Cistercian nuns. Most of the stones were incorporated in the construction of Kirklees Hall during the late 16thC. It is believed that Robin Hood died whilst at the priory but before so doing he shot two arrows from the window to mark his burial place. One landed in the River Calder and floated away, the other landed in the grounds of the park. A tablet marks the spot thought to be his grave.
Brighouse
W. Yorks. EC Tue. MD Wed, Sat. All services (but no BR station). A woollen textile producing village transformed into an important canal port with the building of the Calder & Hebble Navigation. In the 19thC silk and cotton were also spun here. Now there seems to be plenty of thriving new industry. The canal bisects the town, passing very close to the market place. A large Victorian church at the top of the hill is surrounded by trees and flowers.

PUBS AND RESTAURANTS
◖ **Pear Tree Inn** Near Battyeford Lock. Pleasant pub with a real fire and a collection of plates. Webster's real ale, family room. Food *lunchtime and evenings*. Moorings at the bottom of its garden, on the river at the top of the lock.
◖ **Red Rooster** 123 Elland Road, north of Brookfoot Lock. Real ale enthusiasts' pub, with a real fire as well. Boddingtons, Marston's, Theakston and guest beers. Garden.
◖ **New Tavern** Near Brighouse Basin (0484 712755). Comfortable modern pub with a restaurant. Whitbread real ale.
◖✕ **Anchor Bridge Restaurant and Inn** Brighouse. Webster's real ale.
◖ **Prince of Wales** North of the bridge, Brighouse. A handsome black and white half-timbered pub rebuilt in 1926 with timber from *HMS Donegal*, a wooden battleship launched in 1858. The Tudor-style interior is compromised by two TVs, a juke box and a battery of fruit machines. Webster's real ale.

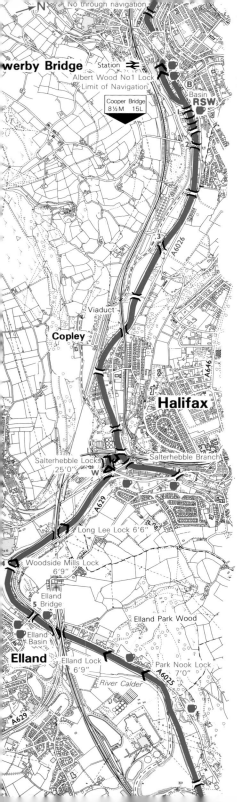

Sowerby Bridge

A milestone right by Park Nook Lock (*off-licence and grocers nearby*) reveals that you are now 18 miles from Fall Ing, with just a short distance to travel to Sowerby Bridge. Elland Basin, with its tastefully restored buildings and gardens, is worth more than a fleeting glance, however, and makes a good stopping place en route. There are several pubs close by. Have a look at the fine converted warehouse with its covered dock, before pressing on to the three superbly kept and picturesque Salterhebble Locks. The bottom lock here has an electrically-powered guillotine gate operated with a British Waterways key. This was installed when the road was widened in the 1930s. The towpath passes separately through its own narrow tunnel. Immediately after this first lock the canal passes over a small aqueduct before climbing the top two. To the right is the Salterhebble Branch (where the old Salterhebble Basin is being restored), to the left the route to Sowerby Bridge. The canal, now relatively narrow, clings to the side of a wooded hill, its clean water alive with small fish. A conspicuous building to the north is Wainhouse Tower, built in 1875 as a 253ft dyeworks chimney but converted into a viewing tower. A superb example of stonemasonry, it is *opened on Bank Holidays* (400 steps to the top). The buildings close in as the navigation approaches the basins at Sowerby Bridge, where the Rochdale Canal once branched off to cross the Pennines. Once restoration of the whole length is completed it will again be possible to make this trip. The towpath throughout this section is excellent.

Elland
W. Yorks. EC Tue. MD Fri. PO, tel, stores, bank. Elland has an enviable position on the steep south side of the Calder Valley, its narrow streets discourage through traffic, and its handsome church and terraces of stone houses give an air of tranquillity. The well-restored canal basin makes an excellent stopping point.

Halifax
W. Yorks. EC Thur. MD Fri, Sat, Sun. All services. Well known as the home of the Halifax Building Society, founded in 1853, which now has ultra-modern offices in Portland Place; it is worth the journey north from the canal to visit this industrial town. The splendid Piece Hall, rebuilt in 1770, is the last remaining manufacturers' hall in the country. Here weavers traded their products, the continuation of an industry that dates back to 1275 in Halifax. Now restored, the hall houses arts and craft shops, a museum, restaurant and the **Tourist Information Centre**. The parish church of St John the Baptist is Perpendicular in style, battlemented and with a mass of pinnacles, parapets and gargoyles.

Calderdale Industrial Museum Next door to the Piece Hall, Halifax (0422 358087). Steam engines, a Spinning Jenny, a Flying Shuttle loom and toffee wrapping machines, all working. Re-creation of 19thC Halifax, coal mines and clay mines. *Open 10.00-17.00 Tue-Sat, 14.00-17.00 Sun.* Small charge.

Shibden Hall Folk Museum Shibden Park, Halifax (0422 352246). A 15thC building with 17thC furniture and extensive folk exhibits. *Open Mar-Nov 10.00-16.45 Mon-Sat, 12.00-16.45 Sun. Closed Dec & Jan, and Mon-Sat in Feb.* Charge.

Sowerby Bridge
W. Yorks. EC Wed. MD Tue, Fri. All services. Although this is an industrial town, the scale and grandeur of the surrounding landscape dominates the mill chimneys and factory roofs that are dotted about. This rare subservience to nature makes the town human and attractive. The 19thC classical church is in a good position, overlooking the present canal terminus.

Sowerby Bridge Basin
PO, tel, stores. This great canal centre is a classic example of the functional tradition in industrial architecture, and has thankfully

survived to be given a new life in restoration, while many other such examples have disappeared. The Rochdale Canal was built to accommodate vessels up to 72ft in length, so goods had to be transhipped here into the shorter Calder & Hebble craft before they could continue their journey; hence this important centre grew in stature.

Rochdale Canal
One of three canal routes across the Pennines, its 92 wide locks over a distance of 33 miles virtually guaranteed its ultimate commercial failure. Long stretches have now been restored, including the section from Sowerby Bridge (which starts behind the Kwiksave supermarket) to Littleborough. It is also worth taking the 10-minute train ride from Sowerby Bridge to Hebden Bridge to see the canal there.

BOATYARDS
Ⓑ **Shire Cruisers** The Wharf, Sowerby Bridge, Halifax (0422 832712). Facilities either here or in the basin. Ⓡ Ⓢ Ⓦ Gas, pump-out, narrowboat hire (also from Hebden Bridge on the restored section of the Rochdale Canal), overnight mooring, long-term mooring, winter storage, chandlery, books and maps, boat building, engine sales and repairs, wet dock, toilets.
Ⓑ **Sowerby Marine and Chandlery** The Wharf, Sowerby Halifax (0422 832922). Ⓡ Ⓢ Ⓦ Ⓓ Ⓔ Overnight mooring, long-term mooring, winter storage, slipway, crane, chandlery, books and maps, boat building, boat sales, engine sales and repairs, breakdown service.

BOAT TRIPS
Calder Valley Cruising From Hebden Bridge Marina (trains from Sowerby Bridge). Trips along a restored section of the Rochdale Canal, and visits to the Clog Factory. Details from 0422 844833.

PUBS AND RESTAURANTS
🍺 **Rawson Arms** Signposted half a mile below Park Nook Lock near picnic tables in the woods. Food *lunchtime and Sat evenings*.
🍺 **Colliers Arms** Between Elland and Park Nook locks. Traditional canalside pub offering Sam Smith real ale, food *lunchtime and evenings*, an open fire and a waterside garden.
🍺 **Barge & Barrel** Elland Basin. An interesting choice of real ales in a comfortable Victorian pub. *Lunchtime* food, real fire, garden. Families welcome.
🍺 **Royal** South of Elland Bridge. Webster's real ale in an attractive stone-built pub. *Lunchtime* food.
🍺 **Malt Shovels** Next to The Royal. Sam Smith real ale, garden. These two pubs are separated by an extravagant neo-Grecian workshop.
🍺 **Calder & Hebble Inn** East of Salterhebble Locks.
🍺 **Jenny Dee** A new pub at the terminus of the Salterhebble Branch.
🍺 **Punch Bowl Inn** By the Salterhebble Branch.
🍺 **Navigation Inn** By bridge 1. Friendly 17thC canalside pub with a collection of Buckby cans. Tetley's real ale and an extensive bar menu. Garden.
🍺✕ **Moorings** No 1 Warehouse, Sowerby Bridge Basin (0422 833940). A good choice of bar food and real ale in this attractive conversion. Wide range of foreign lagers and beers. Restaurant *open Tue-Sat evenings*. Patio, family room.
🍺✕ **Ash Tree** Wharf Street, by the basin. (0422 831654). A pub/restaurant specialising in Indonesian food (*evenings only*). Good choice of real ale, including Old Mill and Stones. Bar food (*lunchtime*).
🍺 **Engineers** and the **William IV** are also very close to the basin.

Sowerby Bridge Basin, Calder & Hebble Navigation. *Derek Pratt.*

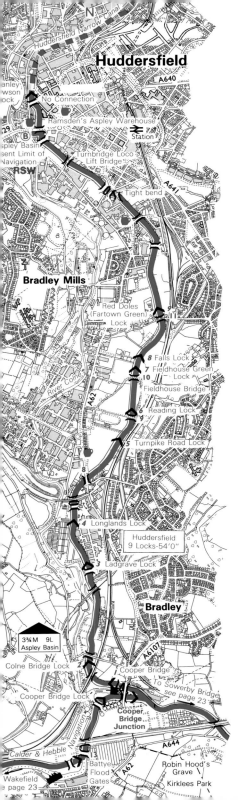

Huddersfield

Also known as Sir John Ramsden's Canal, this navigation was authorised in 1774. It leaves the Calder & Hebble at Cooper Bridge and makes a very rewarding short diversion off the main line. Brick-arched bridges and a succession of locks maintain interest, and although industry is omnipresent, there are plenty of green patches, and a vast expanse of sports fields, to bring light relief. After climbing Red Doles Lock, the last of the nine, a tight bend under three bridges brings you to the remarkable Turnbridge loco lift bridge. Dated 1865, you will need a British Waterways key to unlock it. Aspley Basin is effectively the limit of navigation, although the new Wakefield Road Bridge means that the link with the Huddersfield Narrow Canal has once again been made navigable for craft of 7ft beam. It is well worth exploring this end of the narrow canal, especially to have a look at the warehouse south of the bridge. Built prior to 1778 it is probably the oldest surviving example of such a building, demonstrating an early stage in the development of the large multi-storey warehouses of the 19thC. It has now been converted into dwellings. The crane beside it dates from the early 19thC. Further along, beyond Huddersfield University, is the first restored lock on the narrow canal. The towpath on the Huddersfield Broad Canal is good.

Navigational notes
1 When joining the Huddersfield Broad Canal at Cooper Bridge, take care to avoid the weir on the river just beyond the entrance lock (1).
2 Although there are mooring rings on the Huddersfield Narrow Canal south of Aspley Basin, turning here may be difficult.

Huddersfield
W. Yorks. EC Wed. MD Mon. All services.
Huddersfield is in the best tradition of Victorian industrial towns: all built to a grand scale of dark local stone, in a happy mixture of 19thC styles. The most striking part of the town is around the railway station, built in 1847 with its powerful classical façade of Corinthian columns, considered one of the finest examples of railway architecture. The renowned Huddersfield Choral Society operates from the 19thC Town Hall.
Huddersfield Narrow Canal
One of three Pennine canal crossings, and noted for the length of its summit tunnel at Standedge, fully 5698yds end to end. Authorised in 1794 and completed in 1811, this canal packs 74 locks into its 20 miles between here and Manchester. Active restoration is afoot at both ends.

BOATYARDS
Ⓑ **Aspley Wharf Marina** Aspley Basin, Huddersfield (0484 514123). Ⓡ Ⓢ Ⓦ Ⓓ Gas, overnight mooring, long-term mooring, slipway, groceries, chandlery, books and maps, boat sales, engine sales and repairs, toilets.

PUBS AND RESTAURANTS
🍺 **White Horse Inn** South of bridge 8. Handy pub by the cricket pitches. Food.
🍺 **Spinners Arms** East of the canal, approaching Turnbridge. Roadside pub serving bar meals.
🍺🍴 **Ramsden's Landing** Aspley Basin, Huddersfield (0484 544250). Café-bar, brasserie and waterfront restaurant with a wide variety of cuisines and strong family atmosphere. Free moorings.
🍺 **Wharf** Just across the busy road from the basin (access along the towpath through the Wakefield Road Bridge is preferable to the traffic). Take-away food close by.
🍺 **College Arms** 33 Queensgate, Huddersfield. Close to the basin. Webster's and Wilson's real ales in this unusual pub, formerly the Dog & Gun. Bar meals *lunchtime and evenings.*

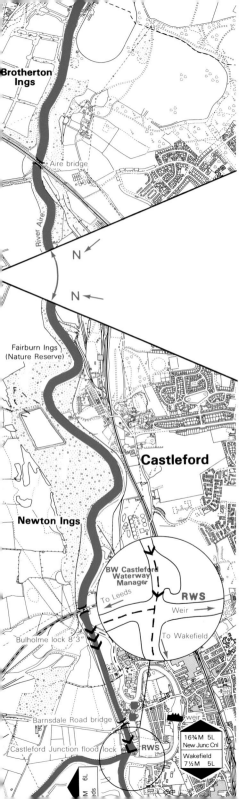

Castleford Junction

Leaving Castleford Junction the canal is dominated by the extensive works of Hickson and Welch. The company, founded in 1905 by a Mr Hickson, is now a multi-national chemical giant best known in this country for developing the pressure treatment process used to preserve timber. Also in the vicinity of the basin is the maintenance depot of Cawood Hargreaves, one of the largest haulage companies on the Aire & Calder. At Bulholme Lock is a sign directing walkers to Newton. This walk should not be attempted in wet weather as the footpath becomes waterlogged. The lock keeper's bungalow, built on stilts, replaces a traditional canal-side cottage. At this point the canal enters the river which is surrounded by large areas of derelict land. Landscaping of the now abandoned Fryston and Wheldale collieries is still being undertaken but will, no doubt, lead to the establishment of plants and trees in the area. The lower land to the north of the navigation forms the 'Ings', a word dating back to Viking times which denotes areas of riverside water meadows which are subject to seasonal flooding. Mining subsidence in the area, particularly over the last fifty years, has meant that much of this land has now become permanently waterlogged, resulting in the loss of a considerable area of agricultural land. These wetlands have, however, provided a habitat to all forms of wildlife, the area between the river and the village of Airburn being recognised as a nature reserve since 1957. Owned by the NCB and leased to the RSPB, the 618-acre site was designated a statutory Bird Sanctuary in 1968. 251 species of birds have been recorded, of which about 170 are regular visitors. Originally the land was acquired in order to provide space for tipping spoil from the collieries. British Coal still retains tipping rights in the area but, in the interest of wildlife, has restricted its activities. Continued work on the spoil heaps prevents the natural establishment of vegetation, although tree planting on the mature spoil heaps between Castleford and Ferrybridge has proved most effective. The river eventually traces a surprisingly pretty course as it meanders through banks now well established with silver birch, larch and alder. Just before the skew railway bridge are some sluice gates, installed in order to regulate the water levels within the washland areas of the reserve. These levels can vary considerably, often having a disastrous effect on nesting birds. Boaters should note that the only recognised access to the reserve is from the Fairburn to Allerton Bywater road to the north of Castleford. On no account should visitors try to gain access from the river, as the land here is the property of British Coal and is prone to subsidence. The village of Fairburn is a good walk from Castleford but would provide a useful refreshment point for anyone visiting the Bird Sanctuary.

Navigational notes
1 Boaters should be on the alert for large commercial craft, often heavily laden, especially on the many bends that the river prescribes on this stretch. There is nowhere suitable to moor on this part of the navigation.
2 The power stations of Ferrybridge are not far away and navigators should be prepared for the sudden activity in that area.

The towpath
At the present time there is no recognisable towpath beyond Bulholme Lock. It is possible that when British Coal reclamation is completed the towpath will be reinstated on the north bank.

Fairburn
W. Yorks. PO, tel, stores. Limestone and alabaster were once quarried here. There is also a record of a tunnel, 350yds long, which extended under the village connecting it to the river. Perched on the hillside above the Ings, the village has several pubs and shops.

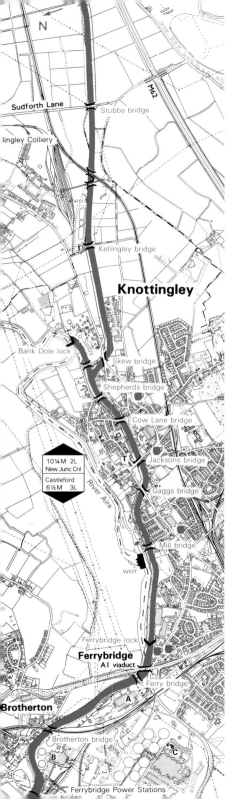

Ferrybridge/ Knottingley

On arrival at the Ferrybridge Power Stations the river suddenly resumes its industrial character as the massive cooling towers overpower the landscape. Coal is transported to Ferrybridge from over thirty collieries throughout the north east, approximately twenty-five per cent of this being carried by water. Hargreaves alone carry over 1,000,000 tonnes of coal to Ferrybridge C each year. Navigators should therefore be prepared for the movement of heavily-laden commercial craft in the area. ¼ mile upstream of Brotherton Railway Bridge there is a build-up of traffic as coal barges and trains of compartment boats manoeuvre in the stream waiting to unload. Once alongside the wharf a large overhead gantry takes over, propelling individual 'pans', each holding approximately 170 tons, into position under a giant hoist capable of handling 1000 tonnes of coal an hour. This in turn lifts the pan 40 feet into the air, tipping it into a concrete hopper. Coal to Ferrybridge B wharf still arrives by conventional motor and dumb barge pairs. Leaving behind the frantic activity of the power stations the graceful 18thC bridge which once carried the Great North Road comes into sight. This has now been superseded by the concrete viaduct which carries the A1 dual carriageway. Here the River Aire leaves the navigation, flowing off to the left, as the canal traces a more southerly course through Knottingley. All craft should bear right and await the traffic lights controlling the entrance to the Ferrybridge Flood Lock. Moorings immediately beneath the viaduct are for the use of boats waiting to enter the lock only. Long-stay moorings are to be found on the river to the left of the lock. Care should be exercised on this section as the river terminates in a weir. Pubs and shops in Ferrybridge can be reached from the lock. The navigation now enters an artificial cut which continues all the way to Goole. The canal skirts an industrial complex on the right and passes the tall gaunt buildings of King's Flour Mills on the left, before entering a pleasantly green, wooded cutting. Here is evidence of limestone quarrying over and above the need to make passage for the waterway and indeed the approaches to both Gaggs and Jacksons Bridges remain as solid rock. The left bank here is lovingly tended by some of the local residents who have encouraged plants to grow alongside the water's edge. Immediately through Shepherds Bridge the navigation forks; straight ahead to Bank Dole Lock into the River Aire and thence to the Selby Canal, while the main line bends right hugging the glassworks and boat-repair yard. Care should be exercised here on account of both moored commercial craft and laden coal pans approaching under Skew Bridge. They require first call on the available water to line up for Shepherds Bridge. From here on the drama diminishes as the navigation passes another chemical works. The wharves of Kellingley Colliery, a mile further on, are a hive of activity and the source of a great bulk of the coal travelling to the Ferrybridge power stations.

Ferrybridge
W. Yorks. PO, tel, stores, garage. The town takes its name from the bridge over the River Aire which was built at the point where, for many centuries, travellers were ferried across the water. Possession of the site has been contested in the past by the Romans and much later by the armies of York and Lancaster. The area is now dominated by the three power stations, Ferrybridge A, B and C. Ferrybridge A is now given over to workshops devoted to the repair and testing of machinery whilst B and C produce electricity for the national grid. The power stations are open to visitors by telephoning 0977 674188.

Knottingley
W. Yorks. EC Thur. All services. Once famous

for the making of clay tobacco pipes and for its pottery, Knottingley now depends on the manufacture of synthetic chemicals, hydrocarbons, cosmetics and glassware. The famous Rockware Glass Works produce the majority of the glass containers in our homes and supermarkets. Jam, salad cream, pickle and perfume are all likely to be contained in Rockware glass. The company also supplies bottles to the beer, cider, wine and spirit industries as well as being the sole UK supplier to the cosmetics trade. A more unusual product is the white opal glass characteristic of certain bottles used for spirits or aftershave. The pretty church of St Botolph can be seen at the north end of Jacksons Bridge. The church has some impressive carvings around the doorway and an interesting campanile tower. The area next to the church was once the site of Knottingley Old Hall, an Elizabethan residence owned by the Wildbore family. According to a plaque to commemorate the site, the building was sadly demolished in 1830 'for the sake of the limestone beneath it'.

BOAT TRIPS
PA Sunshine Cruises 'Nosille', Hollygarth Lane, Beal, Nr Goole, North Humberside (0977 678136). Scheduled *2-hour* cruises from Ferrybridge Lock aboard *The Enterprise*, a 96-seater passenger vessel. Bar, commentary and music. No booking required. *Wed & Fri 19.00, Sun 14.30 & 19.00.*

PUBS
🍺 **Golden Lion** Riverside at Ferrybridge Lock. A friendly pub overlooking the River Aire. Bar snacks served *lunchtime and evenings Mon-Sun.* Restaurant open *Wed-Sat evenings and Sun lunch.* Vegetarians catered for. Children welcome.
🍺 **Magnet Inn** 100yds south of Ferrybridge Lock. A basic John Smith's real ale pub, popular with the locals. Bar food. Pub games. *Extended opening hours throughout the week.*
🍺 **Bay Horse** Main Street, Knottingley. A simple Whitbread real ale pub serving bar food.
🍺 **Anvil Inn** Knottingley. 100yds south of Jacksons Bridge. Bar food and take-away pizzas. Pool and darts.
🍺 **Lamb Inn** Lamb Inn Road, Knottingley.

An empty oil tanker leaves Ferrybridge, Aire & Calder Navigation. *Derek Pratt.*

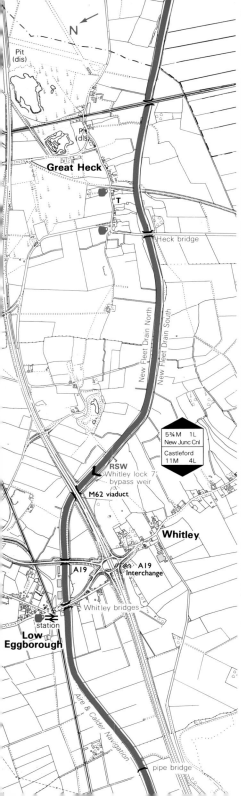

Heck Bridge

The navigation continues its journey
accompanied to the north by the railway and
to the south by the M62. The flat, featureless
landscape is broken only by the landscaped
spoil heap of a local colliery and the
interchange of the A19 with the motorway. In
the distance stand the giant cooling towers of
Eggborough Power Station. The waterway
provides an element of calm amidst the
hurried activity of the other transport systems.
At Whitley Bridge access can be gained to
shops, pubs and a fish and chip shop. There is
also a station. Just beyond the A19
interchange the canal is joined by two
drainage ditches which accompany the
navigation to the Southfield Reservoir. For
much of this journey the canal is steel-piled,
thus preventing the softening of its banks by
vegetation. Moorings are available at both
ends of Whitley Lock. Boaters should keep left
to enter the lock and avoid the bypass weir.
After a straight stretch Heck Bridge appears.
Here local pubs and the quaint village shop
can be reached. Only the sign outside the shop
gives the visitor any indication of its function
and inside it becomes apparent that the shop is
no more than a room set aside in someone's
house. Just beyond Heck Bridge is the home of
the South Yorkshire Boat Club. The site
makes use of the basin once excavated to
provide transhipment of stone to Goole from
the local quarry. Immediately beyond the
village the east coast main railway from
London to Edinburgh crosses the navigation.
Recently electrified, this line carries the new
Class 91 Electra locomotives capable of
hauling passenger trains at speeds up to
140 mph, but until an automatic in-cab
signalling system has been approved these
trains will continue to travel at a maximum
speed of 125 mph. To the north stand the twin
chimneys of the disused quarry, now the site of
a concrete pipe works. Also on the skyline
stand great quantities of straw bales, stacked
into huge walls which, from a distance,
resemble fortifications. These are to be used in
the making of strawboard, another local
industry.

Whitley Bridge
N. Yorks. PO, tel, stores. The original
settlement of Whitley Bridge has now been
lost amidst a sprawling development of new
housing in Low Eggborough. There are two
feed mills in the area. Eggborough Power
Station, one of the largest in Yorkshire, is
situated half way between the canal and the
old course of the River Aire.

Great Heck
W. Yorks. Tel, stores. A small, friendly village
consisting of a long line of irregularly built
houses following the course of the canal.

PUBS
● **Jolly Miller** Whitley Bridge. An attractive
pub next to the station, 100yds north of the
canal. Bar food. Pool.
● **Bay Horse** Heck. 300yds north of Heck
Bridge. A cosy pub, popular with boaters,
serving Tetley's real ales. Bar snacks. Children
welcome. Music *Wed.* Quiz night *Thur.*
● **New Inn** Heck. On the Pollington Road
out of the village.

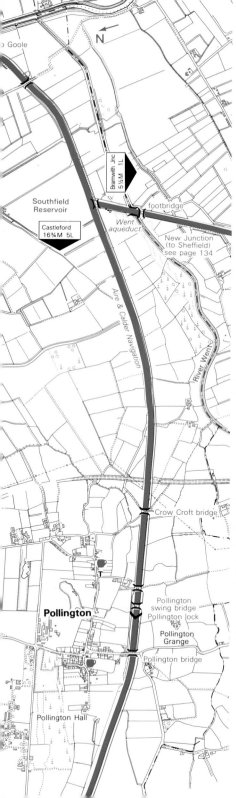

Pollington

The navigation now adopts a fairly bleak and monotonous course through a flat but fertile landscape. Trees are scarce, and hedges and livestock are nowhere to be seen. There are numerous drainage ditches. The straggling village of Pollington lies to the north of Pollington bridge; there is a post office and two pubs. The school and a brick-built chapel with a bell tower are on the south side of the bridge. To the west of the village, facing the canal, stands Pollington Hall, an attractive 18thC house with pleasingly proportioned narrow windows and a door canopy. Beyond the lock is Manor Farm where there is evidence of a moat. These buildings, along with Pollington Grange to the south of the navigation, indicate a former prosperity. At Pollington Lock the lock keeper's pretty cottage is one of the best examples of its type, with attractively rounded brick arches above the windows and a particularly deep overhang to the roof at the gable ends. Beyond Crow Croft Bridge the demolished abutments of an old railway bridge can be seen, unusual in that it once pivoted upwards at one end. At this point the River Went draws close and follows the line of the navigation towards Goole. The dinghies of the Beaver Sailing Club at Southfield Reservoir add an unexpected and welcome splash of colour to the landscape. The 110-acre reservoir, built at the turn of the century, marks the beginning of the New Junction Canal leading south to Sheffield. Its construction provided a water supply to meet the needs of the much larger locks installed on the navigation and effectively maintains the water levels of the docks at Goole.

Navigational notes
1 Both Whitley and Pollington Locks are boater operated outside normal working hours. A single 'Castell' key, available from either keeper against a refundable deposit, opens a lockside control panel. This allows the boater to operate the hydraulic paddle gear and the lock gates by pressing a series of buttons. Those anxious about operating these controls should consult the lock keeper during duty hours.
2 It is BW's long term strategy to make all locks on the Aire & Calder navigation, except flood locks, boater operated over the next few years. Flood locks, for obvious reasons of safety, will remain under the control of keepers, but under normal river conditions will be left open. Telemetry equipment is currently being installed to monitor river levels and automatically signal to BW staff should rising water levels dictate that the gates be closed. Under these conditions boaters should stay put until they are advised by a lock keeper that it is safe to proceed.

Pollington
Humberside. PO, tel, stores. A sprawling village, about ½ mile from the canal, providing basic facilities.

PUBS
◗ **George & Dragon** Pollington. In the square directly north of Pollington Bridge. A basic Tetley's real ale pub, popular with the local youngsters. Garden. B & B.
◗ **King's Head** Pollington. A Whitbread real ale pub at the east end of the village. Bar snacks. Garden and play area.

BRIDGEWATER CANAL

Maximum dimensions

Length: 70'
Beam: 14'
Headroom: 8'
Draught: 3'

Licences

Estates Officer, Manchester Ship Canal
Company, Property Division, Quay West,
Trafford Wharf Road, Manchester M1 2HG.
Enquiries: 061-872 2411.
All craft using the canal must be licensed and
insured against normal third party risks. Any
boat holding a normal British Waterways
licence may cruise on the Bridgewater for three
consecutive days.

Mileage

PRESTON BROOK to
Lymm: 9¾
Waters Meeting, junction with
Leigh Branch: 20½
Hulme Locks Branch: 23¼
CASTLEFIELD JUNCTION, start of
Rochdale Canal: 23½

No locks

DUCIE STREET JUNCTION, start of
Ashton Canal: 25 (Rochdale Canal, 9 locks)

Preston Brook to Runcorn: 5¾, no locks

Leigh Branch: 8½, no locks

The Bridgewater Canal, which received the
Royal Assent on 23 March 1759, was the
forerunner of all modern canals, following a
route that was independent of all existing natural
watercourses. It was built by Francis Egerton,
third Duke of Bridgewater, to enable coal
from his mines at Worsley to be transported
to Manchester and sold cheaply. His engineers
were James Brindley and John Gilbert, who
designed a lockless contour canal which crossed
the River Irwell on a stone aqueduct – a
revolutionary concept and one that was ridiculed
by many sceptics. However, the line was open
to Stretford by the end of 1765.

While the canal was under construction,
there began the excavation of a remarkable
system of underground canals to serve the
Duke's mines, reached through two entrances
at Worsley Delph. Eventually 46 miles of
underground canal were built, some on different
levels and linked by an ingenious inclined plane
built along a fault in the sandstone. The craft
used in the mines were known as 'starvationers',
double-ended tub boats which could carry
up to 12 tons of coal. This whole system
remained in use until the late 19thC.

In 1762 the Duke received sanction to
extend the canal to the Liverpool tideway at
Runcorn – this was later amended in order
to connect with the new Trent & Mersey Canal
at Preston Brook. The route between Liverpool
and Manchester was opened in 1776, although
Brindley did not live to see its completion.
In 1795 the Duke, then 60 years old, received
the Royal Assent for the final part of the network,
which linked Worsley to the Leeds & Liverpool
Canal at Leigh. As a result of this enterprise the
Duke spent much of his life heavily in debt,
although he finally recouped his investments
to die, in 1803, a rich man.

The coming of the railways did not initially
affect the prosperity of the canal, the Trustees
going to great lengths in Parliament to protect
their position. In 1872 the newly formed
Bridgewater Navigation Company purchased
the canal for £1,120,000, and they in turn
sold it to the Manchester Ship Canal Company
in 1885. The building of the new Ship Canal
meant that Brindley's original stone aqueduct
over the River Irwell would need to be replaced.
Its successor, the Barton Swing Aqueduct, was
no less outstanding than the original, being
a steel trough closed by gates at each end,
pivoting on an island in the Ship Canal. The
weight of water carried by the new aqueduct
is 1500 tons.

The Bridgewater Canal is a tribute to
its builders in that it continued to carry
commercial traffic until 1974 – indeed its wide
gauge, lock-free course and frequent use of
aqueducts makes many later canals seem
retrograde.

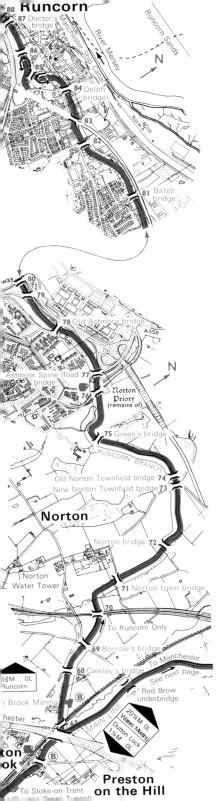

Preston Brook

Although the main line of the Bridgewater was originally to Runcorn, where it locked down to the Mersey, this is now a dead end, reached through the dull acres of the new town's expanding housing estates. There are, however, some attractive terraces and elegant iron bridges to enliven the journey. The locks down to the Mersey were closed in 1966. The route to Manchester bears to the right immediately after the big motorway bridge, and the canal's direct course to the south of the Mersey affords interesting views of the Manchester Ship Canal and industry to the north.

Runcorn
Ches. EC Wed. MD Tue, Thur, Sat. All services.
Runcorn's industrial growth began with the completion of the Bridgewater Canal in the latter part of the 18thC. The old town is to be found down by the docks, where the elegant curved 1092-ft single span of the steel road bridge (built 1961), with the railway beside, leaps over the Ship Canal and the Mersey. West of the bridge, by the Ship Canal, is Bridgewater House where the 'Canal Duke' spent much of his time while the docks were being built – it is now occupied by the Manchester Ship Canal Company. The massive flight of 10 double locks which connect the canal to the Mersey was finally abandoned in 1966, and filled in, much to the dismay of thousands of industrial archaeologists and canal enthusiasts. Since 1964 Runcorn has been a 'new town', its rapid growth being carefully planned. It is interesting to note that Runcorn, following local government reorganisation, is now part of Halton (which includes Widnes on the north bank of the Mersey), an echo of the time following the Norman Conquest when it was a dependent manor of the Barony of Halton.
Tourist Information Centre 57-61 Church Street, Runcorn (0928 576776).
Norton Priory The remains of a priory c1200, set in woodland, with a picnic area and museum. *Open Mon-Wed, Sat, Sun & B. Hol afternoons in summer – also Thur & Fri in Aug.*
Preston Brook
Ches. PO, tel, stores. A village that grew up to serve the canal, where goods were transhipped from the wide beam craft of the north west to the narrowboats of the Midlands. There is now little left to remind us of this activity, and a very different means of transport, the M56 motorway, dominates the area. To the south, on the Trent & Mersey Canal, is the 1239-yard-long Preston Brook Tunnel (see page 177).

BOATYARDS

Ⓑ **Claymoore Navigation** The Wharf, Preston Brook (0928 717273). Ⓡ Ⓦ Ⓓ Ⓔ Pump-out, gas, narrowboat hire, day hire craft, overnight mooring, long-term mooring, crane, groceries, chandlery, books and maps, boat sales, engine repairs, gifts, toilets.
Ⓑ **Preston Brook Marina** Preston Brook (0928 719081). Ⓡ Ⓢ Ⓦ Gas, overnight mooring, long-term mooring, slipway, boat sales, toilets, showers.

PUBS

Plenty of pubs in Runcorn, including:
● **Clarendon** Church Street, Runcorn.
● **Egerton Arms** Bridge Street, Runcorn.
● **Barge Hotel** Norton. By bridge 77.
● **Red Lion** Preston Brook.

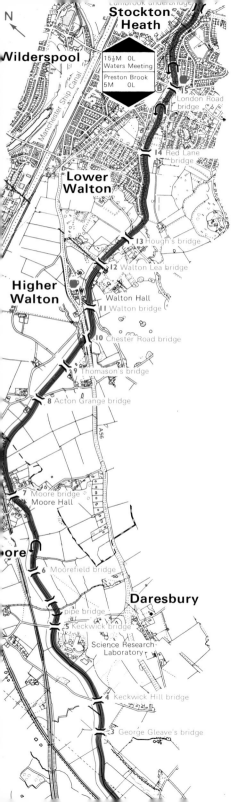

Daresbury

Industry is far enough away to the north to remain an interesting diversion rather than an ugly intrusion as the canal passes through pleasant countryside, punctuated initially by the tall white tower and pleasant landscaped grounds of the Daresbury Laboratories, where the government conducts science and engineering research. By Moorefield Bridge there is one of the small cranes used to hoist stop planks into position, should a section of the canal need to be drained. The canal frontage at Moore is attractive, with moored boats, a shop and a phone right by the canal, followed by a group of interesting red-brick, bow-fronted cottages. A short rural stretch is interrupted by the estate village of Higher Walton, which can be seen among trees, and this is followed by a secluded tree-lined length in a shallow cutting before the outskirts of Stockton Heath are approached. There follows a pleasant example of urban canal, busy with fishermen and walkers. There are useful services at London Bridge.

Stockton Heath
Ches. EC Thur. Shops and services north of London Bridge. An outer suburb of Warrington, England's centre for vodka distilling. A useful place to victual.
Stockton Quay Bridge 15. The terminus of the canal from 1771 to 1776, before the Duke of Bridgewater completed his route from Manchester to Runcorn, and consequently a major transhipment point with stables, yards, wharves, warehouses and a canal company office. Passenger packet boat services also ran from here from 1771 to the mid 1880s, one of the craft being the renowned *Duchess-Countess.*
Higher Walton
Ches. PO, tel, stores. A pretty, late-Victorian estate village among trees. The gardens of Walton Hall are open to the public.
Daresbury
Ches. PO, tel, stores. Half-a-mile up the road from Keckwick Bridge. An appealing village, where Charles Lutwidge Dodgson, better known as Lewis Carroll, was born in 1832. His father was vicar of Daresbury (pronounced Darzby) and they lived until 1843 in the Old Parsonage, Newton-by-Daresbury, 2 miles south of the church. The house was burnt down in 1883 – the site is now marked by a plaque with a quotation from Carroll's poem *The Three Sunsets*, standing in an open field on Glebe Farm. The church has a pretty Lewis Carroll memorial window, bright and cheerful, where he is shown with characters from *Alice in Wonderland.* Viewing is by prior appointment only – ring 0925 740348.

BOATYARDS
Ⓑ **Thorn Marine** London Bridge, Stockton Heath (0925 265129). Ⓢ Ⓦ Gas, overnight mooring, slipway, groceries, chandlery, books and maps, engine sales and repairs, toilets. Gifts and crafts next door.

PUBS
🍺 **London Bridge** Stockton Heath. Canalside.
🍺 **Walton Arms** Higher Walton. Food, garden.
🍺 **Ring o'Bells** Daresbury. A spacious old pub serving Greenalls real ale, and excellent food in a charming dining room. Garden with swings.

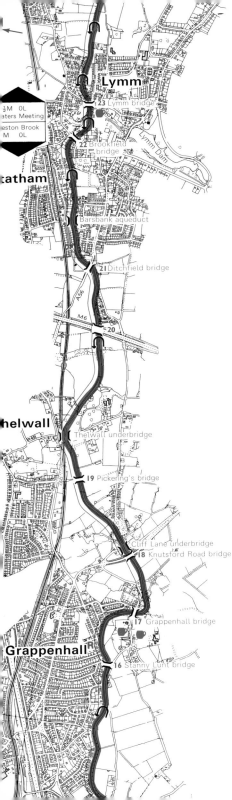

Lymm

Where the canal comes to within a ¼ mile of the Manchester Ship Canal, the houses of Stockton Heath merge into those of Grappenhall crowded to the north, while to the south the old village survives. The canal makes a dog-leg turn past Thelwall and under the M6 Motorway south of the vast and infamous Thelwall Viaduct which climbs laboriously over the Ship Canal. There are fine views of the distant Pennines to the north before the canal makes a very pleasing passage through the heart of Lymm, whose streets come down almost to the water's edge. There are convenient temporary moorings here.

Lymm
Ches. PO, tel, stores, banks, fish & chips, launderette. The l7thC Lymm Cross, with replica wooden stocks close by, stands on a rock outcrop just a few yards from the canal in the centre of this hilly and attractive little town, which has retained its intimate character in spite of its proximity to Warrington. Craft of the Lymm Cruising Club line the banks, and there are several fine canalside residences.
Thelwall
Ches. A short walk north from Thelwall underbridge will bring you to a ferry where, for a minimal charge, you will be rowed across the Ship Canal.
Grappenhall
Ches. PO, tel, stores. A fine group of buildings on cobbled streets survive around the church of St Wilfred, where the village stocks remain. There are two pubs.

PUBS

There are plenty of pubs in Lymm.
● **Golden Fleece** Lymm. Canalside. Food *lunchtime and evenings*, real ale, children's room, garden with swings.
● **Bull's Head** By Lymm Bridge. A cosy red plush pub serving Hydes' real ale and food *lunchtime and evenings.*
● **Ram's Head** Grappenhall. Food.
● **Parr Arms** Grappenhall. Food.

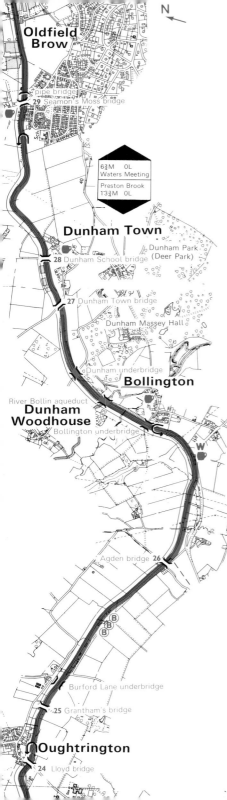

Bollington

The canal leaves Lymm, passes the village of
Oughtrington to the north and a row of smart
new houses to the south, each with a canalside
garden and barking dog, before entering
surroundings which are surprisingly rural.
Rows of moored boats, some in an advanced
state of decay, announce the presence of three
useful boatyards. The fields then gently fall
away into the valley of the River Bollin, which
the Bridgewater crosses on a large
embankment, with fine views of the
Manchester Ship Canal and Dunham Park,
the last greenery before Sale and Manchester.
Dunham Underbridge is a new concrete and
steel construction, built to replace the original
stone trough which breached disastrously in
August 1971 and resulted in a 2-year closure.
It cost £125,000 to repair. *PO, stores, fish and
chips* are south of Seamons Moss Bridge.
There are good moorings by Dunham Town
Bridge.

Dunham Town
Gt Manchester. PO, tel, stores. A small,
scattered, farming village with a pub.
Dunham Massey Hall Until recently the
seat of the Earl of Stamford, now owned by
the National Trust. The beautiful 18thC
house stands in a wooded park, with deer and
an Elizabethan mill. Access is via Bollington,
over the footbridge near the Swan with Two
Nicks. *Open daily except Fri, Apr-Oct.*
Restaurant & shop. Admission charge,
although access to the park is free.
Bollington
Ches. A compact and attractive village, with a
fine old pub and a converted mill.
Oughtrington
Ches. PO, tel, stores. A good place for supplies.

BOATYARDS

Ⓑ **Lymm Marina** Warrington Lane, Lymm
(092 575 2945). Ⓡ Ⓦ Ⓓ Gas, long-term
mooring, winter storage, slipway, dry dock,
chandlery, books and maps, boat building,
boat and engine sales, toilets.
Ⓑ **Hesford Marine** Warrington Lane, Lymm
(092 575 4639). Ⓦ Ⓓ Gas, overnight
mooring, long-term mooring, winter storage,
slipway, crane, chandlery, books and maps,
boat building, boat sales, engine sales and
repairs, toilets.
Ⓑ **Wharfage Boat Co** Agden Wharf, Lymm
(092 575 4900). Ⓡ Ⓢ Ⓦ Ⓓ Pump-out, gas,
narrowboat hire, crane, books and maps, boat
building, boat sales, engine sales and repairs,
toilets.

BOAT TRIPS

Lymm Bargee is a 42-seater restaurant trip-
boat, operating from Agden Wharf, Lymm.
Phone 092 575 4900 for details.

PUBS

■ **Bay Malton** By Seamons Moss Bridge.
Food, bowling green, overnight mooring, Ⓡ.
■ **Axe & Cleaver** Dunham Town. A Chef &
Brewer pub serving Wilson's real ale and food
lunchtime and evenings. Family room, garden.
■ **Swan with Two Nicks** Bollington. A very
fine, comfortable and cosy pub with a friendly
atmosphere, serving Boddingtons and Castle
Eden real ale. Extensive menu for food
lunchtime and evenings. Collections of key
rings, bottles and bottle openers. Garden.
■ **Ye Olde No 3** Bollington Wharf. A very
pretty canalside pub serving John Smith's real
ale and good food *lunchtime and evenings.*
Garden.

Sale

Beyond Seamons Moss Bridge the buildings close in on the canal, and the countryside disappears from view. Among the derelict buildings and graffiti stands the superb Victorian Linotype Factory, dated 1897, where metal printing type was manufactured. Moored by Timperley Bridge are assorted craft of the Sale Cruising Club. The electric suburban railway closes in from the south east and escorts the canal all the way through Sale and on into Stretford – as the trains hurry by you can enjoy a more relaxing 3 mph. There are two convenient canalside pubs before the canal is crossed by the M63 motorway, and then itself crosses the River Mersey. A large expanse of graves heralds the entrance to Stretford, followed by the moorings of the Stretford Boat Club.

Sale
Gt Manchester. EC Wed. All services. A residential suburb of Manchester, transformed from a farming community by the building in 1849 of the Altrincham to Manchester Railway – hence most of its buildings are Victorian or later. St Martin's Church is, however, 18thC and has a hammerbeam roof. The clock tower of the town hall, built in 1914, is a prominent landmark. There are shops close to Sale Bridge (35). The northern part of Sale merges into Ashton Upon Mersey, unremarkable except as the birthplace of Stanley Houghton (1881-1913) who wrote *The Dear Departed* in 1908 and *Hindle Wakes* in 1912.

Altrincham
Gt Manchester. EC Wed. A few black and white half-timbered buildings remain in the market square of what was once a small market town. Later in the 18thC it became a textile manufacturing centre, and is now, inevitably, a dormitory town.

PUBS
🍺 **Bridge Inn** Canalside at Dane Road Bridge. *Shop & launderette nearby.*
🍺 **Railway** Canalside at Sale Bridge. Food.

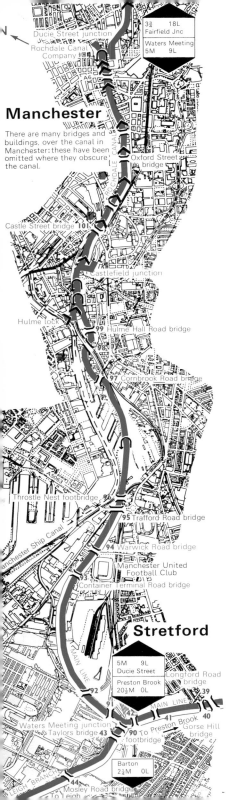

Manchester

At Waters Meeting the original main line of
the canal is joined – to the north west is
Barton, Leigh and the connection with the
Leeds & Liverpool Canal which crosses the
Pennines to Leeds; to the east is the centre of
the Manchester & Rochdale Canal, which
itself, as the name implies, once crossed the
hills to Rochdale before it fell into disuse. The
Bridgewater's route is now hemmed in by
factory walls and fences, passing close to the
Manchester United football ground. The
floodlights of this famous football club tower
above the canal, which passes between the
ground and the massive (and empty) docks of
the Ship Canal. Old Trafford cricket ground,
the home of Lancashire Cricket Club and a
Test Match venue is a little further south. The
Ship Canal is now very close – more empty
docks are passed before Hulme Lock Branch,
which connects the two canals, is reached.
There are moorings here on a narrow isthmus
isolated from the surrounding factories and
roads – it is not particularly attractive, and
trains pass frequently high above, but it is a
safe spot to spend the night before tackling the
locks of the Rochdale and Ashton canals (after
Castlefield Junction the next safe overnight
moorings are at locks 1 & 2 on the Ashton
Canal, or at Portland Basin). The Bridgewater
ends and the short navigable stretch of the
Rochdale begins at Castlefield Junction,
where you pass Britain's first Urban Heritage
Park. The first of the nine wide locks is just
after the bridge. The gear is anti-vandal locked
so you will need to use the British Waterways
anti-vandal key. The canal now passes
between the backs of tall buildings and
beneath elaborate railway arches, all of which
have a certain faded grandeur. Tantalising
glimpses of Victorian buildings invite
exploration, but there is really nowhere to
leave an unattended boat. You can, however,
moor for a rest at the picnic area above the
second lock. Finally the canal crawls under an
18-storey office block where a lock lurks
amidst concrete pillars. The Rochdale Canal
Office is next to the top lock, so if you haven't
already done so, you must pay your licence fee
here, or at the third lock down. Sharp right
and sharp left turns bring you to the start of
the Ashton Canal, and the climb to Fairfield
Junction (see page 132).

Manchester
All services. One of Britain's finest Victorian
cities, a monument to 19thC commerce and the
textile boom. There is an incredible wealth
of Victorian buildings still surviving in spite of
redevelopment – the Town Hall and the
surrounding streets being a particularly rich
area (north of Oxford Street Bridge). St
Peter's Square, by the Town Hall, was the site
of the 'Peterloo Massacre' in 1819, when a
meeting demanding political reform was
brutally dispersed by troops carrying drawn
sabres. Eleven people were killed and many
more were injured. The Free Trade Hall,
home of the Hallé Orchestra, is a little further
along the road. Built in 1856 on the site of the
original Free Trade Hall, it was badly
damaged in World War II, but was
subsequently rebuilt to its original Palladian
design. The old Central Station has now been
converted into a £20 million conference and
exhibition centre called GMex. There is
theatre, ballet and cinema, art galleries, and a
wealth of interesting buildings as well as
Victorian shopping arcades, many pubs with
an excellent choice of good beer, many
excellent restaurants – one being an Indian
tandoori house, in Sackville Street, between
the sixth and seventh lock up – all a short walk
from the canal.
Tourist Information Centre Town Hall
Extension, Lloyd Street, to the north of
Oxford Street Bridge (061-234 3157). Call in
for details of the many attractions in this great
city.
Museum of Science and Industry Liverpool
Road, off Deansgate, to the north of the
bottom lock (061-832 2244). Located on the
site of the world's first passenger railway

station, this exciting 'hands-on' museum has 14 galleries covering everything from steam to space, transport to textiles, and includes a working steam train, a reconstructed Victorian sewer (complete with smells!) and an interactive science centre. *Open daily (except 23 – 25 Dec) 10.00–17.00.* Charge. Coffee shop.

Granada Studios Water Street, close to the Museum of Science and Industry (061-833 0880). An extremely popular attraction, where you can visit Coronation Street, 'Baker Street', '10 Downing Street', The Giants Room, 3D shows, Motion Master cinema and many other highlights. Restaurants and shops. *Open daily 09.45-last entry 16.00 (15.00 Mon-Fri in winter).* Charge.

Metrolink The new electric 'supertram'. Deansgate is the station closest to the canal, near to the second lock, if you fancy a ride. Information on 061-228 1228.

Manchester Ship Canal
The Harbour Master, The Port of Manchester, Manchester Ship Canal Co, Dock Office, Manchester (061-872 2411). The canal was opened in 1894 at a cost of £15 ½ million and carries ships up to 15,000 tonnes displacement. It is 36 miles long and connects the tidal Mersey at Eastham to Manchester. The Weaver Navigation, the Bridgewater and the Shropshire Union connect with it. Pleasure craft wishing to navigate on the Ship Canal must complete an application form demanding stringent standards of seaworthiness (and third party insurance for £50,000), and return it to the Harbour-master at the above address at least *48 hours* before entering the canal.

BOATYARDS

Ⓑ **Lorenz Canal Services** Potato Wharf, Castlefield Basin (061-789 5977). Ⓡ Ⓦ Ⓓ Boat building and repairs, engine repairs. Narrowboat hire from Egerton Narrowboats.

LICENCES

Rochdale Canal Company 75 Dale Street, Manchester (061-236 2456). By the top lock. A licence must be purchased for these important 2 miles of canal, which are usually open during the cruising season from *09.00-17.00 every day.*

PUBS AND RESTAURANTS

There are many fine pubs in Manchester.

🍺 **Peveril of the Peak** Great Bridgewater Street, Manchester. A superbly restored building close to the old entrance to the now abandoned Manchester & Salford Junction Canal. Wilson's and Webster's real ale and good *lunchtime* bar snacks. Children welcome, outdoor drinking area.

🍺 **Crown** Deansgate, Manchester. Comfortable and well appointed pub offering a good choice of *lunchtime* meals and snacks at all times, Wilson's and Webster's real ale. Handy for the Castlefield Heritage Centre and museums.

✕ ❢ **Kathmandu Tandoori** 42-44 Sackville Street, Manchester (061-236 4684). An excellent and reliable Indian restaurant, decorated with Kama Sutra murals. *L & D. Closed B. Hols.*

🍺 **Ordsall** Ordsall Lane, Salford. West of Hulme Locks. A good basic city pub with many others close by. Wilson's real ale, *lunchtime* meals and snacks at all times. Children welcome.

Castlefield, Manchester. *Derek Pratt.*

Worsley

This is a very interesting section of canal, well worth visiting. What was the original line of the canal leaves Waters Meeting through the vast Trafford Park Industrial Estate to cross the Manchester Ship Canal on the impressive Barton Swing Aqueduct (*open 09.00-17.00 every day*). There is a useful boatyard just to the north of the aqueduct – the closest canal services to the city centre. Curving through the suburbs of Salford the navigation reaches the village of Worsley and the entrance to the underground mines which provided its *raison d'être*. It is now possible for small shallow-draughted craft to navigate into the Delph to view the entrance tunnels where iron ore colours the water bright ochre. After Worsley the M62 motorway and its attendant slip roads cross the canal, which then heads west through parkland on its way to Leigh. The winding hole at Boothstown Bridge is full of sunken boats so take care when winding.

Worsley
Gt Manchester. EC Wed. PO, tel, stores, garage. Originally an estate village dating from the 18th-19thC, now recognised as the birthplace of British canals. Coal had been mined in Worsley since the 14thC, originally from the surface, and later by sinking shafts. It is thought that a drainage sough, common in underground workings, may have provided the germ of the idea for an underground canal network to bring the coal out. John Gilbert, the Duke of Bridgewater's agent, probably designed the system, which included an inclined plane on a 1 in 4 gradient. Work started at the same time as the building of the canal to Manchester, and eventually 46 miles of tunnels were hewn out. A particular kind of double-ended tub boat was used underground, called a 'starvationer', carrying up to 12 tons of coal. The old canal basin at Worsley Delph, with its entrance tunnels to the mines, is still intact, and full-length narrowboats can enter the wind – smaller craft can navigate the entrance tunnels. The basin is overlooked by Worsley Old Hall (now a restaurant), the half-timbered Court House and the Lantern Gallery. The church, by George Gilbert Scott, 1846, has a spire decorated with crockets and gargoyles – inside there is a rich collection of monuments to the Dukes of Bridgewater.

Salford
Gt Manchester. Although now merged with Manchester, Salford was granted its charter 80 years before that of its now larger neighbour. It has a fine new university, built in 1967, and a Roman Catholic cathedral dating from 1855. It is, however, most widely known as being the subject of many paintings by the artist L. S. Lowry (1887-1976). It is less widely known that he gained his inspiration by walking the streets of Salford for many years as a rent collector, only painting in the evenings and at weekends – a fact to which he would never willingly admit. There is a wonderful collection of his paintings in Salford Art Gallery, Peel Park.

Eccles
Gt Manchester. EC Wed. All services. Monks Hall Museum, Wellington Road, contains an important collection of Nasmyth machine tools and relics. *Closed Sun.*

Patricroft
Gt Manchester. All services. Here are the Bridgewater Mills, established in 1836 by Nasmyth, who invented the steam hammer.

Barton upon Irwell
Gt Manchester. PO, tel, stores, garage. In an interesting position overlooking the two canals. The richly decorated Catholic church is by Pugin, 1867.

Barton Aqueduct
One of the wonders of the waterways, it carries the Bridgewater Canal over the Manchester Ship Canal. Designed by Sir Edward Leader Williams, it was built in the early 1890s. Gates seal off the 234ft-long 800-ton section that swings at right angles to the Ship Canal over a central island. It replaced Brindley's earlier aqueduct over the Irwell. The aqueduct

operates *daily 09.00-19.00 Mon-Thur, to 21.00 Fri-Sun.*

BOATYARDS

Ⓑ **Worsley Dry Docks** The Boatyard, Worsley (061-793 6767). Ⓦ Moorings, dry dock. Egerton Narrowboats operate from here.

Ⓑ **Brinks Boats** The Old Boatyard, Worsley (061-728 1184). Ⓓ Pump-out (*weekend afternoons*), gas, narrowboat hire.

BOAT TRIPS

Bridgewater Packet Boat Service Operate public trips on *Sun & B. Hols* from Worsley, Timperley and Manchester. Also private charter. Ring 061-748 2680 for details.

PUBS AND RESTAURANTS

🍺 **Bridgewater Hotel** Worsley. Canalside.

✕ ❢ **Worsley Old Hall** Old Lane, Worsley (061-799 5644). Choose from a French à la carte restaurant, or a 17thC-style Jacobean banquet. James Brindley stayed in this building while working on the new canal. *L (not Sat) & D (not Sun).*

🍺 **Bridgewater Packet House** By bridge 47. A cosy corner pub serving Boddingtons real ale and *lunchtime* bar meals. *Open 19.00 Sat.*

🍺 **Dutton Arms** Barton Road, Barton. A large canalside pub which features original plans for the Manchester Ship Canal. Boddingtons real ale and *lunchtime* bar meals. Children allowed in at lunchtime (ask).

🍺 **King's Head Hotel** 535 Barton Lane, Eccles. Near the swing aqueduct. Large open-plan pub offering good home-cooked food at *lunchtime*. Boddingtons real ale, outside dining area. *Opens 19.00 Sat.*

🍺✕ **Bargee Inn and Pearl River Cantonese Restaurant** By bridge 50 (061-788 8788). A canalside pub with restaurant attached offering Cantonese and English food *lunchtime and evenings*. Hartleys and Robinson's real ales. Children's play area and canalside patio.

Worsley, on the Bridgewater Canal. Iron ore colours the water bright ochre here. *Derek Pratt.*

Leigh

After the excitement of Barton and Worsley, the canal now passes through open farmland towards the mill town of Leigh, and its junction with the Leeds & Liverpool Canal. Raised canal banks beyond Boothshall Bridge reveal the problems of subsidence in this area, caused by mine workings. The old colliery village of Astley Green is passed, and at Leigh the canal becomes the Leeds & Liverpool. The familiar stop plank cranes of the Bridgewater finish here, and signs announce you are back in British Waterways territory. Wigan is 7¼ miles away (see page 94).

Leigh
Gt Manchester. EC Wed. All services. Once the archetypal mill town, most of the tall buildings and chimneys have now been demolished. In the market place you can see the fine Edwardian baroque Town Hall, built 1904-7, facing the battlemented church of St Mary.

Astley Green
Gt Manchester. PO, tel, stores. Canalside mining village dominated by a gaunt red-brick Victorian church.

PUBS

● **Bull's Head** Butts Bridge, Leigh. Canalside local serving John Smith's real ale and *lunchtime* meals. Garden, accommodation.

● **Foundry** 276 Chapel Street, Butts Bridge, Leigh. Autograph hunters' pub run by ex-England footballer, Alex Lindsay. Greenall Whitley real ale.

● **Railway Hotel** Twist Lane, Leigh. A beer enthusiast's pub offering Tetley's, Jennings and Ind Coope (Burton) real ales. *Opens 12.00 & 19.00 (sometimes later).*

● **Bridge Inn** 7 St Helen's Road, Leigh. The licensee of this large, quiet and comfortable pub is a waterways enthusiast. Greenall Whitley real ale and a good range of *lunchtime* food.

● **George & Dragon** King Street, Leigh. A recently refurbished pub with a wide choice of food at *lunchtime*. Greenall Whitley real ale. Can be busy in the evening.

● **Cart & Horses** Town Lane, north of bridge 59. Holt real ale in a friendly pub.

● **Boat House Inn** By bridge 58.

CHESTERFIELD

Maximum dimensions

Length: 72'
Beam: 7'
Headroom: 7' 6"
(Craft of 8'6" beam *may* be able to proceed as far as Clayworth, depending on the height of the superstructure).

Manager

(0636 704481)

Mileage

WEST STOCKWITH to
Drakeholes Tunnel: 6½
Haydon: 12
Retford Lock: 15¼
Osberton Lock: 22¼
WORKSOP Town Lock: 25½

Locks: 16

The Chesterfield Canal was initially surveyed, in 1768, by John Varley to follow a line between Chesterfield and Bawtry on the River Idle, as an improvement on the trade route already in use. However, both Worksop and Retford were anxious to benefit from the proposed waterway, so Varley undertook a second survey, a year later, along a route to West Stockwith that bypassed the Idle altogether.

In 1769 James Brindley who had, due to pressure of other work, delegated the initial survey to Varley, called a public meeting at the Red Lion in Worksop. Here he proposed a draft line, terminating near Gainsborough and costing £105,000. This was later re-amended, on the grounds of cost and speed of construction, to meet the Trent at West Stockwith.

Work started in October 1771 with John Varley as resident engineer, Brindley being still too busy with other schemes to be permanently on site. Most of the work, including digging the 2893yd long Norwood Tunnel, constructing the summit level reservoir, and building the lock flights, was let as separate contracts and carried out by individual contractors. Brindley's method was to make each section of the canal navigable as soon as it was completed to enable the company to benefit from the carriage of the heavy construction materials.

Brindley's death in September 1772 was a sad blow to the project and led to Varley being placed in overall charge of this, his first large project. Ultimately Hugh Henshall, Brindley's brother-in-law, was made inspector of works, later to become chief engineer with a salary of £250 per annum. In the following year he discovered work, carried out by John Varley's father and two brothers, in the construction of Norwood Tunnel, to be unsatisfactory. Soon other examples of dubious contractual arrangements and slack management came to light, all reflecting badly on the Varley family. The extent of John Varley's complicity in these matters remains to this day a matter for debate.

On 4th June 1777 the canal was officially opened from West Stockwith to Chesterfield. Norwood Tunnel caused problems from the outset, as did the shortage of water to the summit pound. Boats travelling less than 12 miles empty, or lightly ladened, were penalised when using a lock. Over the next 25 years a more satisfactory solution was provided by the building of three large reservoirs at Killamarsh, Woodhall and Harthill.

As had always been envisaged by the canal's promoters, coal was the principal cargo carried, followed by stone, corn, lime, lead, timber and iron. Pottery and ale were also regular cargoes. Traffic peaked at over 200,000 tons in 1848, while records show the average load as 22 tons. Early in 1840 a cargo of Anston Stone, bound for the construction of the new Houses of Parliament, was carried for transhipment at West Stockwith: the first of approximately 250,000 tons despatched altogether. As always, amalgamation with a railway com-pany, in this case the Manchester & Lincoln Union Railway, led to a steady decline in the canal's fortunes and a reduction in maintenance. By 1904 it was reported that the minimum headroom in Norwood Tunnel was reduced to 4' 10", owing to subsidence, while a roof collapse in 1907 led to its final closure.

Between the wars, now under LNER ownership, the canal was reasonably maintained, while the tidal lock into the Trent was enlarged and repaired in 1923-5. Attempts were also made to reduce the weed which had appeared in 1852 and remains, to some extent, a problem today. The navigation was temporarily resuscitated by the transport of munitions during the Second World War, but traffic virtually came to an end in 1955 when the small trade from Walkeringham brickworks (near Gringley) to the Trent finished. One cargo that did linger on into the early 1960s was that of 'warp': a fine natural silt dredged from the Trent at Idle Mouth and used as a metal polishing material in the Sheffield cutlery trade. To the end all boats remained horse-drawn.

On 24th May 1960 a public enquiry into the canal's future was held in Chesterfield at which BW proposed the retention of the waterway from the Trent to Worksop for pleasure boating. The remainder was to be either utilised for water supply or infilled. The 1968 Transport act finally confirmed its status as a cruiseway.

By 1976 it was generally considered desirable that the waterway be restored beyond Worksop and the Chesterfield Canal Society was formed with the ultimate aim of full restoration to Chesterfield. Work on the western end is moving on rapidly, aided by a great deal of volunteer work, together with industrial and European Community money. The major difficulties remaining are the restoration of Norwood Tunnel and by-passing the houses built on the infilled line at Killamarsh.

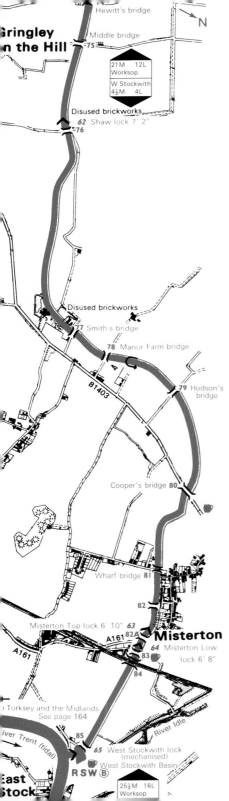

Map labels:

Hewitt's bridge

Gringley on the Hill

Middle bridge

75

N

21M 12L
Worksop

W Stockwith
4½M 4L

Disused brickworks

62 Shaw lock 7' 2"

76

Disused brickworks

77 Smith's bridge

78 Manor Farm bridge

B1403

79 Hodson's bridge

Cooper's bridge 80

Wharf bridge 81

82

Misterton Top lock 6' 10" 63

A161 82A

A161

Misterton

83 64 Misterton Low lock 6' 8"

84

To Torksey and the Midlands
See page 164

85

River Idle

River Trent (tidal)

65 West Stockwith lock (mechanised)

R S W B West Stockwith Basin

East Stock

25½M 16L
Worksop

West Stockwith

The church spire of East Stockwith stands opposite the entrance to the Chesterfield Canal, just downstream of a sharp bend in the River Trent. The lock here is power-operated. Just above the lock is a basin housing a boatyard, a boat club, a slipway (apply to the lock keeper), and plenty of moored pleasure boats. A pub is nearby. This is obviously an excellent safe mooring to keep a sea-going boat. Leaving the basin for the gradual 15-lock rise to Worksop, the navigator must notice the tremendous contrast between the great tideway of the River Trent and this little canal, picking its way through the countryside. At Misterton there are two locks close together, with a canalside pub at the bottom. The canal's passage through the village is a pleasant one. At the new Cooper's Bridge the canal emerges into quiet farmland, heading south towards and then along the ridge of low hills that is capped by the village of Gringley. There are two disused brickyards along here – they supplied the canal with its last commercial traffic, sending bricks to Stockwith for the Trent Navigation. The yards were closed down in 1955. The course of the canal is entirely rural and pleasant, passing well-established but often decaying farm buildings that are mostly built of the rich red brick that is so common in north Nottinghamshire.

Navigational note
Entering the canal from the Trent can be tricky due to the tidal flow across the entrance to the lock. Whilst it is possible to turn into the tide and steer across into the mouth of the lock, the simplest way is to come alongside the wall on the upstream (Torksey) side of the lock where there is current-free water and a ladder. Once the lock is set ready it is easy, with the aid of a line, to walk the boat into the chamber. The lock is keeper operated (give as much prior notice as possible by ringing 0427 890204) and passage can usually be made 2½ hours before to 4½ hours after high water. By coincidence Flood at Stockwith (when the tide ceases ebbing and turns to come back in) is the same time as high water at Hull. The Flood runs for approximately 2½ hours and the direction of flow changes very rapidly. VHF radio frequencies: calling channel 16, working channel 74. The radio is not constantly manned.

Gringley on the Hill
Notts. PO, tel, stores. Situated along the top of a ridge of hills, the village is about a mile's walk up from the canal. Its high situation is emphasised by the tower of the old windmill. Gringley is a quiet and attractive place with plenty of handsome, mellow houses. The pretty stone church commands the village. Its most striking aspect inside is probably the north side of the nave, whose arches are leaning drastically outwards. A small rise on a level with the church tower gives a good view – over the flat lands to the north and the hills of Nottinghamshire to the south. On a clear day the pinnacles of Lincoln Cathedral can sometimes be seen, nearly 20 miles to the south east.

Misterton
Notts. PO, tel, stores, garage. Although attractive from the canal, this village is not really very fascinating. The pub is in the older part, which surrounds the curiously shaped church; a stubby spire stands heavily beside its rather low, flat nave roof. It was rebuilt in the 19thC after being struck by lightning. The village also has a thriving Methodist church, as do most of the places in this area. John Wesley came from nearby Epworth.

West Stockwith
Notts. PO, tel, stores. An interesting riverside village at the junction not only of the Chesterfield Canal with the Trent but also of the River Idle with the Trent. The Idle was once a busy navigation up to Bawtry, so West Stockwith must have been a very prosperous port in days gone by. The village extends along the west bank of the River Trent, although bank raising measures over the years have shut out a view of the river from ground level. The houses are old, and remind one of a typical

coastal village. The plain 18thC brick church preserves the illusion. East Stockwith is just across the river, tantalisingly out of reach. The two communities used to be connected by a ferry, but, as so often on this river, the ferry has vanished. In a way, the total lack of communication with the other village, only 50yds away, serves to enhance the magical sense of remoteness that Stockwith possesses – especially when one sees the big barges appearing round the bend on every tide, churning past the two villages and then as quickly disappearing again.

Miniature World Museum West Stockwith (0427 890450). A fascinating collection of more than 40 dolls houses dating back over three centuries, together with a whole world in miniature, occupying the entire ground floor of a private house. Will captivate even the most hard bitten. Also home-made teas. *Closed Jan.* Charge.

PUBS

🍺 **Blue Bell** 1 mile from the canal, in Gringley. Small and simple local serving Stones, Bass and Tetley's real ale. Snacks, games room. Children welcome in the garden where there are animals and games. *Closed Mon to Thur lunchtime.*

🍺 **Red Hart** Misterton, near the church. John Smith's and Ruddles real ale. Patio area. Pool table. Snacks *(not Sun, Mon, Tue evenings).*

🍺 **Packet Inn** Canalside at Misterton Low Lock. A lively and welcoming pub dispensing Tetley's and Bass real ale. Good choice of reasonably priced meals available, including vegetarian, *lunchtime and evenings (not Mon lunchtime).* Beer garden. Music *Thur evenings.*

🍺 **Crown** Canalside at West Stockwith Basin.

🍺 **White Hart** West Stockwith by the junction of the rivers Idle and Trent.

🍺 **Waterfront Inn** Canalside at West Stockwith Basin. A smart pub serving Ruddles, Webster's and Theakston real ale together with excellent food and their own organically grown vegetables. *(No food Sun evenings).*

Drakeholes Tunnel on the Chesterfield Canal. *Derek Pratt.*

Clayworth

This is a thoroughly delightful stretch of canal. Leaving Gringley Top Lock, the navigation goes along the bottom of the ridge of hills, before turning sharply south east and heading for Drakeholes Tunnel (154yds). All the way from Gringley to Drakeholes the canal is heavily overhung by trees. Plenty of wildlife lives here near the water's edge, especially coots, moorhens, water rats, and bats. It is very secluded, but the intimate feeling of the thickly wooded cutting preceding the tunnel has been ruined by the construction of a large road bridge. The tunnel is cut through rock and is mostly unlined. At the south end one emerges to find a sharp corner at a mooring site, where there is also a turning place for full-length narrowboats, and a slipway owned by the Retford & Worksop Boat Club. A handsome pub stands nearby. Leaving Drakeholes, the canal is still accompanied by woods as it reaches Wiseton Park, passing the stern features of a bearded man on the parapet of Old Man Bridge. The canal now skirts an attractive courtyard housing development built on the site of the park's old walled kitchen garden. The brick from the enclosing walls has been put to good use in the construction of many of the houses. The straight road that crosses the canal at Gray's Bridge is of Roman origin. The navigation circles round the village, ending with a sharp turn to the right at Clayworth Bridge. The white building by the bridge used to be a pub (The White Hart). It is now a boat club base, so a good look-out for other boats should be maintained when negotiating the bridge.

Clayworth
Notts. PO, tel, stores. A quiet and pleasant village extending along a single main street. The houses are of all periods, the new blending well with the old. The Retford & Worksop Boat Club is based at the old pub at Clayworth and welcomes visitors to the clubhouse. There are good moorings and a water tap here. In the old days a passenger boat used to run every Saturday from this pub to Retford, so that the villagers of Clayworth, Hayton and Clarborough could take their produce to Retford Market. The goods were loaded into the 'packet' boat on the Friday night, then the people would return early on Saturday morning, leaving at 06.30 to reach Retford by 08.30. The boat used to return in the evening when the market closed. A handsome sundial sits over the porch of the pretty village church inscribed with the words 'Our days on earth are as a shadow'. Inside there is a series of beautiful wall paintings.

Wiseton
Notts. Tel. A superbly elegant estate village set in a landscaped park, still clearly fulfilling its original manorial function. Trees and grass separate the various buildings, of which the large stable with its handsome clock tower is the most significant. The hall, a modern red brick building, which replaced the original in 1962, is well hidden behind high walls.

PUBS

🍺 **Brewers Arms** Clayworth. Unadulterated village local serving Tolly Cobbold and Everards real ale. Bar snacks available (*not Mon*).

🍺 **Blacksmith's Arms** Clayworth. A nicely kept village pub with a good choice of real ale including Stones, Bass, Tetley's and Castle Eden. Meals are available *lunchtime and evenings* in both the bar and restaurant, both of which offer an interesting choice, including vegetarian. Children welcome.

🍺 **Griff Inn** Canalside at Drakeholes Tunnel. A smart and fairly pricey establishment serving Castle Eden and Tetley's real ale. There is an extensive bar menu, offering a good choice for vegetarians, as well as a carvery and restaurant. *Food available lunchtime and evenings (Carvery closed Mon-Wed evenings).* Outside seating. Children welcome.

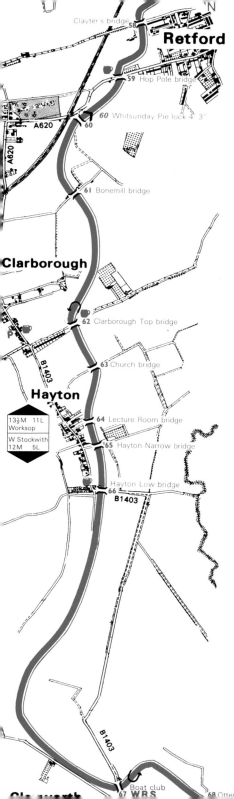

Hayton

The canal now leaves the woods and low hills to the north and heads southwards through more open farmland towards Retford. From Clayworth to Hayton there is a 2-mile stretch without a single bridge, only green fields and hedgerows accompanying the navigation on its quiet course. Approaching Hayton, there is a pub by the bridge and a succession of old farms and bridges – one of them extremely narrow. Near one of these bridges is the very ancient stone church. At Clarborough Wharf there is another canalside pub, with good moorings. South of here the railway embankment draws near as the canal arrives at the first lock for 9 miles. Whitsunday Pie Lock is apparently so called because a local farmer's wife baked a vast pie on Whit Sunday for the navvies who had that day completed construction of the lock. This lock is the last wide lock on the canal as one travels towards Worksop. The cottage near the lock was built this century, of bricks fired at the brickyards near Gringley and, naturally, brought to this site by canal boat. Sadly its charm is now cloaked in render and concrete roofing tiles, set off by picture windows and a flat roofed extension. Yet another canalside pub is soon encountered, before the navigation begins to follow its circuitous course round East Retford.

Clarborough
Notts. PO, tel, stores, garage. An unexciting village straggling along the main road.
Hayton
Notts. Tel. Once a quiet farming village, stretching along the road parallel to the canal, it is fast becoming a dormitory area of housing estates for Retford. The church, with its sandstone tower now badly eroded, stands on a quiet lane, near Church bridge No. 63 and dates from 1120. In nearby Bolham, where the local inhabitants once lived in caves hewn in the rock, there are the remains of an ancient chapel.

PUBS

🍺 **Hop Pole Inn** Canalside at Hop Pole Bridge (A620). Stones real ale. Snacks *lunchtime Mon-Sat.* Carvery *lunchtime and evenings.* Garden and play park. Good moorings for patrons.
🍺 **Gate** Canalside at Clarborough, offering Flowers, Castle Eden, Boddingtons and a guest real ale. Bar snacks available *lunchtime and evenings (not Sun evenings).* Attractive outside seating and play area. Regular quiz nights and bingo. Overnight moorings for patrons.
🍺 **Kings Arms** Clarborough. Small village local serving Castle Eden and Whitbread real ale. Bar meals *lunchtime and evenings.* Garden and play area. Quiz night is *Thur.* Fish & chips opposite.
🍺 **Boat Inn** Canalside near Hayton Low Bridge. A popular, nicely kept pub offering Bass, Stones and Castle Eden real ale. A wide range of reasonably priced food (including vegetarian) is available in the bar and carvery *lunchtime and evenings (carvery closed Mon evenings).* Garden and play area.

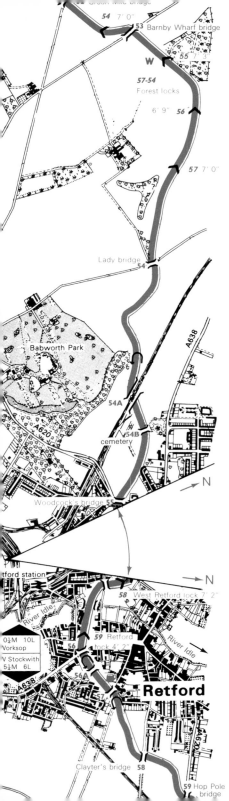

Retford

The canal's twisting passage through Retford
is outstandingly pleasant – though not by
design. It just happens that almost all the way
through the town, the canal is accompanied by
green – either grazing fields, or common land,
or water meadows (however unkempt), or at
the west end of the town by a long and
treelined cemetery. In the town centre one
encounters the first of the narrow locks, with a
large canal warehouse beside it. West of here
the canal crosses three minute aqueducts, then
a double bend and an old iron footbridge lead
to West Retford Lock, overlooked by large
trees and old houses. Beyond the main road
bridge the canal is still lined by trees and
bushes as it invades the very middle of the
extensive cemetery. The busy East Coast
railway line crosses here, and while the
navigation now begins to meander through
open farmland, the noise of the frequent
express trains thundering along the track takes
a long time to recede. In the open countryside
along here are the four Forest Locks. At the
third one up is a British Waterways permanent
mooring site; and there is a water point right
beside the top gate. The straight road crossing
at the nearby Barnby Wharf Bridge was a
Roman highway. It was, in fact, the original
course of the Great North Road; but 200 years
ago the citizens of Retford got the road
diverted to pass through their town, thereby
increasing its importance and prosperity.
They must now be equally relieved to have rid
themselves of it again.

East Retford
Notts. EC Mon, Wed. MD Sat. All services. A
market town with good railway connections
(passenger services in four directions) and
light industry. There is a funfair held on *23
March* and a sheep fair on *2 October.* The
market square is the only area of any interest
in Retford, and this is indeed superb, with lots
of cheerfully uneven Georgian terraced houses
jumbled up with lesser, newer buildings. All
are put to shame by the flamboyant Town
Hall, built in 1868. In front of it is a stone
called the Broad Stone, and when a plague
raged in the town many years ago people
making cash transactions would put their
coins into a vinegar-filled vessel on this
pedestal. The vendor picking the money out of
the vinegar thus ran less risk of catching the
disease from the purchaser, it was thought.
East Retford Church A splendid cruciform
structure of great dignity and elegance, all set
about with battlements, pinnacles, and fine
foliate ornament. The nave is tall, and
incorporates a generous clerestory giving light
to the interior, while there is a peal of 10 bells
in the tower. Outside, the church is guarded
by a mean-looking black 24-pounder cannon,
captured at Sebastopol in 1858.
Bessetlaw Museum 40 Grove Street,
Retford (0777 706741). Local history. *Open
10.00-17.00 Mon-Sat. Closed Sun & B. Hols.*

PUBS AND RESTAURANTS

🍺 **Clinton Arms** Retford. Not far from
Retford Lock. John Smith's real ale and bar
snacks. Family room.
✕🍺 **White Hart Hotel** The Market Place,
Retford (0777 703671). A 17thC posting
house serving real ale. Bar snacks available
Mon-Sat lunchtime only.
🍺 **Hop Pole** Canalside, Welham Road,
Retford. Stones and Bass real ale. Snacks and
meals available *lunchtime and evenings.*
Children welcome.
🍺 **Packet Inn** Canalside at Gas House
Bridge, Retford. This used to be the terminus
for the weekly market boat from Clayworth. A
basic but friendly local with pub games.
✕🍺 **Mississippi** Canalside at Gas House
Bridge. Restaurant and bars serving Stones
and Tetley's real ale.
🍺 **Market Hotel** West Carr Road, Retford.
Real ale enthusiasts will have difficulty
choosing at a bar which offers 18 different
brews. Food available in the bar and
restaurant *lunchtime and evenings.* Vegetarians
catered for.

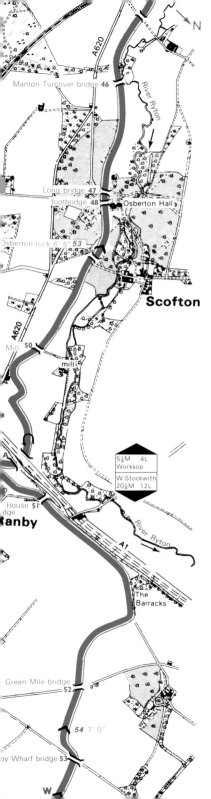

Osberton Park

Leaving Forest Top Lock, the canal now wanders westwards before turning sharply south as it meets the noisy A1 road. There used to be a big army barracks here during the 1914-18 War, but now only a small cottage survives as a reminder. The road follows the canal very closely for over ½ a mile, and its presence is deafening. Fortunately a thick hedge serves to screen it. At Ranby the canal begins once again to follow a winding course, passing under the A1 before making for the haven of Osberton Park. The little lock here, where the towpath crosses over, introduces one of the most attractive stretches of the whole canal, passing through a country estate, which looks as carefully maintained now as it doubtless did in the 18thC. The canal goes straight past the stables at Osberton Hall. Manton railway viaduct, consisting of low but heavily braced red-brick arches, dwarfs the little accommodation bridge over the canal. Nearby the long-standing pit heaps of Manton Colliery have been landscaped and grassed.

Osberton Hall Built in 1806 by James Wyatt and enlarged and altered in 1853 (Private).
Scofton
Notts. This is the tiny estate village for Osberton Hall. It looks decayed now, but the old stable block is impressive, and this is surmounted by a clock tower. The church, built in 1830, has been completely restored, at great expense. All the roof lead has been renewed, the windows have been rebuilt, a new red carpet has been laid, and central heating has been installed. The inside of the church now looks brand new, and for the visitor is a refreshing sight.
Ranby
Notts. Tel, garage (on A1). A small rambling village which manages to retain some charm in spite of being practically on top of the A1. The willow trees that line the canal bank near the village are the gesture of a local tree-loving landowner. There is a pub on the canal, the only one for miles in either direction.

PUBS AND RESTAURANTS

✗ ▭ **Chequers** Canalside at Ranby. A smart, newly furbished pub dispensing Castle Eden, Boddingtons and Marston's real ale. An interesting menu is offered in both the bar and the attractive restaurant *lunchtime and evenings.* Vegetarians catered for. An outside terrace overlooks the canal. Children welcome in the restaurant.

Worksop

Leaving Manton Colliery the canal now negotiates two locks before reaching Worksop. The canal's course into Worksop is fairly open, as the towpath is also a minor public road. There is a canal pub along here, and a good place to tie up for the Canal Tavern is at either side of the old Pickford's warehouse that straddles the canal. One can still see the trapdoors above the water where the goods used to be hauled straight up out of the boats. Worksop Town Lock is by the yard. Just beyond the lock, the navigation is very narrow for a short stretch. The remaining 20 miles of the canal to Chesterfield is no longer a through navigation although parts have been restored. At the turn of the century there was little trade on the canal, and the 2893yd tunnel on the summit level at Norwood collapsed because of mining subsidence. There is an attractive walk along the towpath of the old canal, and there are good railway connections from Worksop and Retford with the canalside stations of Kiveton Park and

Shireoaks. The unnavigable section of the canal still feeds water into the navigable section.

Navigational note
The winding hole above Worksop Town Lock is suitable for full length (70ft) craft.

Worksop
Notts. EC Thur. MD Wed, Sat. All services. An unlovely town in the centre of the north Nottinghamshire coal field – which has contributed much to the present prosperity and ugliness of the area. However, as if in defiance of this overall description, in 1990 the town won a prestigious national street design award for its pedestrianised centre. Here the crests of the five dukes, that give the area its name, are depicted in mellow stone setts within the paving. Old buildings of note in Worksop are the Priory and its gatehouse.
7 Blythe Grove Worksop. When William and Walter Straw's father died in 1932, the brothers kept his house, which he bought in 1932, as a shrine. They altered nothing. In 1991 William died and left the property, with a legacy of £1.5 million, to the National Trust. They have preserved this time capsule, restoring only as necessary, and opened it to visitors. *Enquire at the TIC for information regarding viewing.*
The Priory Near Prior Well Bridge. The church dates from the 12thC, although it suffered badly under Henry VIII's policy towards monasteries. Much rebuilding has taken place since then: in fact from 1970-2 the superstructure was added to, incorporating a new spire. There are interesting paintings and monuments inside the church, and a gruesome relic from Sherwood Forest – a skull with the tip of an arrow embedded in it.
14thC Gatehouse This was given to the priory under a trust by the Duke of Newcastle.
Tourist Information Centre Worksop Library, Memorial Avenue, Worksop (0909 501148).

Within a few miles of the town there are some interesting places and some beautiful countryside to visit, although a car or a bicycle is needed to reach them. All around are the surviving woods of Sherwood Forest, while to the south of the town is the area called the Dukeries, each of the adjacent estates of Thoresby, Clumber and Welbeck having been owned by a duke. Welbeck is now an army college, Thoresby Hall and Park are open to the public. Clumber House was demolished in 1938, but the Park, owned by the National Trust, is one of its most visited properties. There are superb avenues of trees in this park. Three miles west of Worksop is an outstanding building well worth visiting. This is the tiny Steetley Chapel, which has been described by one expert as 'the most perfect and elaborate specimen of Norman architecture to be found anywhere in Europe'. There is a delightfully elaborate triple rounded porch and a beautiful apse. The windows are very narrow, so the interior is dark. Contact the local vicar if you wish to see it.

BOATYARDS

British Waterways Worksop Yard (0909 472788).

PUBS

🍺 **The Riverside** Just above the town lock, Worksop. An establishment which is popular with young people. Discos, pool table.
🍺 **Canal Tavern** Canalside, Worksop. Originally called the Gas Tavern, as the gas works were close by. Bar meals *lunchtime only.* Pizzas available *evenings.* Moorings for patrons.
🍺 **French Horn** Potter Street, Worksop. ⅓ mile south of Town Lock. A basic town pub with an elaborate Edwardian façade. Stones real ale.
🍺 **Golden Ball** Next to Town Lock. Once known as the Red Lion. It was here that the first public meeting was held to discuss the building of the canal.
🍺 **Fisherman's Arms** Church Walk, Worksop. 100yds south of the BW yard. Home real ale.

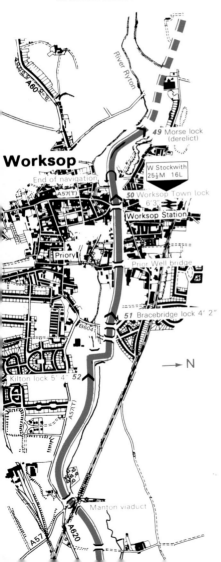

Worksop

EREWASH

Maximum dimensions

Trent Lock to Tamworth Road Bridge
Length: 78'
Beam: 14' 3"
Headroom: 7' 4"
Tamworth Road Bridge to Langley Mill
Length: 72'
Beam: 14' 3"
Headroom: 6'

Mileage

TRENT LOCK to
Sandiacre Lock: 3¼
Hallam Fields Lock: 5½
LANGLEY MILL: 11¾

Locks: 15

Manager

(0509) 212792

The Erewash is one of five canals built towards the end of the 18thC to carry coal from the pits of the Nottinghamshire/Derbyshire coalfield to the towns of the East Midlands. Completed in 1779 by the engineer John Varley, its success encouraged the promotion and construction, during the following decade, of the Cromford, Nottingham, Derby and Nutbrook Canals. The Erewash Canal is navigable for its entire 11¾-mile length from the River Trent to Langley Mill. Unlike its neighbours, the Cromford and Nottingham canals, the Erewash never came under railway control but remained independent until its absorption into the Grand Union system in 1932.

Nationalisation of the canals in 1947 brought the Erewash Canal under the administration of the British Transport Commission, and in 1962 this body closed to navigation the upper section from Gallows Inn to Langley Mill. The need to supply water to the lower section for navigation and industry, however, meant that the upper section had still to be maintained, and boats were allowed to navigate it upon application to the Commission and subsequently to its successor, the British Waterways Board. With the cessation of narrowboat carrying in 1952, such boats had been few, but the growing interest in pleasure boating resulted in more and more craft venturing up the canal from the popular River Trent. With increased use the canal gradually improved, and the news that the major portion of it was to be designated a 'remainder' waterway in the impending 1968 Transport Act was received locally with dismay. A public meeting led to the formation of the Erewash Canal Preservation and Development Association (ECPDA), a body consisting of representatives of boating and fishing interests, residents and local authorities. The need to convince local authorities of the value of the canal as an amenity was recognised at a very early stage, and the association's efforts eventually met with success when in 1972 Derbyshire and Nottinghamshire County Councils agreed to share the cost, with the British Waterways Board, of the restoration of the canal to 'cruising waterway' standards.

Sandiacre Lock. *David Perrott.*

Long Eaton

The Erewash Canal leaves the Trent
Navigation at Trent Lock, a fascinating
waterway junction. A long line of moored boats,
including several houseboats nestling in the
shade of the willow trees, stretches from this
junction for nearly ½ mile. To the south can be
seen the towers of Ratcliffe Power Station,
peeping over the top of Red Hill. At the two
railway bridges is the concealed entrance to an
interesting basin; known as Sheetstores Basin,
this was an important railway depot where the
tarpaulin sheets for covering railway wagons
were made and repaired. Present day synthetic
materials have now rendered tarpaulin obsolete
in this field. The basin was used for
transhipment of coal between boats and trains;
now it is full of pleasure boats, for a boatyard
and a boat club are based here. North of this
basin one sees the first of many canalside
gardens that use the canal as a perfect
background. Approaching Long Eaton, the
canal passes under the A453 and then runs right
beside it, a pleasant, tree-lined urban
boulevard. The centre of Long Eaton is
conveniently close. North of Long Eaton Lock
the old lace mills with their ornamental capped
chimneys overshadow the navigation. To the
east is the little River Erewash, which despite its
name is not joined by the canal at any point. At
Sandiacre is the only surviving lock cottage on
the Erewash Canal (now the base of the
ECPDA), and this lock is particularly
significant because the Derby Canal used to
branch off here. The Derby Canal Company
shared this toll office until 1832, when they
built their own lock house on the opposite bank
of their canal, by the bridge. North of the big
concrete bridge carrying the A52 is Sandiacre;
just through the bridge is a delightfully
landscaped free overnight mooring, with a
properly kept lawn, flower beds and young
trees. All services are nearby. Nearly a mile
further on is Pasture Lock, in a pleasant setting
between the partly hidden railway sidings and
some water meadows. The towpath is in
excellent condition along the whole length of the
navigation.

Navigational note
Trent Lock should always be left *full*, with the
top gates open, except when there is much
traffic about. This will ensure that any flotsam
coming down the canal is able to escape over the
bottom gates.

Derby Canal
The closure of the Derby Canal ended Derby's
link with the navigable waterways which dated
back to the time when the Danes sailed up the
River Derwent to found the settlement of
Deoraby. Navigation of the Derwent was never
easy – the absence of navigation works and,
later, the construction of water mills were
obviously a great handicap – but it was not until
1796, with the completion of the canal, that
navigation on the river ceased. The main line of
the Derby Canal commenced at Swarkestone
on the River Trent. Four locks, which like all
the rest were built to take Upper Trent barges,
lifted the canal to a junction with the Trent &
Mersey Canal. A ¼-mile section of this canal
was then used with the Derby Canal
recommencing just before Swarkestone Lock.
The main line then continued into Derby,
where it crossed the Derwent on the level, and
terminated at Little Eaton. A 9-mile-long
branch ran from Derby to connect with the
Erewash Canal at Sandiacre, and a short
navigable feeder connected with the upper
Derwent. The southern section (from Derby to
the Trent) was an early casualty due to the
double tolls payable on the Trent & Mersey,
and the abandonment of the length to Little
Eaton followed in 1935. The rest of the canal
survived until 1964, when a Warrant of
Abandonment was granted to the Derby Canal
Company.

Long Eaton
Derbs. EC Thur. MD Fri, Sat. All services. The
town is an important junction for canals,
railways and roads, and has little intrinsic

character of its own. Its prosperity was based on the lace trade – nearby Nottingham has for a long time been the national centre of this industry. Long Eaton has an annual festival in *May*.

Trent Lock

An important waterway junction and a long-established boating centre. For motorists, Trent Lock is at the dead end of a narrow lane – but they flock there, for it has great charm and two fine pubs. Sailing clubs on the Trent fill and confuse the scene here; while across the river the steep wooded slopes of Red Hill are overlooked by the steaming towers of Ratcliffe Power Station. The busy railway line to the south disappears into the hill via two splendid blackened portals. Boats navigating the Trent in this rather complicated area should beware of straying too near Thrumpton Weir.

BOATYARDS

Ⓑ **Wyvern Marine** Sheet Stores Basin, Field Farm Road, Long Eaton (0602 726539). Ⓡ Ⓢ Ⓦ Overnight mooring, long-term mooring, crane, slipway, boat building, DIY repair facilities, toilets, licensed club.
Ⓑ **Mills Dockyard** Trent Lock, Long Eaton (0602 733657). Ⓦ Overnight mooring, long-

term mooring, winter storage, dry dock, boat building, boat and engine repairs.
Ⓑ **Sawley Bridge Marina** Trent Lock, Long Eaton (0602 734278). Ⓦ Ⓟ Ⓓ Pump-out, gas, day hire boats, extensive moorings, 2 slipways, 18 ton crane, chandlery, boat sales, engine sales, café, toilet, showers. Maintain a watch on VHF.
Ⓑ **Davison Boat Builders** Trent Lock, Long Eaton (0602 734643). Boat building and fitting out, dry dock, moorings.

PUBS AND RESTAURANTS

◼ **Barge Inn** On the B6540 south of Long Eaton Lock. Friendly games-orientated pub with a skittle alley and several pool tables. Shipstone's real ale.
◼ **Navigation Inn** Trent Lock. Large popular pub with a fine riverside garden. Home real ale and *lunchtime* food.
◼✕ **Steamboat Inn** Trent Lock, on the Erewash Canal (0602 732606). Built by the canal company in 1791, when it was called the Erewash Navigation Inn, it is now a busy and popular venue. The bars have been handsomely restored and decorated with suitably nautical objects. Real ale. Bar and restaurant meals *lunchtime and evenings*. Garden, playground, children welcome.

Long Eaton, Erewash Canal. *Derek Pratt.*

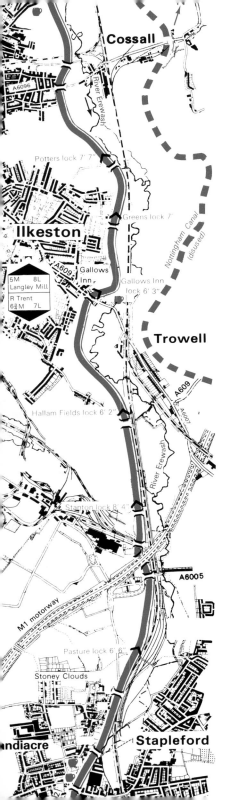

Ilkeston

At Stanton Gate the M1 motorway looms up
and then crosses the canal on its way to
Sheffield. The outskirts of Ilkeston loom up
on the left side while, across the shallow
Erewash valley, the course of the disused
Nottingham Canal appears from the east,
twisting along the contours of the hillside.
Like the Erewash Canal, its course is generally
northerly, but the two waterways do not meet
until Langley Mill. Meanwhile the Erewash
Canal passes extensive low-lying playing fields
before reaching the pub at Gallows Inn Lock
with PO and stores nearby. North of Gallows
Inn, the canal passes housing estates on one
side and water meadows and a main line
railway on the other. The town of Ilkeston is
on the hillside on the west side of the canal. In
spite of its proximity to these built-up areas,
the canal is relatively unspoiled, and
surprisingly rural.

Cossall
Notts. Tel. Cossall is a refreshing contrast to
Ilkeston, an attractive village built on top of a
hill, spreading gently down to the Nottingham
Canal. A narrow street winds among the
houses, all of which seem to be surrounded by
pretty gardens. The little church contains an
oak screen made by village craftsmen: in the
churchyard is a memorial to a soldier killed at
Waterloo. The remains of a moat are to be
found just to the east.

Ilkeston
Derbs. EC Wed. MD Sat. Cinema. A market
and textile town, with a compact main square.
The parish church of St Mary dates from 1150
and has an unusual 14thC stone screen. The
annual 3-day fair is held in the Market Place in
Oct.

Sandiacre
Derbs. PO, tel, stores, garage, bank. These
services are all conveniently near the canal,
but there is not much of interest in this
outskirt, apart from the handsome mill by the
canal, and the church, which is set on a rise
called 'Stoney Clouds' (clearly visible from the
canal at Pasture Lock). The church features
some original Norman work inside, including
carvings. The font is 600 years old.

Nutbrook Canal
This little branch off the Erewash Canal used
to lead for 4½ miles almost parallel to the
Erewash Canal and slightly west of it. But it
has been unnavigable since 1895 and is now
totally abandoned. The short section that used
to pass through the old Stanton Ironworks was
filled in in 1962 and is now quite untraceable.

PUBS AND RESTAURANTS
● **Gallows Inn** Canalside at Gallows Inn
Lock. Nicely refurbished pub. Shipstone's real
ale, food *lunchtime and evenings.*
● **White Cow** Nottingham Road, Ilkeston.
Shipstone's real ale and *lunchtime* food in a
friendly and comfortable pub.
● **Needlemakers Arms** Kensington Street,
Ilkeston. A cheerful local offering Shipstone's
real ale and *lunchtime* food.
● **Warren Arms** Derby Road, Stapleford.
Ansells real ale in a modernised coaching inn.
Lunchtime food.
● **Old Cross** Stapleford, 1 mile east of
B5010 bridge. Named after the Saxon cross
which once stood in the churchyard opposite,
this atmospheric pub dispenses Shipstone's
real ale.
● **Plough** Canalside, Sandiacre. North of the
main road bridge. Fine canalside garden with
good moorings. *Lunchtime food Mon-Sat.*
●✕ **Red Lion Hotel** (0602 399069). By the
Padmoor moorings, Sandiacre. Large
canalside pub and steak bar serving Kimberley
real ale. Food *lunchtime and evenings (booking
required for steak bar),* garden, children's room.
Music at weekends.

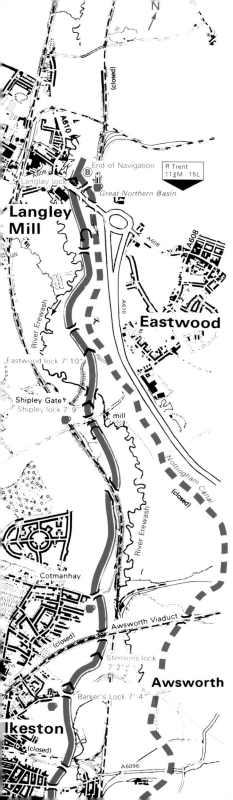

Langley Mill

The northernmost section of the Erewash
Canal is more isolated than the rest, and is
definitely more rural and attractive. As the
tentacles of Ilkeston are left behind, a big
trestle viaduct across the valley is passed; the
inconspicuous River Erewash and beyond it
the Nottingham Canal continue to wind their
ways northwards. There are two splendid old
canal buildings beside Shipley Lock – one was
a stable and the other a slaughterhouse for
worn-out canal horses. Just above the lock, the
River Erewash creeps under the canal, which
is carried above it on a very small aqueduct.
Since this river is the county boundary
between Derbyshire and Nottinghamshire, the
canal now enters Nottinghamshire.
Beyond the next very pleasant rural stretch is
Langley Mill, where the canal terminates at
the Great Northern Basin beyond the final
lock. Boatmen who have navigated the whole
of the Erewash to this point are invited to call
at the cottage just above the old junction in
order to obtain a free facsimile of the old
Erewash Canal Company's bylaws.

Great Northern Basin
This restored basin once formed the junction
of the Erewash, Cromford and Nottingham
canals. A feeder enters here from Moorgreen
reservoir. Since it passed through a coalfield
on its way to the basin, it brought down a lot of
coal silt – which over the years filled up the
Great Northern Basin. Now the Erewash
Canal Preservation & Development
Association has restored the basin and lock, so
that boats may reach a good mooring site with
an enjoyable pub beside it. The Nottingham
and Cromford canals can never be restored
here, for their closure was necessitated by
mining subsidence – although substantial
lengths of both canals are still in water, away
from Langley Mill. Both canals pass through
an interesting mixture of heavily industrial
surroundings and quiet open countryside. The
northern 5 miles of the Cromford Canal, from
Ambergate to Cromford (a length still in
water) is strongly recommended to all walkers,
country lovers and especially industrial
archaeologists. Explorers will find all kinds of
exciting things, including two aqueducts and a
fine old pumping station regularly in steam.
Langley Mill
Derbs. EC Wed. Near the head of the Erewash
Canal, with the little Erewash river going past
it. Langley Mill stoneware pottery is made
here in a very modern works.
Eastwood
Notts. EC Wed. PO, tel, stores, garage, bank. Up
on the hill east of the Great Northern Basin,
this mining town is best known as the
childhood home of D. H. Lawrence. He was
born at 8a Victoria Street, and the early part of
Sons and Lovers is set in the town. At the Sun
Inn a meeting in 1843 between local coal
owners and iron masters led to the
construction of the Midland Railway.

BOATYARDS AND RESTAURANTS

Ⓑ **Langley Mill Boat Co** Great Northern
Basin, Langley Mill (0773 760758).
Ⓡ Ⓢ Ⓦ Ⓓ Overnight mooring, long-term
mooring, winter storage, slipway, dry dock,
chandlery, boat building, engine sales and
repairs, toilet.

PUBS

🍺 **Great Northern** At Great Northern Basin
(the railway company were once owners of the
canal). An excellent local pub serving
Kimberley real ale and food *lunchtime and
evenings.* Canalside garden.
🍺✕ **Shipley Boat Inn** Langley Mill (0773
530313). 100yds west of Shipley Lock. A very
handsome pub/restaurant. Castle Eden real
ale. Garden with swings. *Bar lunches daily, D
Tue-Sat.*
🍺 **Bridge Inn** Awsworth Road, Ilkeston.
Canalside pub with a large garden. Ind Coope
real ale and meals *lunchtime and evenings.*
🍺 **Bridge Inn** Bridge Street, Cotmanhay.
Small canalside local offering Kimberley real
ale and snacks. Garden with swings.

Erewash Canal near Sandiacre. *Derek Pratt.*

FOSSDYKE & WITHAM

Maximum dimensions

Fossdyke Navigation (Torksey to Lincoln)
Length: 75'
Beam: 15' 3"
Headroom: 12'
Witham Navigation (Lincoln to Boston)
Length: 75'
Beam: 15' 3"
Headroom: 9' 2"

Manager

(0636) 704481

Mileage

TORKSEY to
Saxilby: 5½
Brayford Pool, Lincoln: 11
Bardney: 20½
Southrey: 23¼
Kirkstead: 26¾
Dogdyke: 31¾
Anton's Gowt: 40¼
BOSTON Grand Sluice: 42¾

Locks: 3

The Fossdyke Navigation was built in about AD 120 by the Romans, and is the oldest artificially constructed waterway in the country which is still navigable. It was designed to connect the River Witham (made navigable by the Romans) to the Trent and the Humber. The two navigations were used by the Danes when they invaded England, and later by the Normans to carry stone to build Lincoln Cathedral. Subsequently the Fossdyke and the Witham navigations became the responsibility of various riparian landowners, and of the church. They gradually deteriorated and by the beginning of the 17thC were virtually impassable. But King James I transferred the Fossdyke to the Corporation of Lincoln, and from that time conditions improved. Acts of Parliament were passed in 1753 and 1762 for straightening and dredging both navigations, and in 1766 the Grand Sluice at Boston was built, to protect the Witham from the damaging effects of tides and floods. In the 18thC and 19thC further improvements were made, many related to the extensive drainage systems carried out throughout the Fenlands. Thus over a period of centuries the two navigations came to assume the wide, straight course that is so characteristic of them today.

In 1846 the navigations were leased to the Great Northern Railway Company, and immediately their revenue began to fall. Railway competition continued, and by the end of the 19thC both navigations were running at a loss. After a period of dormancy the Witham and Fossdyke navigations became established cruising waterways, as pleasure boats replaced the last surviving commercial operators.

Today their isolation and total lack of development attracts many, while their survival preserves the pleasures of visiting Lincoln by boat; also, Boston is one of the vital links between the inland waterway system and the open sea.

Witham Navigation at Lincoln. *Derek Pratt.*

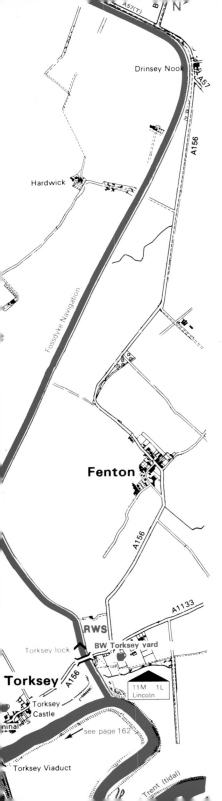

Torksey

The Fossdyke Navigation dates from Roman
times and is the oldest artificial navigation in
Britain. It leaves the tidal Trent at Torksey, ½
mile south of the railway viaduct. The lock
here may be used at nearly all states of tide.
Although the village is some way to the north,
there are plenty of services available at the
lock, including a grocery/chandlery, a garage
and a pub. There is a good restaurant in the
village. A great number of pleasure boats are
moored above the lock. Leaving Torksey the
canal twists slightly before settling down to a
series of long, wide, dead straight reaches
flanked by high banks. This sets the pattern
for the course of the navigation all the way to
Boston, which is 44 miles but only two locks
from Torksey. The long straight reaches make
the navigation somewhat unexciting, as the
banks prevent boatmen from seeing much of
the countryside; but the canal is quiet and
pleasant, and the green banks harbour plenty
of wildlife, while cattle browse by the water. At
Hardwick there used to be a ferry across the
canal. At the end of a very long straight a busy
main road joins, and the canal completely
loses its privacy. They curve together towards
Saxilby, passing a garage and an AA telephone
box.

Navigational note
Torksey Lock may be self-operated during
daylight hours outside normal working hours,
but you must check the gauge board to ensure
a sufficient depth of water over the cill. The
lock keeper can be contacted on 042 771 202,
VHF Channel 74. The lock may be used at
nearly all states of the tide.

Torksey
Lincs. PO, tel. Once a Roman port, but now a
small riverside village quite separate from the
thriving settlement centred on the lock. The
main feature is the ruined castle, whose gaping
Tudor facade is best seen from the Trent. The
17thC pub houses a restaurant. A short
distance north of the railway is the site of
Torksey Pottery, now completely vanished. It
was established in 1802 by William
Billingsley, a noted porcelain decorator who
previously had worked at Pinxton. Although
an excellent decorator, Billingsley was not a
sound business man, and the pottery closed
down after 3 years. Examples of his work can
be seen in Lincoln's Usher Art Gallery.

BOATYARDS

British Waterways Torksey Yard at Torksey
Lock (042 771 202). $\boxed{R}$ $\boxed{S}$ $\boxed{W}$ $\boxed{D}$ Overnight
mooring, toilets, showers.

PUBS AND RESTAURANTS

● **White Swan** Torksey. Near the lock. Also
a caravan and camping site.
●✕ **Hume Arms** Torksey (042 771 613).
An attractive old pub with two bars, situated
300yds from the junction of the Fossdyke and
Trent navigations. À la carte menu with lots of
fish specialities. *L & D every day.*
● **Carpenters Arms** Fenton.

pipe bridge

A57(T)

pipe bridge

Fiddler's
Elbow

Stanley Drain

B1241

pipe bridge

5½M   0L
Lincoln

Torksey
5½M   1L

Saxilby

station

Fossdyke Navigation

A57(T)

Saxilby

The main road clings to the canal all the way
into Saxilby, where it disappears behind
houses. It seems strange that the railway
bridge in Saxilby is the first one after Torksey,
5½ miles away to the north west. Emerging
from the railway bridge one finds the main
street of this attractive village laid out right
beside the navigation. The canal is below the
level of the street, but there are plenty of
excellent moorings, and two pubs just across
the road. Unfortunately the railway makes
quite a lot of noise. Leaving Saxilby, the canal
is rejoined by the busy main road, the A57,
which runs right beside it again for 1½ miles.
As the road finally moves away, the
Gainsborough–Lincoln railway line moves in
to take its place on the other bank, although
separated from the canal for much of the way
by a low hedge. After a few industrial works on
the way out of Saxilby, the canal is entirely in
countryside, green and flat. For most of this
stretch, the towers of the mighty Lincoln
Cathedral are clearly visible in the distance. As
usual the canal's course consists mainly of a
series of dead straight reaches broken up by
occasional corners.

Saxilby
*Lincs. PO, tel, stores, garage, bank, station, fish
& chips.* The presence of the Fossdyke Canal
has clearly determined much of the layout of
the village, although the siting of the church
over ½ mile to the north has obviously
provided another focal point, and as a result
Saxilby extends between the two. All the
buildings in the main street face the waterway,
which is a welcome change for canal veterans,
and a line of cherry trees completes the scene.
The church is pretty, and has a generous
Perpendicular clerestory. Inside the church
are the alabaster figures of a knight and his
lady; they date from the 14thC, but are badly
defaced.

PUBS AND RESTAURANTS

● **Sun** Saxilby. Canalside. *Fish & chips*
nearby.
● **Ship** Saxilby. Canalside, near the Sun.
● **Anglers Hotel** Saxilby.
●✕ **Bridge Hotel** Saxilby (0522 702266).
Near the canal. Restaurant *Wed-Sat.*

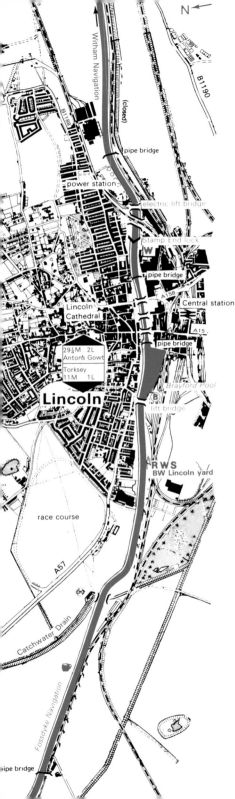

Lincoln

This is in parts a fascinating stretch of
waterway. The approach of Lincoln is marked
by the magnificent towers of the cathedral on
the hill. Passing the remarkable isolated
Pyewipe pub on the canal bank, the Fossdyke
bends briefly as it reaches Lincoln
Racecourse, which is edged by trees. Then a
long line of moored pleasure boats leads to a
lift bridge operated by British Rail. This
bridge is normally left open at night and at
weekends – at other times, just hoot. Beyond
this bridge, the navigation widens out
dramatically into the vast expanse of water
known as Brayford Pool. There is a boatyard
here and boat clubs. Navigators should resist
the temptation to cruise all over this lake, since
much of it is heavily silted: it is advisable to
keep to the north side. Continuing straight
through the pool, the River Witham can be
seen flowing in as an unnavigable stream at the
south corner, and from here onwards
(eastward) the Fossdyke Canal is replaced by
the Witham Navigation. Leaving Brayford
Pool, one passes under the new concrete
bridge; here the channel becomes extremely
narrow and goes straight through the heart of
old Lincoln, passing through the famous and
well-named 'Glory Hole', an ancient half-
timbered building astride the navigation.
Lincoln High Street runs over the heavily
vaulted bridge that carries this house. East of
the Glory Hole the navigation continues its
narrow course along a pleasantly landscaped
stretch before the channel widens out, passing
the old flour mills that once used barges for
shipping the grain. Further on are Stamp End
Lock and sluices: the lock keeper lives across
the road, and will come to operate the lock
and its swing footbridge (see below). The top
gate has no paddles, for it is simply raised *à la
guillotine* into a steel framework to let the water
rush in and the boats pass underneath.
Beyond the next railway bridge is another,
larger bridge with a headroom of about 5ft. An
operator should be summoned by sounding
your horn. One moves out into uncluttered,
flat landscape and wonders at the difference
between the Fossdyke Canal and the River
Witham. To the west is Lincoln Cathedral,
standing proudly on the hill above the town.

Navigational notes
1 Stamp End Lock is *open 08.00-17.00 Mon,
07.00-17.30 Tue-Fri, 07.00-12.00 Sat.* Ring
0522 525749 *before 15.00 (12.00 on Fri) for a
passage outside these times or at weekends.*
2 Water levels on the River Witham can
change rapidly – leave some slack in your lines
when mooring, and use the anchor as an
added precaution.

Lincoln
All services. Lincoln is a very fine city, with a
vast amount for the visitor to see. Once the
Celtic settlement of Lindon, it became
Lindum Colonia, a Roman town; and many
Roman remains have been discovered. Plenty
of these traces can be seen around the town.
The old part of Lincoln is of course grouped
around the cathedral, which sits on a hill to the
north of the river, overawing the city and the
surrounding countryside for miles. There are
some splendid rows of houses in the Close and
just outside it, where the steep and narrow
cobbled streets have remained unchanged for
centuries, and motor traffic can hardly
penetrate.
Lincoln Cathedral This very splendid
building dominates the city and should
certainly be seen by visitors to Lincoln. The
original Norman cathedral was begun in about
1074, but a fire and an earth tremor in the
next century made two extensive restorations
necessary. The present triple-towered
building is the result of rebuilding in Early
English style begun in 1192 after the second
disaster, although the magnificent central
tower (271ft high) was not finished until 1311.
The vast interior contains an abundance of
fine stone monuments and wood carvings, and
in the Cathedral Treasury is one of the original
copies of the Magna Carta.

Lincoln Castle Built as a stronghold for William the Conqueror in 1068, it stands on the crest of the hill close to the cathedral. Over six acres of lawns and trees are enclosed by the thick walls, the two towers and the Cobb Hall – a 14thC addition. The Observatory Tower and the old keep were built on separate mounds on the south side of the castle. The keep is now a mere shell, but the Observatory Tower is in good repair and there is an excellent view of the surrounding area from the top. Cobb Hall, a lower battlemented tower, was built in the north-east corner of the castle and was a place of imprisonment and execution.

Brayford Pool
This great sheet of water separates old Lincoln from industrial Victorian Lincoln. It joins the Fossdyke Canal to the Witham Navigation, and provides the navigator with a welcome relief from the long straight stretches of navigation on either side of Lincoln.

BOATYARDS

British Waterways Lincoln Yard Fosse Bank South, Lincoln (0522 520148). R S W.
Ⓑ **Lincoln Marina, James Kendall & Co** Brayford Pool, Lincoln (0522 526896). R W D Gas, overnight mooring, long-term mooring, winter storage, slipway, dry dock, chandlery, boat sales, toilets, licensed bar.

PUBS AND RESTAURANTS

🍺✕**Green Dragon** Broadgate, Lincoln (0522 524950). By main road bridge 300yds east of the Glory Hole. Medieval pub beside River Witham.
🍺 **Royal William IV** North-east corner of Brayford Pool. Old pub.
🍺✕ **Pyewipe** Canalside. 2 miles west of Lincoln (0522 528708). Very isolated pub, with moorings. Terrace overlooking the Fossdyke.

The 'Glory Hole' in Lincoln. *Derek Pratt.*

Washingborough

Leaving Lincoln, the River Witham heads due
east in a series of straight, wide reaches. The
landscape is similar to that seen from the
Fossdyke, but the river follows the bottom of a
wide valley. To the west, the towers of Lincoln
Cathedral are visible from the river for about
10 miles out of Lincoln. Overhead, RAF
transport planes approach the landing strip at
Waddington airfield, 5 miles south of Lincoln.
There are several villages on the hills
overlooking the Witham; to the south is
Washingborough, all trees and chimneys,
while opposite is Greetwell Hall and its little
stone church. Further east is the unappealing
sprawl of Cherry Willingham, and then
Fiskerton. There is an overnight stop jetty at
Washingborough.

Fiskerton
Lincs. PO, tel, stores, garage. The name of this
village comes from 'fisher's town', for in the
old days it was a fishing village. Once, fishing
boats could sail right up to Fiskerton Church
on the tide. Later, the fens here were drained
and the river diverted into its present straight
course. Since then Fiskerton has stood back
from the river. However when the river
breached its banks in 1962, the water once
again reached the church. The village is full of
new housing. The church is curious, having
the only round tower in Lincolnshire.
Washingborough
Lincs. PO, tel, stores, garage. A pretty village on
the south side of the Witham valley. There are
some attractive stone terraced cottages and
many trees. This has clearly become a smart
commuter village.

PUBS
🍺 **Carpenter's Arms** Fiskerton.
🍺 **Five Mile House** Fiskerton (in the village,
not on the river).
There are several pubs in Washingborough.

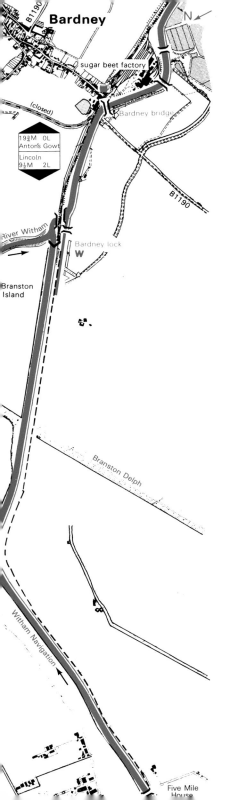

Branston Island

Leaving Five Mile House, where, paradoxically, no house stands, the river continues eastwards for nearly 2 miles through the unchanging flat and empty landscape. Then it turns south east and maintains this general course right through to Boston. There is a small pumping station at the point where the old course of the river branches off round a loop to the north, forming a large island known as Branston Island. Meanwhile the navigation runs in a straight line to Bardney Lock, the only lock between Lincoln and Boston. Below the lock, the old course of the river flows in again from the north, the railway crosses and a river-sized drain enters from the north west. (Boats heading *upstream* at this point should be sure to pass under the railway bridge and turn immediately left.) The village of Bardney is near the next bridge; pubs and fish & chips are close here, and there is an overnight stop jetty.

Bardney
Lincs. PO, tel, stores, garage, banks. A small village to the east of the river, on a slight rise. Bardney is attractive, with a mellow 15thC church and a pleasant village green. The parish almshouses by the green were built in 1712. There are the remains of a Cistercian abbey to the north of the village. Bardney has become well known in recent years as the scene of music festivals; in fact the site is to the south east of the village, towards Southrey.

PUBS AND RESTAURANTS
◖ **Railway** Bardney, by the old station. Telephone outside, and *fish & chips* nearby.
◖ **Jolly Sailor** Bardney. Near the railway.
◖✗ **Nags Head** Bardney (0526 398402). In the village centre. Food.
◖ **Angel Hotel** Bardney.
◖ **Tyrwhitt Arms** Short Ferry, between Bardney and Fiskerton. Snacks, caravan site. Access for boats by sailing north from Bardney Lock up the old course of the Witham.

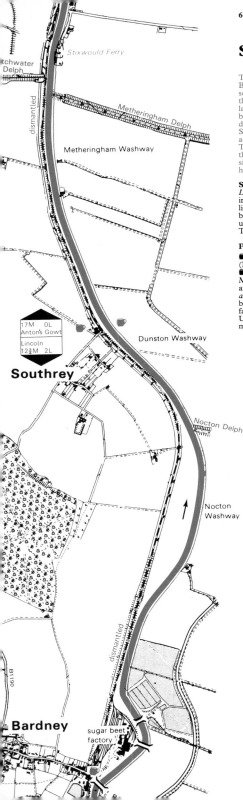

Southrey

Two bridges over the river connect the
Bardney sugar-beet works with its associated
settling ponds. The big ungainly buildings of
the factory continue to dominate the flat
landscape for several miles. The river flows
between high banks to Southrey, passing the
drain (or field dyke) called Nocton Delph. At
Southrey there are two pubs facing each other
across the water, connected by a small ferry.
There are occasional farms on the south bank;
the closed railway continues to hug the other
side of the navigation to Stixwould. Southrey
has an overnight stop jetty.

Southrey
Lincs. Tel. A small village of little intrinsic
interest, but with reasonable river access. The
little wooden church, with its belfry, was built
by the villagers in 1898. A mile to the north, in
undulating countryside, are the ruins of
Tupholme Abbey, founded in 1160.

PUBS
🍺 **Copper Hood** Southrey. On north
(Lindsey) side of river.
🍺 **White Horse Inn** Dunston Fen,
Metheringham (0526 398341). This homely
and welcoming pub offers bar meals *lunchtime
and evenings,* and a variety of services for
boaters, including: moorings, children's
facilities, games room, showers, laundry,
Unigas butane, telephone. Floating pontoon
moorings.

Kirkstead Bridge

The river continues on its straight course through the quiet flat Lincolnshire countryside. At Kirkstead there is a large new bridge – virtually a viaduct – built in 1968 to replace an older, low-level bridge. South of Kirkstead, the river is flanked on one side by the old railway line and on the other by a minor road linking many old farms and cottages along the river bank. There is an overnight stop jetty at Kirkstead Bridge.

Woodhall Spa
Lincs. EC Wed. PO, tel, stores, garage, bank, cinema. A curious resort town in the woods a mile north east of Kirkstead Bridge. The town grew up in Victorian times after waters rich in mineral salts were discovered in 1824. It has the characteristic atmosphere of most English 'spa towns'. There is a very popular 'Kinema' tucked away in the woods; also the town boasts Lincolnshire's only championship golf course.

Kirkstead Abbey ¼ mile east of Kirkstead Bridge is a solitary finger of masonry about 30ft high. This is all that remains of the enormous Cistercian monastery known as Kirkstead Abbey, founded in 1139. The trained eye can recognise the former fishponds attached to the monastery ground.

St Leonard's Church, Kirkstead Originally an extramural chapel of the abbey, the church was built in the mid 13thC, and survives largely intact. It contains a 13thC wooden screen, one of the oldest in the country, and an effigy of a knight of the same period. The church is just a few hundred yards north east of the bridge.

PUBS
🍺 **King's Arms** Kirkstead. On the west bank of the river.
🍺 **Railway Hotel** Kirkstead. On east bank near the station.

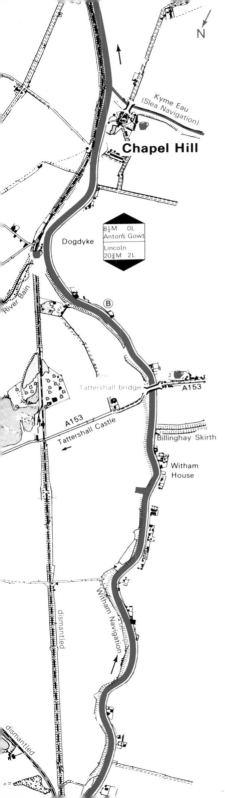

Dogdyke

The river continues southward on a winding course, providing a pleasant contrast to the former straight navigation. The old railway line runs in a straight line over to the east. Along the Kesteven bank are a number of farm cottages served by a minor road. The old Junction with the Horncastle Canal can be seen as a slight dent in the east bank. Less than a mile from Tattershall Bridge is Dogdyke beyond the old steam pump, an attractive place where there is a marina, a restaurant and a riverside pub. Coningsby airfield is nearby: one end of the runway is near the river, so navigators may find aircraft screaming over them at a height of perhaps 100ft. This can be disconcerting on an otherwise quiet summer's afternoon. South of Dogdyke there is a small landing stage on the west bank; this marks a caravan site with facilities useful to those on boats (shop, shower, gas, W etc). Beyond it are the houses of Chapel Hill, where the Kyme Eau or Sleaford Navigation joins (see below). Beyond Chapel Hill, the river becomes straight and wide once again, with piling to protect and strengthen the bank on one side and reeds on the other. Boston Stump, the tower of the church, can be seen from here. It is 9 miles away. There is an overnight stop jetty at Tattershall Bridge.

Chapel Hill
Lincs. PO, tel, stores, garage. A pleasantly compact tiny village.
Dogdyke
Lincs. Tel. A riverside settlement close to a signpost which indicates 2½ miles to New York and 12 miles to Boston. One is reminded that the names of two settlements in the New World originated here.
Dogdyke Pumping Station Between Tattershall Bridge and Dogdyke. An 1855 steam beam-engine and scoop-wheel. *Open 13.30–17.00 first Sun in each month May–Oct.* Admission charge.
Tattershall Castle 1 mile north east of Tattershall Bridge. Only the keep of this superb building remains, which was rebuilt in brick in the 15thC for Ralph Cromwell, Treasurer of England 1434-5.
Horncastle Canal This navigation, 10 miles long, was built 1792-1802 to serve the small country town of Horncastle. It left the River Witham ½ mile upstream of Tattershall Bridge, but now an embankment has been built over the junction in the cause of flood prevention, so those travelling on the river must look carefully to discover any trace of the junction. The remains of the first lock are about 300yds from the river. Nearer Horncastle parts of the canal are still in water, and the town basin survives. It was abandoned in 1885.
Kyme Eau Sleaford Navigation Society, Red Gables Farm, Pointon Fen, Sleaford (0529 240501). Now navigable through Kyme Lock (BW key needed) for over 4 miles to Cobblers Lock, where it is possible to wind. Maximum dimensions are 72ft x 14ft 6in, with headroom of 6ft 6in. From *Oct–Mar* the gates at Kyme Eau Lower Lock are chained back for flood prevention reasons. *Navigation is difficult in winter.* Full restoration to Sleaford is planned.

BOATYARDS

ⓑ **Belle Isle Marina** Dogdyke (0526 42124). R S W D E Pump-out, narrowboat hire, day hire craft, overnight mooring, long-term mooring, winter storage, slipway, crane, chandlery, books and maps, boat building, boat sales, engine repairs, restaurant, toilets, showers.

PUBS AND RESTAURANTS

🍺 **Crown** Chapel Hill.
🍺 **Packet Inn** Dogdyke. Riverside.
✗ ❢ **Captain's Table** Dogdyke. Riverside restaurant. Mooring.
🍺 **Royal Oak** Tattershall Bridge. Shop nearby.
🍺✗ **Hume Arms** South Kyme, on the Slea Navigation (0526 861004). A comfortable waterside pub serving Wards and Tetley's real ale, and food.

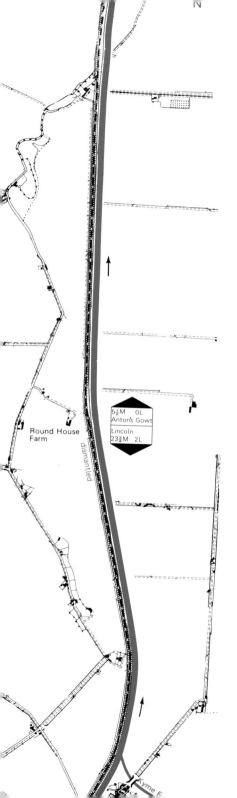

Round House Farm

The river continues south east in familiar
straight, wide reaches with occasional bends of
a few degrees, accompanied by the disused
railway line on one side and high grassy banks
on the other. Cattle graze on the banks. All
around, but hidden from those in boats by the
high bank, is a flat fenland landscape.

N

Round House
Farm

dismantled

5½M   0L
Anton's Gowt

Lincoln
23¾M   2L

Kyme E

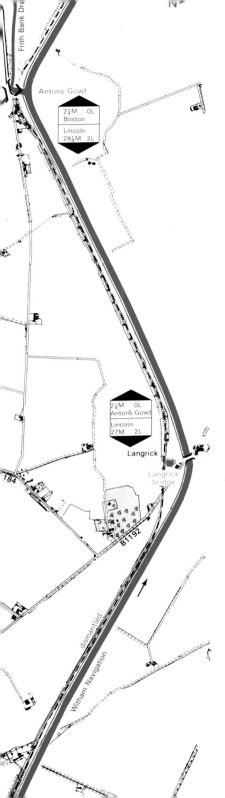

Langrick

At Langrick the river is crossed by a big iron girder bridge as it curves round to head due east for 2 miles. At the end of this reach is Anton's Gowt; there is a lock and its cottage here, for this is the entrance into the great network of waterways knows as the Witham Navigable Drains, and navigators with time to spare can easily continue through to Boston by this alternative route and will, as a reward, find good moorings in the *centre* of Boston. At Anton's Gowt there is a sailing club near the lock. The river turns here on its final course to Boston and the sea.

Witham Navigable Drains
This remarkable network of waterways north of Boston exists to drain and irrigate the flat and highly vulnerable tract of fenland. The network is a vital part of the local economy and of the defence of the area against the encroachment of the North Sea. Castle Dyke Drain, Houghbridge Drain, Newham Drain, West Fen Drain, Medlam Drain, Stonebridge Drain and the Maud Foster Drain are usually navigable *early May–mid Sep*. Craft of 75ft x 18ft can pass through Anton's Gowt Lock, the limiting size at Cowbridge is 62ft x 11ft 5in. Information regarding water level should be obtained by ringing the Witham Fourth Internal Drainage Board on 0205 310099 before you venture in. The key to Cowbridge Lock is held by the Drainage Board foreman. Ring 0205 310099 *during office hours*, 0205 353758 *evenings & weekends*. However, one should always remember that navigation is not the top priority of the drainage authority: sometimes a navigator is brought up sharply by a low bridge, often in a place where the channel is no wider than 30ft for several miles. Anton's Gowt Lock is the only entrance to these waterways. The best (widest) course is to head east from here, along Frith Bank Drain for 2 miles, to the great junction of waterways at Cowbridge Lock. From here one may go north towards the Lincolnshire Wolds, or south into Boston along the Maud Foster Drain. (But note that there is no longer a connection with the tidal Witham this way).
Langrick
Lincs. Stores, garage. This tiny settlement grew to serve the ferry crossing, replaced by an iron bridge in 1907. There is an old jetty facing Witham Lodge, an attractive house where the ferry used to be. The pub is nearby. The late Georgian brick church was built in 1828.

PUBS AND RESTAURANTS

🍺 **Malcolm Arms** Anton's Gowt, on north side of Frith Bank Drain.
🍺✕ **Ferry Boat Inn** Langrick, on north side of river (0205 73273). Snacks, meals *L & D*.

Boston

The River Witham now completes its journey to Boston, aiming straight for Boston Stump, the tower of St Botolph's Church. A low black iron railway bridge crosses at the Boston Grand Sluice, which marks the end of the non-tidal Witham. Boats should keep away from the powerful 'draw' of the sluices on the south-west side of this structure (the lock is at the north-east end of it). The river here is a very attractive scene, and a fitting end to the trip from Torksey. On either side of the river is a line of town houses; these are particularly elegant on the north bank. There are two boat clubs: Boston Sailing Club and Boston Motor Yacht Club, also a rowing club, a boatyard and a riverside pub. There are good moorings here. The centre of Boston is a short walk away.

Navigational note

At Boston Grand Sluice the River Witham becomes tidal, leading down through Boston past the docks and into the Wash. It is most inadvisable to venture down the tideway unless you have a suitable, sea-going boat and are familiar with the currents and shallows in the Wash. The Grand Sluice is of course a sea lock, with gates facing both ways, but what is particularly interesting about it is that, unlike most tidal locks, the sea gates (referred to locally as 'doors') here are actually used at every tide. In other words the North Sea at high water is always above the level of the non-tidal Witham, and the sea gates close automatically twice a day to keep out the tide. This makes locking through the Grand Sluice somewhat complicated as far as times are concerned. It is not possible to lock up into the tide, since there is only one pair of outward facing gates, but on the other hand the tidal river practically dries out at low water. The best time to lock through is in fact 2 to 3 hours either side of high water. The lock will take boats up to 50ft long by 30ft wide. A lock keeper is on duty in the nearby office: his telephone number is 0205 64864 (VHF Channel 74) and you should give him at least *24 hrs* notice if you intend to pass through (answerphone).

Boston

Lincs. EC Thur. MD Wed. All services. An immensely attractive town at the mouth of the Witham, Boston has been an important seaport for over 800 years. There are many splendid buildings in the town, but of course the most conspicuous among them is the famous Boston Stump – the 272ft tower of the parish church. There are two large market places, virtually contiguous. This area is the scene of much revelry in the spring, when the May Fair takes place. Under a charter of Elizabeth I dated 1573 the fair is held from *3-10 May.*

St Botolph's Church beside the Witham. This enormous building is a magnificent example of the late Decorated architecture, and reflects the prosperity of Boston following the rise of its wool trade in the 13thC. The thriving guilds paid for the church, into which were built their respective chapels. Inside, the church is immensely spacious, the tall roof carried by slender quatrefoil columns. There are plenty of interesting things to look at here. The main south door is a remarkable piece of dovetailing, the pulpit is an elaborate Jacobean affair and the choir stalls are an excellent example of 14thC carving. There are some good brasses and other monuments. The 272ft tower may be ascended, at a small charge; with hundreds of steps up a claustrophobic narrow turret, this can be heavy going, but one may walk right around a balcony near the top and of course the view over the fenland is unbeatable – on a clear day Lincoln, 32 miles away, is visible. The church is much loved by the inhabitants of Boston, Massachusetts, who have largely financed its structural repairs this century.

The Guildhall South Street (0205 365954). An ancient and fascinating building, now a museum illustrating Boston's history. It contains the cells that in 1607 held William Brewster and his friends after their unsuccessful attempt to leave the country. They were tried in the courtroom above. On the ground floor of this dark but historic building is the original kitchen. The roasting spit is self-propelled; the heat rising from the fire drives simple fans connected to a chain that operates the turning gear. This remarkably useful device is over 500 years old. *Open Mon-Sat and Sun afternoon.*

Fydell House next to the Guildhall. A superb town house built in 1726 by William Fydell, a successful wine merchant who was three times Mayor of Boston. The building was saved from demolition in 1935 by the pioneering Boston Preservation Trust, who have fully restored this and many other venerable buildings hereabouts. Fydell House is now partly financed and used by Nottingham University as a college for Americans (Pilgrim College). *Open daily until sunset.*

Blackfriars Spain Lane, next to the Guildhall. This was once part of a 13thC Dominican friary, and much of the old stone structure remains. But the building has now been skilfully converted by the Boston Preservation Trust into Boston's only theatre. It backs onto Spain Court, a charming little square.

BOATYARDS

Ⓑ **Boston Marina** Witham Bank, Boston (0205 354420). Ⓡ Ⓢ Ⓦ Ⓓ Ⓔ Gas, overnight mooring, long-term mooring, chandlery, books and maps, boat and engine sales, shop. *Moorings closed in winter.*

PUBS

⬤ **Witham Tavern** Boston. Riverside, above the Grand Sluice.
⬤ **Barge** Boston, near the Grand Sluice.
There are plenty more pubs and restaurants in the town.

St Botolph's Church, known as the 'Boston Stump', beside the tidal River Witham. *Derek Pratt.*

LANCASTER

Maximum dimensions

Preston to Tewitfield
Length: 75'
Beam: 14'
Headroom: 7' 6"
Glasson Branch
Length: 70'
Beam: 14'
Headroom: 8'

Manager

(0524) 32712

Mileage

PRESTON to
Garstang: 16¼
Junction with Glasson Branch: 24
Lancaster: 29¼
Carnforth: 37¼
CANAL TERMINUS: 41¼

No locks

Glasson Branch: 2¾ miles, 6 locks

The city of Lancaster has always been slightly unfortunate in being situated a little too far up the Lune estuary to allow easy navigation. By the late 18thC industrial developments in north-west England created a great demand for better access from Lancaster to Preston, Manchester and the busy manufacturing areas near the River Mersey. A link such as a canal would enable much needed coal to be brought up from the pits around Wigan, while farm produce from the fertile plains of north Lancashire could be sent back to feed the teeming town workers to the south.

After various proposals had been aired, including suggestions for a ship canal up the Lune estuary and a canal along the coast, a smaller canal was promoted to run from Kendal to Westhoughton (a few miles east of Wigan). This was authorised as the Lancaster Canal by Parliament, and construction began in 1792, after a survey by John Rennie, the company's engineer. He designed the new navigation as a 'broad' canal, with locks 72ft long by 14ft wide, to take barges with a 50-ton carrying capacity. The water supply for the canal was – and still is – drawn from a reservoir at Killington (between Sedburgh and Kendal).

The route chosen included only eight locks (at Tewitfield), but several aqueducts, the most important being across the River Lune at Lancaster. It was intended that the Ribble should be crossed at Preston by locking down to the river and up the other side, but this plan was constantly shelved because of lack of capital. By 1799 the canal was open from Tewitfield to Preston (including the great Lune Aqueduct), and from Clayton to Chorley. There remained a 5-mile gap between the two sections, which became known as the North and South Ends respectively. The gap was closed in 1803 by a horse tramway from Walton Summit to Preston, which was carried over the River Ribble by a wooden trestle bridge. This tramway was intended only as a cheap, temporary solution to the gap, but it was never replaced by a proper canal line, so the North End was doomed to be separated for ever from the rest of the country's inland waterways. (The tramway was closed in 1857.)

On the South End, the Lancaster Canal Company agreed with the Leeds & Liverpool Canal Company to extend the former's line past Chorley to Wigan (they never continued it to Westhoughton). The L & L then shared the Lancaster Canal for 10 miles – for a substantial consideration. Meanwhile the North End was extended from Tewitfield to Kendal and opened in 1819. The branch down to Glasson Dock, near Lancaster, was opened in 1826 as the canal's only direct outlet to the sea.

There are several unusual aspects about the Lancaster Canal and its history. One is that the 75-mile-long main line was constructed with only eight locks, at Tewitfield. (There are of course also six locks on the Glasson branch.) This was naturally a great benefit to traders and helped to counteract the disadvantage imposed by the tramway at Preston. One may also notice that the towpath is on the same side all the way along the canal, except for a short stretch in Lancaster. This fostered the growth in the 1820s of an express passenger service along the canal. Using special 'fly-boats', a constant change of horses at special staging posts, and precedence over all other craft, this service lived up to its name, averaging up to 10 mph along the run from Preston to Kendal.

Another interesting aspect of the Lancaster Canal was the extraordinary but canny interest the company took in the new railway companies, alternately leasing whole lines and then being leased by the railways. Eventually, in 1885, the Canal Company sold out altogether to the London & North Western Railway – except for the South End, which was already leased in perpetuity to the Leeds & Liverpool Canal Company.

Since the 1930s the canal has been progressively shortened from the Kendal end; and in 1968, after Tewitfield locks had been disused for several years, the canal north of Tewitfield was closed so that the M6 motorway could be driven across the canal. In Preston the canal has been shortened by over half a mile.

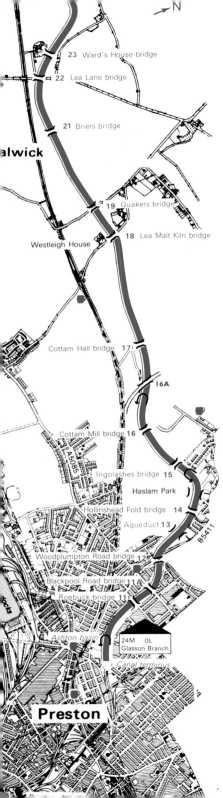

Preston

The canal in Preston, shortened many years ago by over ½ mile, now starts in the middle of nowhere, on an embankment by the old Ashton Basin. (There is not much left of the original line, although pubs in Preston like the Lamb & Packet recall the days when passenger 'fly boats' or 'packet boats' used to leave Preston to do the trip to Kendal in eight hours – a remarkable speed.) From Ashton Basin, the canal runs through dull urban areas for a short while. However, the attractive Haslam Park appears at bridge 12 and, while housing estates line the offside bank for a mile, the towpath side of the canal is effectively already in the countryside. Soon Preston is left behind and the canal runs through flat and featureless but always green, open, agricultural countryside; the first of many sheep and cows are seen grazing along here. Passing Westleigh House and several farms, one begins to see the large industrial works at Salwick where fuel elements are made for atomic power stations. Farm eggs may be bought at bridge 18.

Navigational notes
1 You will need a special key to use the locks on this canal. These can be purchased from British Waterways, Aldcliffe Road, Lancaster, or from Lodge Hills or Glasson locks.
2 Overnight mooring in Preston is not recommended.

Salwick
Lancs. PO, tel, stores, station. A village scattered over a large area. The school, post office, telephone and pub are just ¼ mile south of bridge 22: the station is ¼ mile south west of bridge 25.

Preston
Lancs. MD Mon, Wed, Sat. All services. A large industrial town which prospered as a cotton manufacturing centre. The teetotal movement was founded in Preston in 1834, and Joseph Livesey's Temperance Hotel (the world's first) used to stand at the corner of Church Street and North Road. The Market Place is dominated by the huge classical building of the Harris Public Library and Museum. There are many churches whose tall spires are a distinctive feature of the town. Attempts to redevelop the centre of the town have resulted in a good new shopping precinct and a large modern bus station housed in a remarkably long multi-storey car park. With the end of commercial use, the huge basin of Preston Dock has been developed as a marina complex, with the turbine steamer *Manxman* as the centrepiece.

Harris Museum & Art Gallery Market Square, Preston (0772 58248). The museum has a specialised collection of the Devis family of painters in addition to exhibits illustrating 18thC and 19thC art, including ceramics, porcelain, glass, toys, stamps and costume. *Closed Sun.*

Tourist Information Centre The Guildhall, Lancaster Road, Preston (0772 53731).

PUBS
● **Smith's Arms** Lea Lane Town. South of bridge 22. Thwaites real ale in a village pub next door to British Nuclear Fuels works. *Lunchtime* food.
● **Cotty Brook** South of bridge 18. McEwan and Younger real ale and *lunchtime* food.
● **John O'Gaunt** Cottam Avenue. North of bridge 16. Boddingtons real ale in a large estate pub.
● **Lane Ends Hotel** 442 Blackpool Road. South of bridge 12 (no access from bridge 11A). Large popular Boddingtons real ale pub. *Lunchtime* snacks.
● **Wheatsheaf** Water Lane. ¼ mile south west of Ashton Basin. A basic pub serving Tetley's and Jennings real ales.
● **Maudland** 1 Pedder Street. ⅓ mile south east of Ashton Basin via Fylde Road and Ashton Street. In the shadow of the third tallest spire in the country, this popular local offers Matthew Brown real ale. Pedder Street is named after one of the sponsors of the Lancaster Canal.

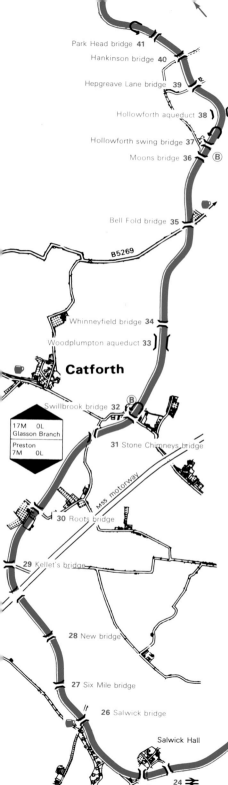

Catforth

The canal now reaches Salwick Wharf, where
the moorings are administered by the Duchy
of Lancaster. On one side of the wharf is the
moated Salwick Hall, screened by trees; on the
other side is Salwick station, on the Preston–
Blackpool line, and a disused windmill
beyond. Here the canal turns north into a
wooded cutting, passing a canalside pub –
unfortunately a rare sight on this canal. At
Kellet's Bridge the navigation turns sharply
east to Catforth (*PO, tel, stores*). All along this
section the countryside is soft, open
pastureland dotted with dairy farms; entirely
peaceful and untouched by busy roads. At
Swillbrook Bridge there is one of the few
boatyards on this canal: the proprietor's house
was formerly the old canal cottage with stables
for the towing horses.

The Fylde
A large flat area of north-west Lancashire
(west of the canal) which is the 'market
garden' of the many industrial towns in the
area. There used to be a wonderful array of
windmills covering the land, but nearly all of
these are gone now.

BOATYARDS
Ⓑ **Preston Hire Cruisers** Moons Bridge
Wharf, Hollowforth Lane, Woodplumpton,
Preston (0772 690627). Ⓡ Ⓦ Ⓓ Gas, hire
craft, long-term mooring, winter storage,
crane.
Ⓑ **Adventure Cruisers** The Jolly Roger,
Catforth (0772 690232). Ⓦ Ⓓ Pump-out,
gas, narrowboat hire, day hire boats, overnight
mooring, long-term mooring, winter storage,
slipway, chandlery, books and maps, boat and
engine sales and repairs, gift shop, tea shop,
off licence, toilet, showers.

PUBS
🍺 **Plough** Woodplumpton, east of bridge 35.
Matthew Brown real ale and food at *lunchtime,
also evenings Wed–Sat, with a buffet Sun.*
Garden with children's play area.
🍺 **Bay Horse Hotel** Catforth. North of
bridge 32. Matthew Brown real ale and bar
meals *lunchtime and evenings Mon–Fri.*
🍺 **Running Pump** Catforth. North of bridge
31. A popular pub serving snacks at *lunchtime*
every day, and full lunches *Sun & Tue–Fri.*
Robinson's real ale.
🍺 **Hand & Dagger** Canalside at bridge 26.
Once the Clifton Arms, this pub was nick-
named the Hand & Dagger because of its
signs. It was renamed when modernised.
Greenall Whitley real ale and *lunchtime* food.

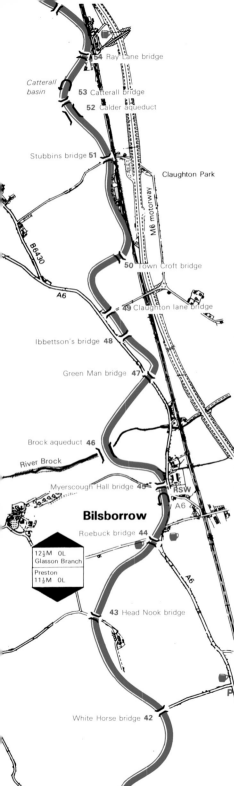

Bilsborrow

Starting at White Horse Bridge (¼ mile to the east of which is a pub, garage, post office and telephone kiosk), the canal sweeps round to enter the village of Bilsborrow on a minor embankment: the A6 joins the canal here and continues to dog it for many miles, as does the main railway line to Scotland, and the M6. When these rival transport routes keep their distance the canal is again delightfully quiet, still passing through peaceful green farmland, while the foothills of the Pennines begin to converge from the east. Just south of Stubbins Bridge can be seen the canal cottage and stable which was one of the places where towing horses were exchanged for fresh teams to pull the express passenger boats between Preston and Kendal. Near the former Garstang and Catterall station is Catterall Basin; both are now disused.

Claughton Hall ¼ mile east of the canal. This hall was originally an Elizabethan mansion built next to the village church for the Croft family, but in 1932-5 the whole house, except for one wing, was dismantled and reassembled on top of the moor north of the village. It was quite a remarkable undertaking and still stands there in defiant isolation.
Bilsborrow
Lancs. PO, tel, stores, garage. A village straggling along the A6, which must have been very noisy before the M6 was built. The church is set apart, up on a hill: there are three pubs very close to the canal.

PUBS
🍺 **Kenlis Arms** Garstang, 100yds east of bridge 54. Boddingtons real ale and food *lunchtime and Fri, Sat & Sun evenings.* Children welcome.
🍺 **Roebuck** Garstang Road, 30yds east of bridge 44. *Lunchtime* food and Matthew Brown real ale in a large modernised pub with a children's room and bowling green.
🍺 **White Bull** Canalside at bridge 44. Friendly village local dispensing Matthew Brown real ale, and *lunchtime* snacks.
🍺✗ **Owd Nell's** Canalside at bridge 44 (0995 40010). Newly built farmhouse-style thatched pub and restaurant. Bar food *lunchtime and evenings,* meals *L & D until 20.00.* Boddingtons, Tetley's and Whitbread real ales.
🍺 **White Horse** ¼ mile east of bridge 42. Small, comfortable pub serving home-made food *lunchtime and evenings* and Matthew Brown real ale.

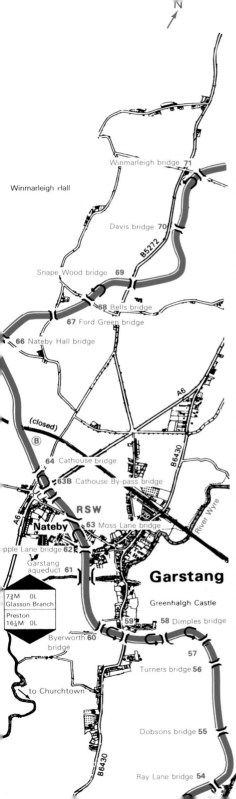

Garstang

The canal moves away from the hills and the
remains of Greenhalgh Castle, crossing the
River Wyre on a fine stone aqueduct and
passing the attractive town of Garstang;
Garstang Basin is a popular mooring for
pleasure boats. There is a restaurant and
museum in the restored wharf buildings here.
The canal then winds through countryside
that is as green and pleasant as ever, but which
is now overlooked by the steep slopes of the
Pennines. Those who walk up the hills will be
rewarded with splendid views over
Cockerham Sands and the Fylde.

Winmarleigh Hall ½ mile west of bridges 68
and 70. A red-brick hall built in 1871 for Lord
Winmarleigh. It was largely rebuilt after a fire
in 1927. It is now an agricultural college.
Garstang
Lancs. PO, tel, stores, bank, garage. A friendly
place, touching the canal, which retains the
feeling of a small market town. Just near the
canal is the 18thC church of St Thomas
surrounded by a tidy churchyard. Opposite
the cobbled market place is an interesting little
town hall with its diminutive bell-tower. The
Town Hall, built in 1680 to acknowledge its
promotion by the king to borough status, was
rebuilt in 1939. There used to be a dozen ale
houses in the town; but the present six seem
quite enough.
Greenhalgh Castle Just north of the canal on
a grassy knoll are the modest ruins of
Greenhalgh Castle. It was built in 1490 by the
Earl of Derby, who placed Richard III's crown
on Henry Tudor's head after the victory at
Bosworth Field. In the 17thC it was destroyed
by the Roundheads during the Civil War when
the Royalists made a final stand there. Ask at
the adjacent farm to visit the ruins.
St Helen's Church 1½ miles south west of
the canal at Churchtown, west of the A6. A
magnificent parish church known as the
'Cathedral of the Fylde', in an attractive
setting of a shady churchyard near the River
Wyre. Parts of the building date from c1300
and inside are 15thC arches on Norman
pillars with the Creed written on them. The
massive beams in the roof are from the four
oaks that Henry IV granted to Churchtown
when forests were the property of the
monarch.

BOATYARDS
ⓑ **Bridge House Marina** Nateby, Garstang
(099 52 3207). Between bridges 64 & 65.
Ⓡ Ⓢ Ⓦ Ⓓ Gas, long-term mooring, winter
storage, slipway, chandlery, boat sales, engine
repairs, toilets, showers, grocery shop,
telephone, laundry.

PUBS AND RESTAURANTS
🍺 **Patten Arms** Winmarleigh, north of
bridge 71. Whitbread real ale and bar food
lunchtime and Sat & Sun evenings.
🍺✕ **Chequered Flag** Nateby, 200yds south
of bridge 64 (099 52 2126). Bass and Stones
real ales and bar meals *lunchtime and evenings.*
🍺 **Eagle & Child** High Street, Garstang.
Lunchtime bar meals.
🍺 **Farmer's Arms** Church Street, Garstang.
Tetley's and Jennings real ales, meals
lunchtime and evenings. Children's room.
🍺✕Royal Oak Hotel Market Place, Garstang
(099 52 3318). Robinson's real ale, bar meals
lunchtime and evenings.
🍺 **Crown** Garstang, east of bridge 62.
Thwaites real ale, bar meals *lunchtime and
evenings.*

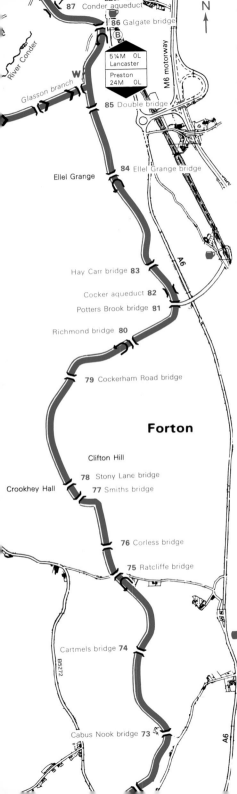

Galgate

Continuing northwards through quiet, modest and unspoilt pastureland, the canal passes countryside that is empty of villages but full of farms and houses dotted about the landscape. The absence of any locks certainly makes this an ideal waterway for restful cruising, while the wildlife and the generously proportioned stone-arched bridges always supply interest along the way. Near Forton, a sharp S-bend carries the canal between Clifton Hill and Crookhey Hall, while from Potters Brook Bridge a lane across the A6 leads to a post office, telephone and hotel beside what used to be Bay Horse Station. Just north of Potters Brook is the Ellel Grange estate with its remarkable spired church, ornamental canal bridge and the Grange itself, shrouded by tall trees; unfortunately the estate is private. Double Bridge is worth a closer look; beyond the rocky cutting that it spans is the junction with the Glasson Branch, and round the corner is Galgate and a large boatyard and mooring site.

Galgate
Lancs. PO, tel, stores, garage. An unassuming village on the A6 but dominated by the main railway to Scotland, which strides through the place on a high embankment and an impressive viaduct. The back of the village up the hill is quiet; by the church of St John are the buildings of what is apparently the oldest surviving silk spinning mill in England (built in 1792).

Ellel Grange On the banks of the canal. A very fine Italianate villa built for a merchant in 1857-9. It is a large mansion with two broad towers that compete in vain with the graceful spire of the charming little church of St Mary that stands in the grounds of the house. Both are private.

BOATYARD

Ⓑ **Marina Park** Canal Wharf, Galgate, Lancaster (0524 751368). Ⓡ Ⓢ Ⓦ Ⓓ Gas, long-term mooring, winter storage, slipway, dry dock, chandlery, books, boat sales, toilets, showers, launderette.

PUBS AND RESTAURANTS

🍺 **Plough Inn** Galgate, near bridge 86. *Lunchtime* bar food and Boddingtons real ale.
🍺 **Green Dragon** Galgate. Thwaites real ale in a village pub. Food *lunchtime and evenings.*
🍺 **New Inn** Galgate, in the village. Mitchell's real ale and food at *lunchtime.*
🍺 **Bay Horse** North east of bridge 81, across the A6. Mitchell's real ale and bar meals *lunchtime (not Mon) and Sat & Sun evenings* in a cosy pub which has its own rugby team. Family room, open fire, garden.
🍺✕ **Hamilton Arms** North east of bridge 73 (0524 791257). Matthew Brown real ale, bar and restaurant meals.

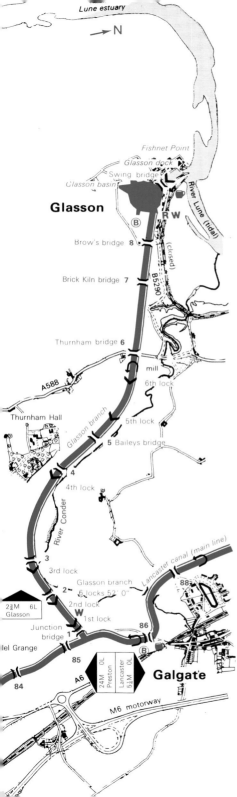

Glasson

Between Ellel Grange and Galgate the
Glasson Branch leads off down to the west to
connect the Lancaster Canal with the Lune
estuary via Glasson Dock. The branch was
finished only in 1826, long after the main line
of the canal was completed, and provided the
canal with its only direct link with the sea.
There are six wide locks whose bottom gates
feature the same excellent type of sliding
paddles as one sees on the Leeds & Liverpool
Canal. The top gates are all kept padlocked for
security reasons: navigators should ensure that
they have the requisite key on board (available
from the British Waterways lock keeper) and
are asked to lock the gates after use, and also
to leave the locks *empty* after use, even when
going up the locks. The arm falls through the
Conder valley, a pleasant, quiet stretch of
countryside whose proximity to the sea is
betrayed by the many seagulls cruising
around. The spire in the trees on the south
bank belongs to Thurnham church;
Thurnham Mill is beside the bottom lock, and
its mill race shows that it still takes water from
the canal. After the bottom lock, the canal
runs in a straight line through saltings and
marshland to Glasson Basin, where there is a
large boatyard, mainly for seagoing yachts,
and British Waterways moorings.

Navigational notes
1 The entrance lock from Glasson Dock up
into Glasson Basin will take boats up to 95ft x
24ft, and 12ft draught, and operates *2hrs*
before high water. Anyone wishing to use the
lock (for which *24hrs* notice is required) or
take up a mooring in the basin should contact
the lock keeper on 0524 751566.
2 The locks on the Glasson Branch will take
boats up to 72ft long, 14ft wide and 4ft
draught. You will need a key to operate them,
available from the lock keeper.

Glasson
Lancs. PO, tel, stores, garage. A fascinating tiny
port that is still busy with trade from coastal
and continental vessels. The canal no longer
contributes to this trade and the huge basin is
only occupied by an assortment of pleasure
boats using its excellent sheltered mooring. In
the tidal dock, however, there are usually
plenty of coasters that discharge into lorries,
since the old railway line from Lancaster has
now been dismantled.
Thurnham Hall On the south-west bank of
the canal. This ancient family home of the
Daltons is a battlemented 16thC mansion that
was given a new façade and beautiful chapel in
the 19thC.

BOATYARDS
Ⓑ **Marina Park** See page 76.
Ⓑ **Glasson Basin Yacht Co** Glasson Dock,
nr Lancaster (0524 751491). Ⓡ Ⓢ Ⓦ Ⓓ Ⓔ
Gas, overnight mooring, long-term mooring,
winter storage, slipway, crane, chandlery,
books and maps, boat building, boat sales,
engine sales and repairs, telephone, toilets,
showers.

PUBS
● **Caribou Hotel** Glasson Dock. Dating
from 1781, this large pub has an open fire and
plenty of cosy corners. Bar food *lunchtime and
evenings,* and Thwaites real ale. Children
welcome.
● **Dalton Arms** Glasson Dock. Thwaites
real ale and food *lunchtime and evenings.*
● **Victoria** Glasson Dock. Mitchell's real ale
and bar meals *lunchtime and evenings.*
● **Plough Inn** Galgate, near bridge 86.
Lunchtime bar food and Boddingtons real ale.
● **Green Dragon** Galgate. Thwaites real ale
in a village pub. Food *lunchtime and evenings.*
● **New Inn** Galgate, in the village. Mitchell's
real ale and food at *lunchtime.*

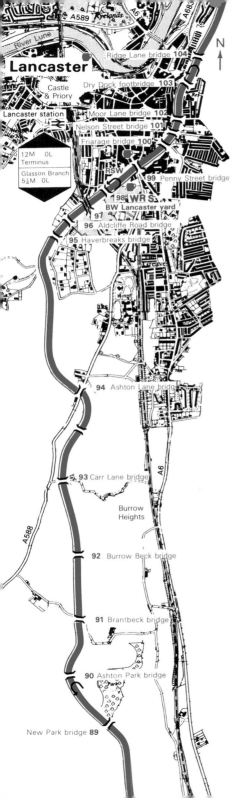

Lancaster

The canal continues northwards through beautiful undulating green countryside, then passes through an unusually long wooded cutting which ends in the outskirts of Lancaster. Going underneath the main line railway, the two-storey building where the old packet boats used to be refitted can be seen: here they were hauled out of the water from pulleys on the beams of the upper floor. The British Waterways maintenance yard is nearby, at the bridge where the towpath changes sides. Past the bridge are the Aldcliffe basins and wharves which were once the headquarters of the canal company. Opposite are some canal stables which have been tastefully converted into a place for punting, eating and drinking. At bridge 101 the towpath returns to the left side of the canal, where it stays for the rest of the journey northwards. The navigation now leaves Lancaster, on the side of the hill that overlooks the Lune estuary.

Lancaster
Lancs. EC Wed. MD Sat. All services. The name Lancaster is derived from a combination of Lune (after the river) and Latin 'castrum' meaning camp, which refers to the Roman fortress that once stood on this site. Today the quay, once a great shipping port handling more cargo than Liverpool, is only a quiet backwater, with a pleasant walk provided by the tree-lined quayside promenade. A large new university was opened at Bailrigg, south of the town, in 1964. The Boat Regatta takes place annually in *May* and the Agricultural show in *Aug.*

Lancaster Castle A handsome but forbidding building on the site of Roman fortifications; mainly 13thC and 14thC construction, except for the Norman keep, which is surmounted by a beacon tower known as John of Gaunt's Chair. The Shire Hall contains an impressive display of over 600 heraldic shields. Most of the castle has reverted to its earlier function as a prison. *Various escorted tours (0524 64998). Closed during the winter, and while Assizes, Quarter Sessions or County Courts are sitting.*

Priory Church of St Mary Vicarage Lane, by the castle. Attractive 15thC church in late Perpendicular style though the original Saxon western doorway still remains and the belfry was added in 1754. Elaborately carved choir stall c1340 and fine Jacobean pulpit.

Town Hall Dalton Square. A very impressive building of classical design, with a grand marble staircase and domed council chamber. It was the generous gift of Lord Ashton to the city of Lancaster in 1909. It is open to visitors, who are shown the magnificent entrance hall, the council chamber and concert hall, as well as the historic charters. To arrange a visit contact the Town Clerk (0524 582000).

Lancaster Museum Old Town Hall, Market Square, Lancaster (0524 64637). Prehistoric, Roman and medieval exhibits; pottery and porcelain, firearms and topographical paintings. *Open weekdays.*

Ashton Memorial Williamson Park, Quernmore Road. The 'Taj Mahal' of the north. Yet another generous gift from Lord Ashton to the city as a memorial to his family. In the centre of a beautiful park, containing a palm-house and ornamental lake, the memorial is a vast structure consisting of two domed chambers, one on top of the other. It was designed in neo-classical style by J. Belcher and constructed of Portland stone in 1907-9.

Maritime Museum Old Customs House, St George's Quay, Lancaster (0524 64637). Walk towards the river from bridge 99, turn left into Damside. Lancaster once handled a greater tonnage of shipping than Liverpool; the display in the 18thC Customs House reflects this maritime heritage. *Open daily 11.00-17.00 (14.00-17.00 in winter).*

Tourist Information Centre 7 Dalton Square, Lancaster (0524 32878).

BOATYARDS

Ⓑ **Canal Cruises** Penny Street Bridge Wharf,

Lancaster (0836 633189). R W D Pump-out, day hire craft.
British Waterways Lancaster Yard At bridge 98 (0524 32712). R S W (nearby). BW keys available here.

BOAT TRIPS

Lady Fiona is a canal motor barge converted and licensed to carry 75 passengers. *Trips Easter–Nov, lasting 3½hrs* leave from near bridge 98. Licensed bar on board. Only party bookings accepted, will run any day of the week. Enquiries to 0524 39279.
Duke of Lancaster Public trips *Easter–Sep*, youth weekends in *winter*, private hire *all year*. Up to 12 passengers. Licensed bar on board. Enquiries to 0836 633189.

PUBS AND RESTAURANTS

There are plenty of pubs in Lancaster.
🍺 **Waterwitch** Canalside between bridge 98 and 99. A choice of real ales and food *lunchtime and evenings.*
🍺✕ **White Cross** Canalside after bridge 99. (0524 841048). Bass and Stones real ales, bar and restaurant meals *lunchtime and evenings.*
🍺 **Farmer's Arms** Lancaster. North west of bridge 99. Thwaites real ale and food *lunchtime and evenings.*
🍺 **Waggon & Horses** 27 St George's Quay, Lancaster. Well worth a look in if you are visiting the Maritime Museum. Good mixed clientele and Hartleys real ale to enjoy. *Lunchtime food,* open fire.

A typical stone bridge on the Lancaster Canal. *Derek Pratt.*

Hest Bank

This is a very interesting and varied section. After crossing a new aqueduct (built in 1961) over the A683, one launches out along the superb aqueduct that carries the canal over the broad River Lune – definitely a high spot on his journey. At the far end of the aqueduct the canal rejoins the side of the valley, turning west then north again through quiet countryside. Gradually one begins to approach the sea: there are good views over the expanse of Morecambe Bay. Past Hest Bank, the navigation winds along to the pretty village of Bolton-le-Sands.

Bolton-le-Sands
Lancs. PO, tel, stores. A village that obviously values its canal. There are some pretty houses, several of them with gardens landscaped down to the water's edge. Ducks, too, are often seen on the canal hereabouts. The village used to be a stop on the Preston–Kendal 'fly-boat' run: the pub survives to remind one of the service.

Hest Bank
Lancs. PO, tel, stores, bank. Until the Glasson Branch was cut, Hest Bank used to be the scene of much transhipment between canal boats and coasters, as Hest Bank was the canal's nearest point to the sea. Now, the village is nondescript, a seaside suburb of Lancaster; but the seashore is only a couple of hundred yards from the navigation, and at low water miles of sandy beach are uncovered. The west coast main railway runs along the shore.

Lune Aqueduct
This splendid edifice, probably the greatest feat of engineering on the Lancaster Canal, carries the navigation for some 600ft across the River Lune, which is 60ft below. A handsome stone aqueduct with an elegant balustrade, it was designed by John Rennie and completed in 1797. The smooth modern lines of the M6 motorway bridge can be seen ¾ mile upstream.

PUBS
● **Blue Anchor** Main Street, Bolton-le-Sands. Mitchell's real ale and bar meals *lunchtime and evenings (not Mon)*.
● **Packet Boat Hotel** Main Street, Bolton-le-Sands. Once a staging post on the canal 'fly-boat' service, it now serves Thwaites real ale and food *lunchtime and evenings*.
● **Hest Bank** Canalside at bridge 118. You can still see the window for the guiding light, which showed the way across the sands. Now this old coaching inn with an open fire is justly popular, offering Boddingtons real ale and *lunchtime* bar food. Canalside garden, children welcome.

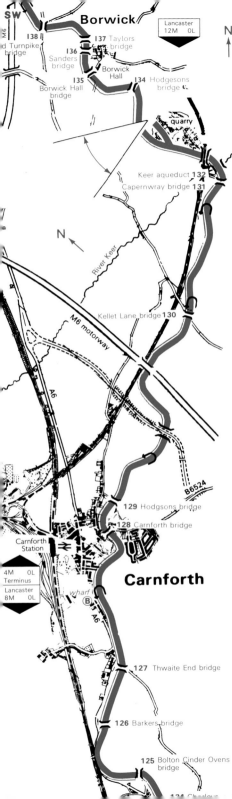

Carnforth

The A6 now runs beside and below the canal
into Carnforth. One may catch occasional
glimpses westward of the distant shores
around Morecambe Bay, then the canal passes
Carnforth, mostly in a cutting. A few small
abandoned quarries are scattered between the
canal and the M6. After passing under the
motorway spur road, the canal finds itself
diverted along a new channel for several
hundred yards before going under the main
line of the M6: this diversion was presumably
cheaper to build than a long, finely angled
skew bridge over the navigation. Beyond the
motorway lies peaceful green countryside
backed, unmistakably, by the foothills of the
Lake District. At Capernwray the canal
crosses the River Keer on a minor aqueduct;
the nearby railway, which goes to Leeds,
crosses the Keer on an impressive viaduct,
framing a tiny old derelict watermill. Past the
railway bridge is a short branch to a worked-
out quarry, then the canal winds round the
hillside to end abruptly just beyond Borwick.
The abandoned Tewitfield locks are just
beyond the terminus. It is possible to walk
from Tewitfield to the original terminus at
Kendal (and get a bus back). Boats can safely
be left at the terminus moorings (facilities
available, and a winding hole).

Borwick
Lancs. Tel. A small, old and attractive village,
spread around a green. Overlooking the canal
is Borwick Hall, a large and sombre
Elizabethan manor house, built around a high
15thC tower. Extensive gardens.

Warton
Lancs. PO, tel, stores. About 2 miles west of
Borwick. Ancestors of George Washington
lived in this village and their family crest
containing the famed Stars and Stripes is to be
seen on the 15thC tower of the church of St
Oswald.

Carnforth
Lancs. PO, tel, stores, garage, bank, station. Not
particularly attractive but of interest as an
important railway junction. One may catch
trains not only north–south but east over the
beautiful green hills to Skipton and Leeds,
west to Barrow and right round the coast to
Carlisle. Carnforth was the last town in the
country to lose its regular British Rail steam
locomotive service in 1968. Since then a
company of steam engine enthusiasts and
volunteers have privately set up the
'Steamtown' museum – a depot with 5 miles
of track along which preserved engines steam
on certain weekends. The collection of motive
power includes the 'Flying Scotsman'. At
Carnforth Wharf are some useful facilities:
moorings, slipway and sanitary station. A
petrol station is nearby.

BOATYARD
Ⓑ **Nu-Way Acorn** Lundsfield, Carnforth
(0524 734457). Ⓡ Ⓦ Ⓔ Pump-out, gas,
narrowboat hire, day hire craft, overnight
mooring, long-term mooring, winter storage,
slipway, boat sales, engine repairs, telephone,
toilets, showers.

PUBS AND RESTAURANTS
🍺 **Longlands Hotel** Tewitfield. 100yds
north east of the canal terminus. Boddingtons
real ale and *evening bar meals (not Mon).*
🍺 **Shovel** Carnforth. West of bridge 128.
Boddingtons real ale and snacks.
🍺✕ **Royal Station Hotel** Carnforth (0524
732033). Mitchell's real ale, bar meals
lunchtime and evenings, and restaurant meals
evenings.
🍺 **Cross Keys** Carnforth. Mitchell's real ale
and snacks.

Greenberfield Locks, Leeds & Liverpool Canal. *Derek Pratt.*

LEEDS & LIVERPOOL

Maximum dimensions

Liverpool to Wigan, and Leigh Branch
Length: 72'
Beam: 14' 3"
Headroom: 8' 6"
Wigan to Leeds
Length: 60'
Beam: 14' 3"
Headroom: 8'
Rufford Branch
Length: 62'
Beam: 14'
Headroom: 8'

Manager

Liverpool to Greenberfield Top Lock: (0942) 42239
Greenberfield Top Lock to Leeds: (0274) 611303

Mileage

LIVERPOOL. Canal terminus to Burscough, junction with Rufford Branch: 24½
Wigan, junction with Leigh Branch: 35
Johnson's Hill Locks: 47¼
Blackburn, Top Lock: 56
Burnley: 72½
Skipton: 98
Bingley Five Rise: 110¾
Apperley Bridge: 118
LEEDS, River Lock: 127

Locks: 91

Leigh Branch: 7¼ miles, 2 locks
Rufford Branch: 7¼ miles, 8 locks

With a length of 127 miles excluding branches, the Leeds & Liverpool Canal is easily the longest single canal in Britain built by a single company. It is hardly suprising that its construction costs amounted to £1.2 million, and that it took well over 40 years before the main line was completed.

The canal has its beginnings in the River Douglas, a little river made navigable by 1740 – well before the canal age – all the way from Wigan to Parbold, Tarleton and the Ribble estuary. The navigation provided a useful outlet for coal from the Wigan area.

After a few years the idea of purely artificial canals as traffic routes became popular among businessmen, and several ambitious trans-Pennine schemes were mooted; one of these was for a canal from Liverpool to Leeds, where it would connect with the head of the Aire & Calder Navigation.

After much predictable argument between the promoters in Yorkshire and those in Lancashire about the actual route of the proposed canal, the Leeds & Liverpool Canal was authorised in 1770, and construction began at once, with John Longbotham as engineer. The first (lock-free) section from Bingley to Skipton was opened within 3 years; by 1777 two long sections were open from the Aire & Calder at Leeds to Gargrave (incorporating many of the dramatic new staircase locks) and from Wigan to Liverpool. The River Douglas navigation had been embarrassingly close to the new canal's line, so the L & L had bought it out at an early stage to gain control of its valuable water supply. It was replaced by a proper canal branch to Rufford and Tarleton, where it joined the (tidal) River Douglas.

Construction was halted at this stage while trade flowed on to the separate lengths of navigation and the company summoned the resources to continue work on the canal. In 1790 a new money-raising Act of Parliament gave fresh impetus to the scheme for completing the difficult middle section of the canal. Work began again, with Robert Whitworth as the company's engineer; but after 1792 and the outbreak of war with France, the nation's purse strings grew steadily tighter and, after the boom year of 1794, investment in canals declined steadily. The canal company did not do badly to finish the whole of the main line from Leeds to Liverpool by 1816 (under a convenient arrangement with the Lancaster Canal Company, the finished L & L line actually *shared* the channel of the Lancaster Canal for 10 miles). This stretch is from Wigan Top Lock to Johnson's Hill Bottom Lock. The Lancaster used then to branch off up what later became the Walton Summit Branch.

In 1820 a branch was opened to join the Bridgewater Canal at Leigh. A short branch (the Springs Branch) was also made to rock quarries at Skipton and an important 3-mile-long canal from Shipley to Bradford. The cut down into the Liverpool Docks was made in 1846.

The prosperity of the company after 1820 was not, at first, greatly affected by the early advent of railways in that part of the country. The scale of the navigation (the locks were built – and remain – as barge locks 62ft by 14ft, allowing big payloads to be carried in each barge along the canal) no doubt contributed to the high dividends paid to shareholders for several years. Water supply was, however, a thorny problem from the very beginning, and in spite of the building of many reservoirs along the summit level, the canal had to be closed for months on end during many dry summers. Although through traffic has never been a very significant proportion of the trade on the canal, this lack of reliability tended, not surprisingly, to drive carriers' custom away to the railways. Use of the navigation for freight has declined throughout this century; the hard winter of 1962-3 finished off many traders. Today there is no large scale commercial traffic at all, although the occasional independent carrier may be seen at the eastern end.

Bootle

Marsh Lane bridge 2C

Bootle
New Strand station

Litherland Road bridge 2B

Stanley Rd
Changeline bridge 2A

Caroline Street
Changeline bridge

Bootle Oriel Road station

Bank Hall station

Liverpool docks

Sandhills station

Liverpool

Boundary Street bridge E

D Athol Street bridge
C Lightbody Street
bridge

Stanley dock
4 locks 44′ 0″

24½M 0L
Burscough

B Burlington Street bridge

A Chisenhale Street bridge
Canal terminus

Liverpool Exchange
station

Liverpool

The first ¼ mile of this canal has been filled in, so the navigation begins now at bridge 'A'. It runs north from the city centre for about 6 miles, parallel and close to Liverpool Docks, before turning east to Aintree, Wigan and the Pennines. Liverpool is not an attractive place from the canal, which is completely shut off from the town by rows and rows of factories with their backs turned to the canal. For much of the way, substantial electricity pylons span the navigation. Access at the bridges to or from the canal is very difficult, because the towpath is officially closed to walkers, but naturally it is often alive with small boys fishing, playing and dropping or throwing things into the canal. The water, however, is surprisingly clear.

Navigational notes

1 Just north of the terminus is the Stanley Dock Branch. This useful connection from the canal down into Liverpool Docks and the River Mersey is nowadays the main *raison d'être* of the west end of the Leeds & Liverpool Canal. There are four locks on the branch: they can be opened only by the resident lock keeper *during working hours Mon–Fri.* Any person wishing to use these locks should give *24hrs notice* to the BW Burscough office (0704 893160). Below the locks, one enters immediately the Stanley Dock: this belongs to the Mersey Docks & Harbour Company, whose permission should be sought before one enters the dock. (Ring 051-200 2079.) The MD & HC is unlikely to refuse such a request, but does not like pleasure boats to tie up in the dock. Navigators are encouraged to move straight on to the big lock down into the tidal River Mersey. The lock is operated *24hrs a day.*
2 Those navigating the Leeds & Liverpool will need, as well as a windlass, a British Waterways anti-vandal key and a sanitary station key.
3 Mooring at unrecognised sites in city centres is not recommended.
4 Please give *24hrs* notice to BW at Burscough (0704 893160) before navigating the Liverpool to Aintree section.

Liverpool
Merseyside. All services. EC Wed. In the first century AD it was 'lifrugpool', a settlement next to a muddy creek; now it is one of Britain's largest ports with a population of over ½ million. Famous worldwide as the place where the Beatles began their march to fame, (in the 'Cavern' club, now demolished), and equally well known for the exploits of Liverpool Football Club, attracting a fanatical and generally good-natured following. There is much to be seen in this ancient port – for example the Anglican Cathedral, begun in 1904 and finished in 1978, is the largest in the world; the Roman Catholic Cathedral is a striking conical structure topped with a lantern tower and illuminated with stained glass by John Piper and Patrick Reyntiens. The Walker Art Gallery has a collection of paintings second only to those in London, and includes the original of Yeames' popular work 'And when did you last see your father?', among works by Reubens, Holbein, Stubbs (born in Ormond Street), Turner and Reynolds. Gladstone, Prime Minister during the reign of Queen Victoria, was born in Rodney Street in one of a row of superb Georgian houses. Down by the Mersey is the Royal Liver Building and Cunard offices, a reminder of the days when the great transatlantic liners used to berth here. Now the superb new Albert Dock development and Liverpool Tate Art Gallery are attracting increasing numbers of tourists to compensate for the decline in trade. Beneath the river are the Queensway Tunnel (opened in 1971). On the pierhead is a memorial to the engineers lost on the *Titanic*, which sank in 1912.
Tourist Information Centre Near Lime Street station (051-709 3631).

PUBS
There are many to be found here.

Litherland

North of Litherland the conurbation thins out
and wastelands and suburbs appear, while the
canal turns east to Aintree. Soon the first of
many swing bridges is encountered; for the
first few miles these bridges have to be
padlocked to combat vandalism, so progress
through them is necessarily slow. All
navigators should ensure that they have the
requisite key before reaching these bridges.
(Keys obtainable from the British Waterways
offices at Burscough, Wigan, Burnley and
Apperley Bridge.)

PUBS
📛 **Tailor's Arms** Canalside, at bridge 4A.

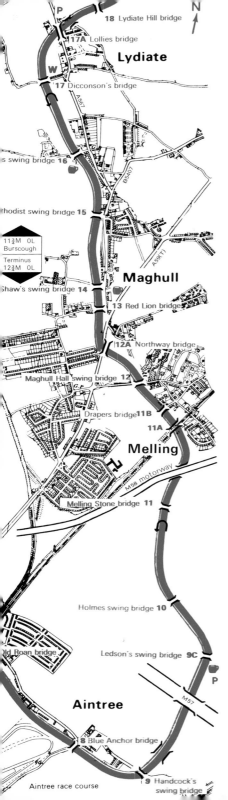

Maghull

Aintree marks the limit of Liverpool's outskirts. The great feature here is of course the Aintree Race Course: the famous Grand National steeplechase is run every year on a spring Saturday. Much of the course lies right beside the canal, but would-be spectators from the canal will have to stand upon their boat's cabin top to see over the fence surrounding the course. At the east end of the racecourse is another swing bridge; this carries a busy main road and traffic lights are installed, but boat crews operate the bridge themselves. Here the canal turns north again, and as the little church tower at Melling comes into view the navigation emerges at long last into open countryside, although Maghull soon looms up to interrupt this with a series of swing bridges.

Navigational note
Those heading towards Liverpool should remember that all the usual city problems with vandals will become apparent beyond bridge 11. There is a winding hole here for those who wish to turn around.

Maghull
Merseyside. EC Wed. All services. A small town astride the canal, convenient for supplies. Since the last war it has greatly expanded, but still maintains its former village atmosphere. **St Andrew's Church** Damfield Lane. Just north of bridge 12A. Though separated from the rest of the town by a dual carriageway, it is well worth a visit: it has a cosy setting among trees that seem to compete with the tower for height. It was built in the late 19thC, but its style is in imitation of that of the 13thC to accord with the tiny 700-year-old chapel known as Old St Andrew's in its grounds. The chapel is a charming little building, said to be the oldest church in the Merseyside area.
Melling
Merseyside. PO, tel. The sight of this little village is like a breath of fresh air to anyone coming along the canal from Liverpool, although southbound travellers probably find it unremarkable. The village stands on an isolated hillock at a safe distance from the big city. The church is a landmark in the area; it was built in the 15thC with rock from an adjacent quarry.

PUBS
• **Running Horses** Maghull. Canalside, at bridge 16. Ind Coope and Walkers real ales.
• **Hare & Hounds** Maghull. Near bridge 14.
• **Bootle Arms** Melling. Burtonwood real ale.
• **Horse & Jockey** Near bridge 9C.
• **Old Roan** Aintree. Near Old Roan Bridge 7D.

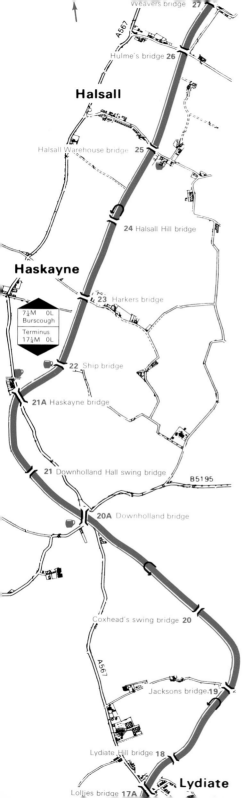

Halsall

The canal now enters continuous open
countryside, which soon establishes itself as
extremely flat and intensively cultivated
lowlands: indeed it is more akin to
Cambridgeshire or Lincolnshire than to the
rest of Lancashire. However, it is pleasant
enough and the canal forms one of its more
important features – a view which is borne out
by the large number of people usually to be
seen walking and boating upon it, as well as
the hundreds of anglers enjoying their sport in
this well-stocked length of canal. As if in
compensation for the unexciting landscape,
the traveller is offered a truly astonishing
number of pubs on or near the canal all the
way from Lydiate to Wigan.

Halsall
Lancs. PO, tel, garage. There is a handsome
tall 14th-15thC church here (St Cuthbert's),
with a fine spire. The choir vestry, erected in
1592, was formerly a grammar school. There
is an interesting pair of pulpits/lecterns. One
of them is generously illuminated by a solitary
overhead window; the other, more sheltered,
gives the occupant the unfortunate air of being
behind bars ...

Haskayne
Lancs. PO, tel, stores. There are just two pretty
houses here: the post office and the old
thatched cottage opposite. No sign of a
church.

PUBS
● **Saracen's Head** Halsall. Canalside, at
Halsall Warehouse Bridge.
● **Ship** Haskayne. Canalside, at Ship Bridge.
A well-known canal pub with a garden serving
Tetley's real ale.
● **King's Arms** Haskayne. 100yds north of
bridge 21A.
● **Scarisbrick Arms** Canalside, at
Downholland Bridge. Greenall Whitley real
ale.
● **Scotch Piper** About 400yds north of
bridge 17A. A beautifully preserved award-
winning pub with no bar, serving Burtonwood
real ale straight from the barrel.

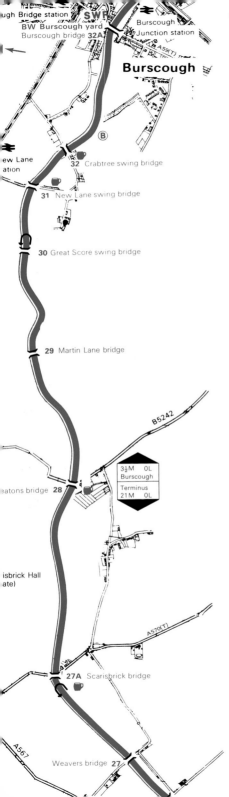

Burscough

One moves now past a massive caravan site on one side and attractive woods containing the private Scarisbrick Hall on the other; then out again into the open flatlands. The Southport–Manchester line converges from the north west; it runs near the canal all the way into Wigan, and has some wonderfully remote stations. A flurry of swing bridges brings the canal into Burscough: just beyond is the junction with the Rufford Branch.

Navigational note
You will need your British Waterways key, and a windlass, to open bridge 32.

Burscough
Lancs. PO, tel, stores, garage, bank, station.
Formerly a canal village and a staging post on the one-time Wigan–Liverpool 'packet boat' run, this place attaches more significance nowadays to the benefits of road and rail transport. It still boasts two stations (one is on the Preston–Liverpool line) and suffers from heavy through traffic. A very convenient place for taking on victuals.

BOATYARDS

Ⓑ **Latham Marina** The Workshop, Crabtree Lane, Burscough (0704 894782). W̄ Gas, long-term mooring, slipway, chandlery, boat and engine sales and repairs, salvage.
British Waterways Burscough Yard (0704 893160). R̄ S̄ W̄ Dry dock.

PUBS AND RESTAURANTS

🍺 **Royal Coaching House** Liverpool Road, Burscough. Boddingtons and Higsons real ales in a pub two minutes' walk from the canal. *Lunchtime* food, children's room, garden.
🍺 **Railway** At New Lane station.
🍺 **Latham Slipway** Canalside at bridge 32. Thwaites real ale and an extensive range of food *lunchtime and evening.* Children allowed in *until 20.30,* garden with play area, good moorings.
🍺 **Farmers Arms** Canalside, by bridge 31. A pub of great character with an open fire and a choice of Jennings, Walkers and Tetley's real ales. Children are allowed in *until 20.00,* and snacks are served. Good moorings.
🍺 **Heatons Bridge** Friendly unspoilt canalside pub, at bridge 28. Tetley's and Walkers real ales, garden.
🍺✖ **Red Lion** Near Scarisbrick Bridge.

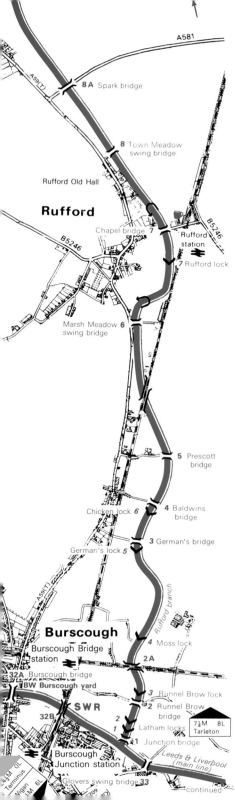

Rufford

The Rufford Branch leaves the Leeds &
Liverpool main line just east of Burscough,
through an imposing arched bridge dated
1816. A little canal settlement surrounds the
top lock and the roomy dry dock for barges
here. The locks come thick and fast to begin
with, as the canal falls through the very fertile
and gently sloping farmland towards the
distant Ribble estuary. The country is
generally quiet, flat and unspectacular but
agreeable. A line of trees and the spire of
Rufford church are followed by the beautiful
Rufford Old Hall, on the west bank.

Navigational notes
1 If you wish to make the diversion off the
main line to visit Tarleton, please note that
craft over 60ft will have difficulty turning at
James Mayor's boatyard.
2 You will need your British Waterways key to
open bridge 33.

Rufford
Lancs. PO, tel, stores, garage, station. Main road
village noted for its Hall. The church is a small
Italianate Victorian building containing many
monuments to the Heskeths who owned
Rufford Hall for many centuries; obviously a
prolific family, judging by one large sculpture
depicting a brood of 11 children, dated c1458.
The family now resides in Northamptonshire.
Rufford Old Hall *NT property* (0704
821254). On the west bank of the canal. A
medieval timber-framed mansion with
Jacobean extensions given to the National
Trust in 1936. The interior is magnificently
decorated and furnished in period style,
especially the great hall with its hammerbeam
roof and 15thC intricately carved movable
screen – one of the few still intact in England.
The Hall also houses a folk museum. *Open
afternoons Apr-Oct (closed Fri).* Admission
charge.
Note: although the Hall is beside the canal, it
is not possible to enter the grounds direct from
the canal. Navigators should therefore tie up
near bridge 7, then walk up to the village and
turn right at the main road. The entrance is a
few hundred yards along the wall on the right.

PUBS

🍺 **Hesketh** Rufford. Greenall Whitley real ale
served via fake handpumps in a cocktail bar
atmosphere.
🍺 **New Fermor Arms** East of bridge 7. An
unremarkable modern pub replacing an earlier
building famous for its tilt which was finally
demolished in 1974. Younger real ale and bar
food. Garden.
🍺 **Ship** Burscough. Near second lock down.
An old canal pub formerly known as the
'Blood Tub' – black puddings were once made
here, and a bucket of pig's blood could be
exchanged for a pint of beer.

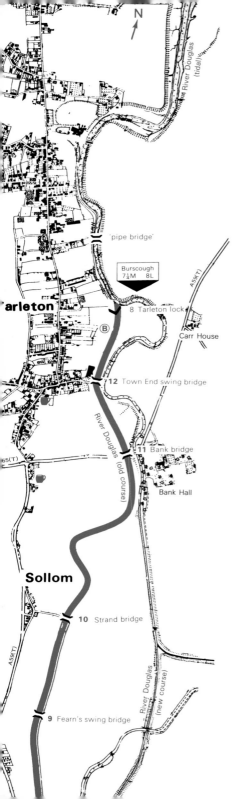

Tarleton

At Sollom there used to be a lock, but now it is
no more. This is where the canal turns into the
old course of the River Douglas, and it twists
and turns as though to prove it. The towpath
has been ploughed up from here onwards. The
'new' course of the Douglas (which was once
navigable from the sea right up to Wigan)
comes alongside the canal at the busy road
bridge near Bank Hall, a house hidden by
trees. From here it is only a short distance to
the final swing bridge and Tarleton Lock,
where the canal connects with the tidal River
Douglas – which in turn flows into the River
Ribble near Preston.

Navigational notes
1 Vessels wishing to enter or leave the Rufford
Branch via Tarleton Lock can only do so at
high water. The Douglas is then a relatively
easy navigation, and since the removal of the
old railway swing bridge a mile downstream,
there has remained only one limitation on
headroom from Tarleton to the open sea. This
is a pipe bridge not far north of Tarleton Lock:
the clearance at normal high water is about
20ft. The boatyard at the lock may help callers
with advice regarding tide times, etc. or ring
BW on 0704 892160.
2 Navigators entering the Rufford Branch
canal from the sea should remember that they
will need a padlock key – as well as a windlass
– to open the locks up the branch.
Arrangements can be made with the British
Waterways Burscough Yard (0704 893160) to
have such key left with James Mayor's
boatyard.

Tarleton
Lancs. PO, tel, stores, garage, bank. A large
village luckily avoided by the A59 road. There
are some useful shops and a good take-away
food shop.

BOATYARDS
Ⓑ **James Mayor** The Boatyard, Tarleton,
Preston (0772 812250). R S W D E
Pump-out, gas, overnight mooring, long-term
mooring, winter storage, chandlery, five
slipways up to 90ft, 3-ton crane, moorings.
Boat and motor sales, motor repairs. Steel and
wood boats built and fitted out. Telephone,
showers, toilets. Extremely helpful people.

PUBS
⬤ **Cock & Bottle** Church Lane, Tarleton.
Thriving village-centre pub dispensing
Thwaites real ale. *Lunchtime* snacks, garden,
children allowed in side rooms *until 21.00.*
⬤ **Ram's Head** West of bridge 11. Large
young people's pub serving Greenall Whitley
real ale and food *at all times.* Garden, children
allowed in *until 20.00.*

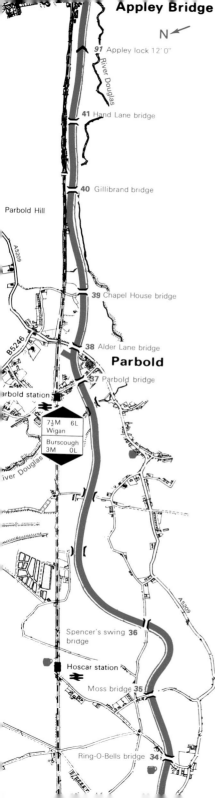

Parbold

East of the junction with the Rufford Branch, the canal meanders through the flat countryside to the village of Parbold with its ancient sail-less windmill. Here the scenery changes completely as the canal crosses the River Douglas and then joins the Douglas Valley. This is a very pretty, narrow wooded valley which the canal shares with the railway: there are several convenient stations along the line. Appley Lock is reached: there are two locks alongside, now restored, and you can choose to use either these or the very deep main lock. The shallower locks were once used as a navigable sidepond for boats passing in opposite directions.

As with all subsequent locks, the gates should be closed and the paddles lowered and padlocked after use to combat vandalism and wastage of water.

Navigational note
You will need your British Waterways key to open bridge 36.

Parbold
Lancs. PO, tel, stores, garage, station. A large village climbing up from the west end of the Douglas Valley. Parbold is prettiest near the canal bridge, where the big brick tower of the old windmill is complemented by an equally attractive pub. Unfortunately the rest of the village is being engulfed by acres of new housing. Local landmarks are the tall spires of Parbold's two churches, and Ashurst's Beacon high on a hill to the south. The latter was built in 1798 by Sir William Ashurst in anticipation of an invasion by the French. (The beacon was intended as a local warning sign.)

Douglas Navigation
The little River Douglas, or Asland, was made navigable in the first half of the 17thC, well before the great spate of canal construction. It provided the Wigan coalfield with a useful outlet to the tidal River Ribble, from which the cargoes could be shipped over to Preston or along the coast. When the Leeds & Liverpool Canal was built to share the Douglas Valley, the old river navigation became superfluous. It was bought up by the new company, who constructed their own branch to the Ribble estuary (the Rufford Branch). Between Parbold and Gathurst it is possible to find many traces of the old navigation, including several locks.

PUBS AND RESTAURANTS

🕭 **Stocks Tavern** Alder Lane, Parbold, south of bridge 37. Very fine traditional country pub serving excellent bar meals *lunchtime and evenings.* Tetley's real ale. Children allowed in *until 20.00.*

🕭 **Railway** Parbold, north of bridge 37. Typical village local. Burtonwood real ale and meals *lunchtime and evenings.* Children allowed in *until 20.00.*

🕭 **Windmill** Parbold, by bridge 37. Old village local dispensing Greenall Whitley real ale, and meals *lunchtime and evenings.* Children allowed in *until 20.00.*

🕭✗ **Ring O'Bells** Canalside at bridge 34. (0704 893157). Tastefully modernised country pub serving bar and restaurant meals (*L & D, not Mon*) along with Higsons and Boddingtons real ales. Canalside tables, children welcome.

🕭 **Railway Tavern** Hoscar Station, north east of bridge 35. Small country pub serving Tetley's and Jennings real ales and snacks. Children allowed into side rooms.

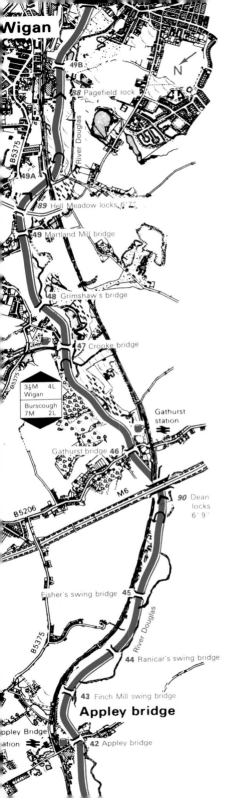

Douglas Valley

The canal now goes through Appley Bridge
and runs up the beautifully rural Douglas
Valley, with the river on one side and the
Wigan–Southport railway on the other.
Passing three consecutive swing bridges, one
soon reaches Dean Locks, a pleasant spot in
spite of the high motorway viaduct nearby.
This used to be a very busy place, for in
addition to the now restored duplicated canal
locks, there used to be a lock down into the
River Douglas Navigation, when this was
navigable before the Rufford Branch was built.
Just east of the locks is a pleasant canalside
pub, then the valley widens out to reveal the
chimneys and factories of Wigan. Hell
Meadow (sometimes mistaken for 'Ell
Meadow') and Pagefield Locks lead the canal
up towards the centre of Wigan.

Navigational note
You will need your British Waterways key to
open bridge 43.

Appley Bridge
Lancs. PO, tel, stores, station. A canalside
hamlet dominated by large mills and works,
the place is nevertheless attractively situated in
the wooded Douglas Valley.

PUBS

⬤ **Crooke Hall Inn** Crooke. Near bridge 47.
Garden, mooring. Greenall Whitley real ale.
⬤ **Navigation** Gathurst. Canalside, at bridge
46. Tetley's real ale.
⬤ **Railway** Appley Bridge by the canal.
Tetley's real ale.

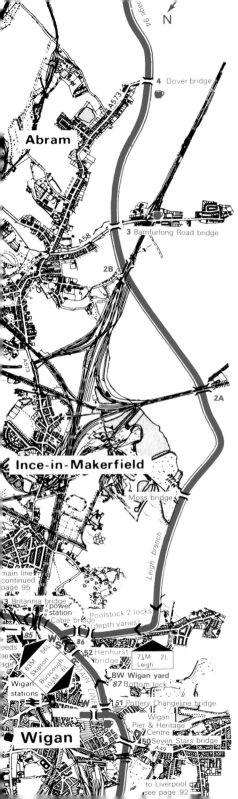

Abram

The Leigh Branch leaves the main line of the Leeds & Liverpool Canal in Wigan, between the big power station and the 22nd lock. The famous 'Wigan Pier', a coal staithe, is by bridge 51 and has been rebuilt. It was made fun of by George Formby Snr, and written about by George Orwell in 'The Road to Wigan Pier', in 1937. Descending through two locks, the canal enters the lock-free level that extends all the way along the Bridgewater Canal to Preston Brook and Runcorn, over 40 miles away, passing through a landscape once spoiled by mining but now painstakingly restored as parkland – a wildlife haven. Most of the way, the canal is on an embankment, well above the level of the surrounding landscape; this is a relatively new situation and is due to severe mining subsidence in the area. (The canal has had to be built up – appropriately with pit waste – while the land on either side has sunk.)

Wigan Pier & Heritage Centre
A wonderful complex of restored and new canalside buildings housing a wide range of superb exhibits and entertainments.
Waterways Gardens By Seven Stars Bridge. Boats, stonemason's blocks and a lock-keeper's garden.
The Way We Were Opposite Wigan Pier, this is a stunning exhibition/museum/theatre illustrating how the local people worked and played, laughed and suffered around the turn of the century.
Orwell Pub and restaurant, see below.
Trencherfield Mill Probably the largest working mill engine in Europe, installed when the mill was built in 1907. Meanufactured by J & E Wood of Bolton it is a horizontal four-cylinder triple expansion engine with a 26½ft diameter flywheel. A magnificent sight. Also textile machinery.
Tourist Information Centre Trencherfield Mill (0942 825677).
Mill at the Pier Concerts, exhibitions, conferences.
Waterbus Operates daily to transport visitors from The Waterways Garden at one end to the Mill at the other.
Café, shops, walks, information centre. *All open daily 10.00-17.00.* Charge. A remarkable initiative.

BOATYARDS

British Waterways Wigan Yard at Wigan Bottom Lock (0942 42239). [R] [W] Chandlery, books and maps. For British Waterways dry dock ring 0942 41563.

PUBS AND RESTAURANTS

🍺 **Dover Lock Inn** Canalside at Dover Bridge on the Leigh Branch. Greenall Whitley real ale, food *lunchtime and evenings* and children's play area in a modernised pub. There used to be two locks nearby: they were removed years ago, becoming unnecessary as the level of the land changed.
🍺 ✕ **Orwell** Wigan (0942 323034). Large pub and restaurant in a warehouse opposite bridge 51. This is a very handsome building, and the conversion has been well done – the pub is spacious, comfortable and restrained. Tetley's and Jennings real ales; bar meals (*lunchtime and evenings*) are available. Outside drinking on canalside verandah. Plenty of moorings close by.
🍺 **Royal Oak** Standish Lower Ground, Wigan. Burtonwood real ale and a wide variety of food *at all times.*
🍺 **Swan & Railway** Wallgate, Wigan. A 5-minute walk from the Orwell towards the town centre. Bass and John Smith's real ales; food *lunchtime and evenings (not Sun).* Children's room.
🍺 **Seven Stars Hotel** Wallgate, canalside. Thwaites real ale and food *lunchtime and evenings* in a friendly and interesting pub.
🍺 **Bamfurlong Hotel** Lily Lane. 200yds south west of bridge no 3 on the Leigh Branch. Walkers real ale.

Leigh

The Leigh Branch continues eastwards
through what was once a wasteland – now
reclaimed and landscaped – towards Plank
Lane swing bridge (actually a lift bridge)
which is mechanically operated (see below).
Past the bridge, in Leigh, the canal suddenly
becomes the Bridgewater Canal (without the
customary stop lock), giving access to
Manchester and the Trent & Mersey via
Preston Brook. This navigation is owned by
the Manchester Ship Canal Company: boats
licensed by British Waterways may use the
Bridgewater without further charge for up to
three consecutive days.

Navigational note
Plank Lane swing bridge is *open summer:
08.00-12.00, 12.45-20.00 daily; winter: 08.00-
12.00, 12.45-14.30 Mon-Fri, 10.00-14.00 Sat
and Sun,* and is operated by a bridge keeper.
Contact British Waterways by ringing 0942
42239 to confirm times.

Leigh
Gt Manchester. EC Wed. All services. Once the
archetypal mill town, most of the tall buildings
and chimneys have now been demolished. In
the market place you can see the fine
Edwardian Baroque Town Hall, built 1904-7,
facing the battlemented church of St Mary.

PUBS
● **Eagle & Hawk** Chapel Street, Leigh.
Walkers real ale and food.
● **Railway Hotel** Twist Lane, Leigh. A beer
enthusiast's pub offering Tetley's, Walkers,
Jennings and Ind Coope (Burton) real ales.
Opens 12.00 and 19.00 (sometimes later).
● **Nevison** Plank Lane. 400yds from the
swing bridge. A comfortable miners' pub
serving Tetley's and Walkers real ales. Snacks
at *lunchtime.*

Wigan Locks

Leaving the junction with the Leigh Branch,
the main line reaches the Wigan flight of 21
locks. It is a long climb to the top by boat, for
these wide, deep locks raise the canal level by
over 200ft. For rest and recuperation, there
are shops and pubs near bridges 53 and 54.
Up at the top lock, however, are two canal
pubs – a comforting sight. Here is a T-
junction as the canal meets what used to be
the southern end of the Lancaster Canal (see
the history section) on its disjointed way to
Johnson's Hill Locks, Walton Summit and
Preston. In the middle of the housing estate
behind the Kirkless Hall is a fish & chip shop,
open for lunch and supper most days except Sun.
Turning left, the traveller is soon aware of the
great height climbed as the navigation winds
along a hill. It soon enters the woods that
precede Haigh Hall and Park.

Navigational notes
1 The locks between Wigan and Leeds are 60ft
long, and therefore cannot accommodate a
full length narrowboat.
2 The Wigan Flight is not quite the daunting
prospect it once was. It is *open mid Mar–mid
Nov 08.00–18.00*, and you can obtain
assistance by ringing 0942 44449. It is
possible to stop on the flight, between locks 77
& 78, which is handy for shops, pubs and take-
aways.
3 You will require a British Waterways anti-
vandal key.

Wigan
Gt Manchester. EC Wed, MD Fri. All services. A
large, heavily industrialised town whose
skyline is now a mixture of industrial chimneys
and towering concrete blocks of offices and
flats. There is a new covered market centre,
good for shopping, and an Olympic-size
swimming pool. It has long been the butt of
many jokes referring to Wigan Pier – not a
Victorian structure devoted to amusement at
sea, but a coal staithe! George Formby Snr
started the confusion, which lasted for years.
See page 93 for details of the Heritage Centre.
All Saints Church A very large and
impressive parish church surrounded by
beautiful rose gardens. Parts of the original
medieval structure remain, but it was largely
rebuilt in 1845-50, still following the rather
ornate design of the former church. There are
several very fine stained-glass windows and
numerous monuments and effigies.
Powell Museum Station Road. Exhibits
include geology, coins and the history of local
industrial development. *Open weekdays.*

BOATYARDS
British Waterways Wigan Yard At Wigan
Bottom Lock (0942 42239). R W
Chandlery, books and maps, information
centre. For British Waterways dry dock ring
0942 41563.
Ⓑ **Wilco Marine** Withington Lane, New
Springs, Wigan (0942 496840). R W D
Pump-out, slipway, engine and boat repairs,
boatbuilding and sales.

PUBS
🍺 **Crown Hotel** West of bridge 59A.
Burtonwood real ale, meals *lunchtime and
evenings (except Tue evenings)*, garden and
children's room.
🍺 **Colliers Arms** Near bridge 59A.
Burtonwood real ale in a charming old pub
overlooking the canal.
🍺 **Kirkless Hall** Canalside, near Wigan Top
Lock. Distinctive black and white building
housing spacious and comfortable bars.
Burtonwood real ale and good bar meals
lunchtime and evenings.
🍺 **Commercial Inn** Canalside, at bridge 57.
A sturdy pub dispensing Tetley's and Walkers
real ales and bar snacks *lunchtime and evenings.*
Payphone here.
🍺 **Shepherds Arms** Tetley's real ale pub at
bridge 53. Good café 100yds north west of this
bridge.

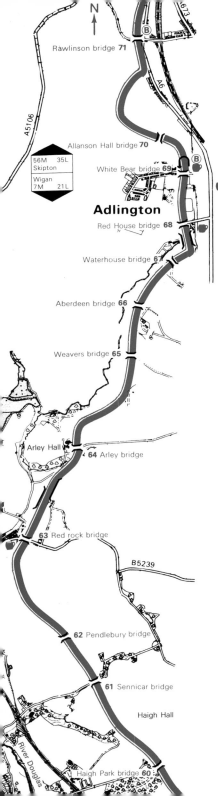

Adlington

The canal continues to run as a 9-mile lock-free pound – known as the 'Lancaster Pool' – along the side of the valley from which the industries surrounding Wigan can be viewed in the distance. It enjoys a pleasant and quiet isolation in this lightly wooded area. Already the navigation is well over 300ft above the sea, and the bleak hills up to the east give a hint of the Pennines that are soon to be crossed. The conspicuous tower east of Adlington stands on a hill that is over 1500ft high. Points of interest on this stretch include Arley Hall, a large and elegant moated house that is now the club house of the local golf club, and the nearby skewed aqueduct over a closed railway track.

Adlington
Gt Manchester. PO, tel, stores, garage, station. A small industrialised town very useful for pubs and supplies – the local licensed store east of bridge 69 is open late most evenings and there is a park nearby.
Haigh Hall (0942 832895). On east bank of the canal. The pre-Tudor mansion was rebuilt by its owner, the 23rd Earl of Crawford, between 1830 and 1849. The reconstruction was designed and directed by the Earl, and all the stone, timber and iron used on the job came from the estate. The Hall is now owned by Wigan Corporation, who allow the citizens to use it for private wedding receptions, etc. There is little to see in the house and it is not normally open to the public. The park and grounds around the hall are *open daily all year,* and contain much that caters for the family: there are children's amusements, glasshouses, a nature trail, a miniature railway, a mini zoo and a golf course.

BOATYARDS
Ⓑ **L & L Cruisers** Rawlinson Lane, Heath Charnock, nr Chorley (0257 480825). Ⓡ Ⓦ Ⓓ Ⓔ Pump-out, gas, narrowboat hire, day hire craft, overnight mooring (*Mon-Fri*), slipway, chandlery, books and maps, boat building, engine sales and repairs, gift shop, ice-cream, toilets.
Ⓑ **White Bear Marina** Park Road, Adlington (0257 481054). Ⓡ Ⓢ Ⓦ Ⓓ Pump-out, slipway, gas, overnight mooring, long-term mooring, winter storage, boat and engine sales and repairs, showers, toilets, chandlery, gifts. Resident night watchman.

PUBS
🍺 **Cardwell Arms** East of bridge 71. Vaux and Wards real ale in a boisterous pub.
🍺 **White Bear** East of bridge 69. An old roadside pub serving Theakston and Matthew Brown real ales. *Lunchtime* food.
🍺 **Bridge Inn** By bridge 69. Greenall Whitley real ale.
🍺 **Waggon & Horses** East of bridge 68. Dark rustic pub offering Whitbread and Hartleys real ale and *lunchtime* food.
🍺 **Crawford Arms** Canalside by Red Rock Bridge (63). Comfortable split-level pub with a garden. Greenall Whitley real ale and meals *lunchtime and evenings.*

Leeds & Liverpool 97

Chorley

This is an initially attractive section as the
canal wanders northwards from Adlington.
Hemmed in for much of the way by woodland,
the canal is undisturbed by the railway and
main roads that for a while follow it closely.
Soon the greenery gives way to views of
Chorley's rows of rooftops across the valley.
The canal crosses this valley, but shuns the
town: it passes instead some large and
resplendent outlying textile mills. The M61
motorway zooms up from Manchester around
the mills and over the navigation before
disappearing in the direction of Preston in a
flurry of flyovers, feeder roads and
roundabouts.

Chorley
Lancs. EC Wed. MD Tue, Fri, Sat. All services.
On the west bank of the canal, a busy town
based on the manufacture of textiles and spare
parts for commercial and public service
vehicles. (Leyland, where the vehicles are
built, is just a few miles away to the north
west.) Chorley has avoided too much
industrial grimness by maintaining its market-
town traditions and extensive new housing
development. Sir Henry Tate, the founder of
the Tate Gallery in London, was born in
Chorley in 1819 and began his career here as a
grocer's assistant.
St Laurence's Church Church Brow.
Surrounded by trees in the centre of the town,
parts of the church date back to the 14thC.
The bones that are enshrined in a recess in the
chancel are believed to have belonged to St
Laurence.
Astley Hall At the north-west end of the town
just over a mile from Botany Bridge. Set in a
large park beside a lake, the appearance of this
Elizabethan mansion is very striking, for in the
17thC the existing timberframing was
replaced by a new façade that is lacking in
symmetry. The interior is very fine with
splendid ceilings, furnishings, tapestries and
pottery. *Open afternoons.*

PUBS AND RESTAURANTS
📖✕ **Railway** Canalside at bridge 78A (025
72 75864). Modernised pub and restaurant
(*L & D*) serving Boddingtons real ale. The
railway line has long disappeared – the viaduct
was blown up to make room for the motorway.
📖 **Bretherton** West of bridge 78. Matthew
Brown real ale in a comfortable lounge bar.
Lunchtime food.
📖 **Seven Stars** 84 Eaves Lane, Chorley.
West of bridges 76 and 77. Basic town local
dispensing Matthew Brown real ale.
📖 **Hop Pocket** Carr Lane, Chorley. West of
bridge 75. Thwaites real ale in a modern estate
pub decorated with hop sacks. Snacks.

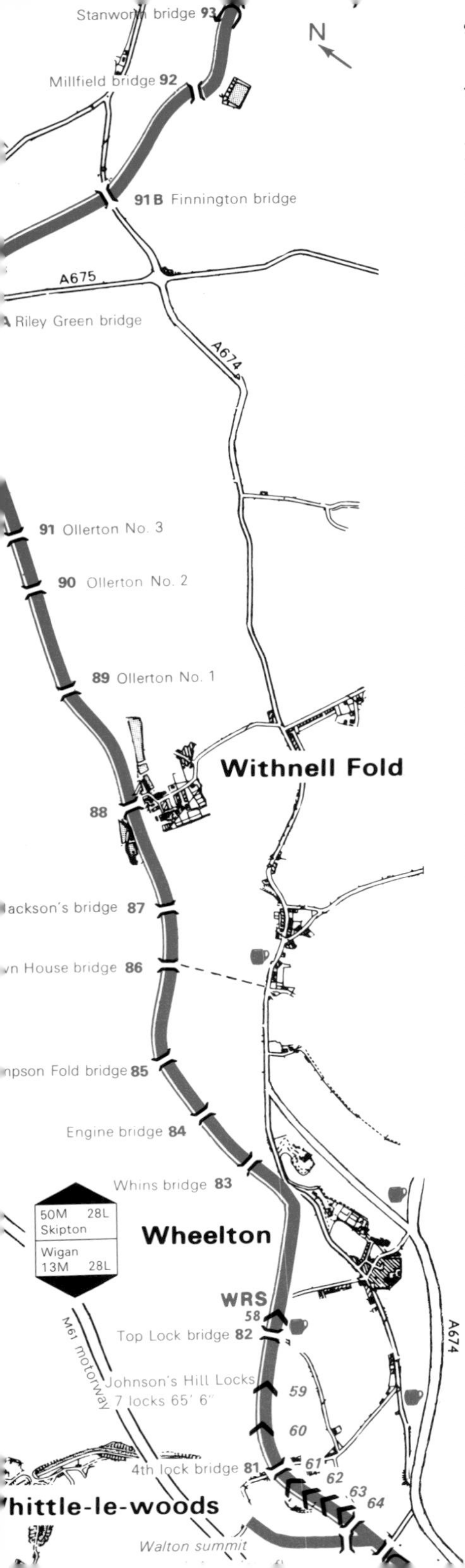
Stanworth bridge 93
N
Millfield bridge 92
91B Finnington bridge
A675
Riley Green bridge
A674
91 Ollerton No. 3
90 Ollerton No. 2
89 Ollerton No. 1
Withnell Fold
88
ackson's bridge 87
n House bridge 86
npson Fold bridge 85
Engine bridge 84
Whins bridge 83
50M 28L
Skipton
Wigan
13M 28L
Wheelton
WRS
58
Top Lock bridge 82
M61 motorway
Johnson's Hill Locks
7 locks 65' 6"
59
60
A674
4th lock bridge 81
61
62
63
64
hittle-le-woods
Walton summit

Withnell Fold

This is a most delightful stretch of waterway. The junction with the old Walton Summit Branch features a canal cottage and the bottom lock in the Johnson's Hill flight. A short but energetic spell of windlass-wielding is required here, for the seven locks are very close together. It is rewarding work, for the steep countryside yields good views, and the locks are tidily maintained and painted. Near the middle lock is an old toll house, a post office, telephone and store; at the top lock is a pub and, usually, a medley of boats (there is a boat club here). The canal now changes course to north east and flows along a beautifully secluded and often wooded valley at a height of over 350ft above sea level. Even the old mills at Withnell Fold, which once brought a glimpse of industry, are gone.

Withnell Fold
Lancs. A remarkable village well worth a short visit. It is a small estate village, built to house workers at the canalside paper mills which are now demolished. They used to export banknote paper all over the world until 'rationalisation' transferred their work elsewhere. Symmetrically grouped around three sides of a spacious square, the terraced cottages present an intimately united front which is almost unnerving to the casual visitor – especially as on the fourth side of the square is an old set of wooden stocks.

Wheelton
Lancs. PO, tel, stores, garage. There are steep terraces and cobbled streets in this village which has been recently bypassed and has thus rid itself of much road traffic.

Walton Summit Branch
The short branch leading off to the north from Johnson's Hill Locks used to be part of the Lancaster Canal, which was originally projected to run south from Preston past Wigan to the Bridgewater Canal. But the Lancaster Canal Company was very short of money and, after arranging with the Leeds & Liverpool Company to share a common course between Johnson's Hill Locks and Wigan Top Lock, was daunted by the prospect of constructing a large and necessarily expensive aqueduct over the River Ribble in Preston. A 'temporary' tramroad was therefore built to connect the two lengths of canal between Preston and Walton Summit about 3 miles north of Johnson's Hill. The tramway, which opened in 1803, featured a short tunnel and a light trestle bridge over the Ribble. Through traffic now began to use the canal, and one may imagine the busy scenes at either end of the tramway as cargoes were transhipped from boats into wagons and back into boats at the far end. The tramroad, although designed only as a short-term measure, was never replaced by a canal; indeed the whole line was closed by 1880. Most of the canal branch has recently been severed by the building of a motorway, although plenty of it still remains in an unnavigable state.

PUBS AND RESTAURANTS

Finnington's At bridge 91A. A smart pub/restaurant.

Royal Oak Preston Old Road, Hoghton. North of bridge 91A. Busy, rambling old pub serving Thwaites real ale, and meals *lunchtime and Wed-Sun evenings.*

Golden Lion Blackburn Road, Higher Wheelton. South of bridge 86. Thwaites real ale in a small, pleasant main road pub.

Dressers Arms Briers Brow, Wheelton (0254 830041). East of bridge 82. An excellent pub with à la carte restaurant upstairs (*L & D*) and a fine choice of real ales and food in the bar.

Top Lock Canalside at Johnson's Hill Top Lock. Good bar food and Matthew Brown real ale in a comfortable pub. Moor below the top lock – there is no room above.

Red Cat Blackburn Road, Heapey (025 72 63966). East of bridge 80. Pizzeria with a small bar area.

Blackburn

The canal now curls round a steep and thickly wooded valley, crossing it on a high embankment before entering the outskirts of Blackburn. Close to bridge 94 there is a useful shop. It seems to take a long time to get through this large town, as there is a flight of six locks here, raising the canal's level to a height of over 400ft above sea level. The lock keeper maintains a tidy flight – indeed most of the passage through the city is now pleasant – there is little rubbish or graffiti, and the views are excellent. A good towpath exists throughout. Of particular interest to those on the canal are the fine canopied wharves of the Depot at Enam Wharf, now converted into a business centre with a pub and visitor centre incorporated.

Navigational note
Gates giving access to the towpath in Blackburn are locked at night. Recommended moorings are by the lock keeper's cottage just above lock 56 and handy for the shops; and at Enam Wharf.

Blackburn
Lancs. EC Thur. All services. Few of the Pennine towns which sprang up with the Industrial Revolution can be described as beautiful, as aesthetic feelings were rarely consulted in the rush to raise mills and cram houses round them. In an attempt to rectify this, Blackburn has taken drastic steps in recent years to construct a new city centre. Nevertheless the most impressive features of the town are still the old cotton mills.
Blackburn Cathedral Dating from 1820-6, the parish church was raised to cathedral status in 1926. Extensive renovations have been made inside. Very striking 13ft sculpture of 'Christ the Worker' in aluminium and black iron by John Hayward. Large churchyard.
Lewis Textile Museum Exchange Street, Blackburn (0254 667130). A series of period rooms demonstrating the development of the textile industry from the 18thC by means of full-size working models, including Hargreaves' 'Spinning Jenny'. *Closed Mon & Sun.*
Museum & Art Gallery Library Street, Blackburn (0254 667130). Exhibits include natural history, pottery, early manuscripts and a large collection of English, Greek and Roman coins. In the art gallery are over 1200 beautiful Japanese prints, as well as English watercolours of the 18thC-20thC. *Closed Mon & Sun.*
Witton park At the western end of the town, north of Cherry Tree station. Nearly 500 acres of magnificent parkland, including the beautiful landmark, Billinge Hill. Splendid rhododendrons and azaleas. *Open daily.*
Tourist Information Centre King George's Hall, Northgate, Blackburn (0254 53277).

PUBS

▬ **Packet House Inn** Near bridge 103A. Bass real ale.
▬ **Wharf** A lively new pub, part of Enam Wharf redevelopment. Choice of real ales, extensive menu *lunchtime and evenings.* Children welcome when eating.
▬ **Angel** Blackburn. By lock 56. Thwaites real ale, good bar food *lunchtime,* children welcome in this down-to-earth pub.
▬ **Navigation** Blackburn. Canalside, at bridge 96A. Thwaites real ale.
▬ **Barge Inn** Blackburn. By bridge 102A. New pub with canal theme serving Thwaites real ale.
▬ **Atlantic** 100yds south of bridge 100. Matthew Brown real ale.
▬ **Royal Oak** 100yds south of bridge 100. Whitbread real ale.
▬ **Moorings** By bridge 99. A large, brand new pub with a large range of food *lunchtime and evenings* and a choice of real ales. Children welcome when eating.

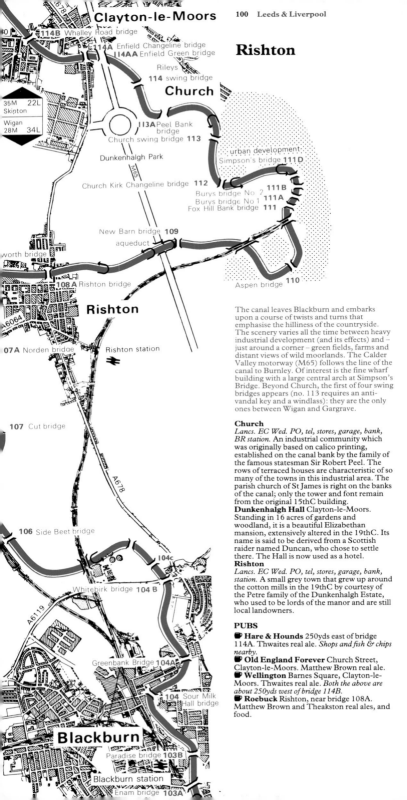

Clayton-le-Moors

114B Whalley Road bridge
114A ─ Enfield Changeline bridge
114AA Enfield Green bridge
Rileys
114 swing bridge

Rishton

Church

35M 22L
Skipton
Wigan
28M 34L

113A Peel Bank bridge
Church swing bridge 113

Dunkenhalgh Park

urban development
Simpson's bridge 111D

Church Kirk Changeline bridge 112

Burys bridge No 2   111B
Burys bridge No 1   111A
Fox Hill Bank bridge 111

New Barn bridge 109
aqueduct

worth bridge

108 A Rishton bridge

Aspen bridge 110

Rishton

07 A Norden bridge

Rishton station

107 Cut bridge

106 Side Beet bridge

104c

Whitebirk bridge 104 B

Greenbank Bridge 104A

104 Sour Milk Hall bridge

Blackburn

Paradise bridge 103B

Blackburn station
Enam bridge 103A

The canal leaves Blackburn and embarks
upon a course of twists and turns that
emphasise the hilliness of the countryside.
The scenery varies all the time between heavy
industrial development (and its effects) and –
just around a corner – green fields, farms and
distant views of wild moorlands. The Calder
Valley motorway (M65) follows the line of the
canal to Burnley. Of interest is the fine wharf
building with a large central arch at Simpson's
Bridge. Beyond Church, the first of four swing
bridges appears (no. 113 requires an anti-
vandal key and a windlass): they are the only
ones between Wigan and Gargrave.

Church
*Lancs. EC Wed. PO, tel, stores, garage, bank,
BR station.* An industrial community which
was originally based on calico printing,
established on the canal bank by the family of
the famous statesman Sir Robert Peel. The
rows of terraced houses are characteristic of so
many of the towns in this industrial area. The
parish church of St James is right on the banks
of the canal; only the tower and font remain
from the original 15thC building.
Dunkenhalgh Hall Clayton-le-Moors.
Standing in 16 acres of gardens and
woodland, it is a beautiful Elizabethan
mansion, extensively altered in the 19thC. Its
name is said to be derived from a Scottish
raider named Duncan, who chose to settle
there. The Hall is now used as a hotel.
Rishton
*Lancs. EC Wed. PO, tel, stores, garage, bank,
station.* A small grey town that grew up
around the cotton mills in the 19thC by courtesy of
the Petre family of the Dunkenhalgh Estate,
who used to be lords of the manor and are still
local landowners.

PUBS
🍺 **Hare & Hounds** 250yds east of bridge
114A. Thwaites real ale. *Shops and fish & chips
nearby.*
🍺 **Old England Forever** Church Street,
Clayton-le-Moors. Matthew Brown real ale.
🍺 **Wellington** Barnes Square, Clayton-le-
Moors. Thwaites real ale. *Both the above are
about 250yds west of bridge 114B.*
🍺 **Roebuck** Rishton, near bridge 108A.
Matthew Brown and Theakston real ales, and
food.

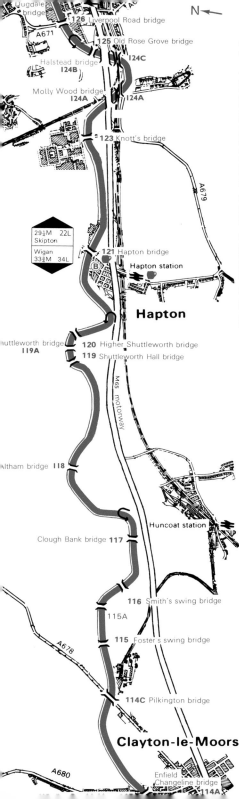

Hapton

The navigation continues to wind eastwards
along the side of what turns out to be the
Calder Valley with the new motorway to the
south. High ground rises on each side of the
valley, and in the distance the summit of
Pendle Hill (1831ft high) can be clearly seen
when it is not obscured by cloud. This is an
attractive length of canal, unspoilt by industry
and greatly enhanced by the ever-changing
views from the side of the hill along which the
canal is cut, although the motorway is
uncomfortably close throughout, and power
station cooling towers are ever present. Soon
the distant mass of dwellings is recognisable as
the suburbs of Burnley.

Hapton
Lancs. PO, tel, stores, station. A small and
unmistakably northern town, with its regular
streets of terraced houses.

BOATYARDS
ⓑ **Hapton Boatyard** Hapton (0282 73178).
Ⓡ Ⓦ Ⓓ Ⓔ Gas. overnight mooring, long-term
mooring, winter storage, slipway, crane, boat
building (and DIY), boat sales, engine repairs.
National boat transporters.

PUBS
🍺 **Bridge House** Hapton, by bridge 121.
Thwaites real ale, *lunchtime* bar snacks.
🍺 **Railway** Hapton. Along the road from the
Bridge House. Thwaites real ale.

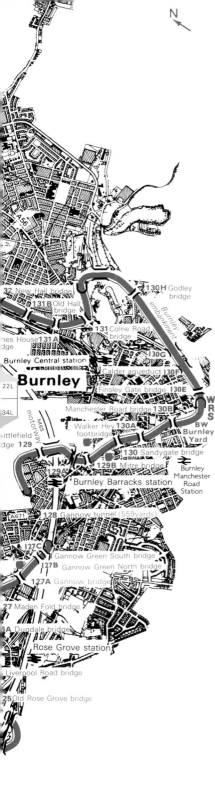

Burnley

The canal now wanders through the suburbs into Gannow Tunnel (559yds long), then round the hillside into Burnley. This is an industrial stretch where the canal was once a main artery for the town and its industries. The area around bridge 130 known as the Weavers' Triangle has been recognised to be of great interest – fine warehouses, tall chimneys and loading bays flank the canal here. There is a museum in the Toll House, and a steam mill engine has been restored. The huge Burnley Embankment carries the navigation across part of the town – called 'the straight mile', it is ¾ mile long, but no less dramatic for that fact; 60ft high, it incorporates an aqueduct over a main road. The whole area of the embankment has been tidied up and the towpath opened and improved: access is now good and this, together with the British Waterways yard, makes a good mooring site. Shops are within easy reach and the attractive Thompsons Park (good play area and boating lake) can be found north of the aqueduct after bridge 130H.

Burnley
Lancs. All services. A large industrial northern town, which has worked hard to improve its appearance. It was once the world centre for cotton weaving. The excellent shopping centre is only 10 minutes' walk from Finsley Gate Bridge, and if you feel like a swim, a sauna or a solarium, the Thompson Recreation Centre is even closer. *Fish & chips* are two minutes' walk south west of the bridge.

Queen Street Mill Museum Harle Syke, Burnley (0282 412555). North east of Burnley Embankment, along Eastern Avenue and Briercliffe Road from the football ground. This is Britain's only working 19thC weaving mill, powered by the 500hp steam engine 'Peace'. Virtually unchanged until it closed in 1982, the mill has now found a new lease of life, with some of the former employees back again to work the looms. Mill shop and café. Ring for details of opening times.

The Weavers' Triangle The area between bridges 129B and 130B is one of the best-preserved 19thC industrial districts in the country – there are weaving sheds with 'north light' roofs, engine houses, spinning mills and well-preserved terraces of 19thC houses. An explanatory leaflet and town trail guide are available from: the Tourist Information Centre or the Toll House Museum of local history and the cotton industry, which is also the information centre for the Weavers' Triangle. *Open 14.00-16.00 Tue, Wed, Sat, Sun & B. Hols Easter-Sep.* Free.

Townley Hall (0282 24213). On the southern outskirts of Burnley, 1¼ miles south east of the BW yard. Set in extensive parkland with a golf course and play area, the grandiose, battlemented house dating from the 14thC was the home of the Townley family until 1902. It is now an art gallery and museum with the rooms lavishly furnished in period style. *Closed Sat & Sun morning.*

Tourist Information Centre Burnley Mechanics, Manchester Road, Burnley (0282 30055).

BOATYARDS

British Waterways Burnley Yard Finsley Gate, Burnley (0282 28680). ⟦R⟧ ⟦S⟧ ⟦W⟧ Pump-out, gas nearby, overnight mooring, slipway, toilet, telephone kiosk, good access to shops.

PUBS

There are plenty of pubs in Burnley.
- 🍺 **Stork** North of bridge 129B. Tetley's ales.
- 🍺 **Mitre Hotel** By bridge 129B. Bass.
- 🍺 **Sparrowhawk** Church Street, Burnley. Moorhouse real ale, brewed in the town.
- 🍺 **Grey Mare** 110 Gannow Lane, Burnley. Typical cosy local serving Bass real ale.
- 🍺 **Gannow Wharf** Canalside at bridge 127A. Bass and bar snacks.

Brierfield

Here again the canal negotiates a landscape which alternates between open country, towns and semi-towns, with the massive distant bulk of Pendle Hill in the background. Cobbled streets of terraced houses run down to the canal, and old wharves lie disused and overgrown. The navigation winds as it follows the hillside; but this ceases at Nelson, where it crosses the valley on a minor aqueduct and begins to climb the pretty Barrowford Locks having finally seen off the new motorway.

Nelson
Lancs. EC Tue. MD Wed, Fri, Sat. All services. Nelson is a conglomerate of a number of small villages that combined in the 19thC to form one industrial town. The centre has been redeveloped with a large covered shopping precinct. One of Nelson's more valuable assets is the easy access to the beautiful moors and Forest of Pendle, behind which looms Pendle Hill.

Brierfield
Lancs. PO, tel, stores, garage, bank, station, cinema. A small industrial town merging into Burnley at one end and into Nelson at the other. The parish church of St Luke in Colne Road is a Victorian building with an unusually designed clock tower culminating in a steep pyramid roof.

PUBS AND RESTAURANTS
✕ ❢ **Greendales Diner** Dale Street, Nelson (0282 697130). Just south of bridge 140. Moorings, handy for the town.
🍺 **Waggon & Horses** Brierfield, up the road from bridge 139. A beautifully restored pub with an open fire, offering Thwaites real ale, and food *lunchtime and evenings.* Garden.
🍺 **Leeds & Liverpool** Brierfield. Up the hill from bridge 137.
🍺 **Reedley Hallows Hotel** 50yds east of bridge 134. Castle Eden real ale.

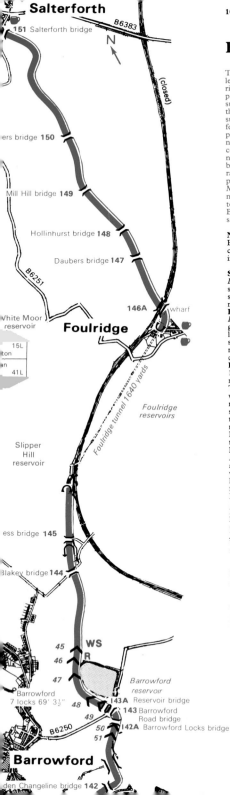

Foulridge

This is a refreshing stretch, in which the canal leaves the succession of industrial towns. It rises through the seven Barrowford Locks, passing Barrowford reservoir (in which the summit level's surplus water is stored), and at the beautifully kept top lock reaches the summit level of the whole canal. Soon various feeder streams can be seen, continuously pouring vital water supplies into the navigation. Meanwhile, distant mountainous country frames beautiful old stone farms nearer at hand. Soon everything is blotted out by Foulridge Tunnel; at the other end, by the railway bridge, is an old wharf where it is possible to moor to visit the village. Meanwhile the navigation continues northward through this very fine countryside to Salterforth, crossing over the little 'Country Brook' between bridges 149 (milk and eggs for sale) and 150.

Navigational note
Entrance to Foulridge Tunnel is restricted and controlled by lights. Please obey signs giving instructions.

Salterforth
Lancs. PO, tel, stores. A small village of narrow streets and terraced houses in an upland setting. Children will enjoy the playground north of bridge 151.
Foulridge
Lancs. PO, tel, stores. Attractive around the green, where alleys festooned with washing lines give the place a homely air. In the surrounding countryside are scattered the reservoirs that feed the summit level of the canal.
Foulridge Tunnel
1640yds long, with no towpath, this tunnel is, not surprisingly, barred to unapproved boats. The hole in the hill sprang to fame in 1912 when a cow fell into the canal near the tunnel mouth and for some reason decided to struggle through to the other end of the tunnel. The gallant but weary swimmer was revived with alcohol at the Foulridge end. Photographs in the Hole in the Wall pub recall the incident. The tunnel roof drips liberally.
Barrowford
Lancs. PO, tel, stores. There are still some attractive terraces of stone cottages in this village, which lie a short walk to the west of the locks. The Toll House, the last intact survivor from the old Marsden (Nelson) to Long Preston turnpike road, together with the 17thC Park Hill (the birthplace of Roger Bannister, the first 'four minute miler') now houses The Pendle Heritage Centre (0282 695366). *Open afternoons; closed Mon,* charge. John Wesley preached from the packhorse bridge in the 1770s; there is a fine park by the river containing traces of a mill dating from 1311.

PUBS

◗ **Anchor** Salterforth. Canalside, at bridge 151. A traditional pub serving Bass Charrington real ale, where a second building was built on top of the first – hence where you now drink was once the bedrooms. The cellar has stalactites. Good moorings, children's room.
◗ **Hole in the Wall** Foulridge. 250yds east of tunnel, north end. Here is recorded the famous cow in the canal incident. Stones real ale is served, and there is a room where children can sit. Steeles stores close by gives genial service and stocks splendid pies – savoury or sweet.
◗ **New Inn** Foulridge. Carry on past the Hole in the Wall and cross the main road. Thwaites real ale, bar food (*not Sun or Mon Oct-Mar*). Children may eat here. Spotlessly clean.
◗ **George & Dragon** Gisburn Road, Barrowford. Large Victorian bar counter and 18thC fireplace in the public bar of this lively village pub opposite the Toll House. John Smith's real ale.

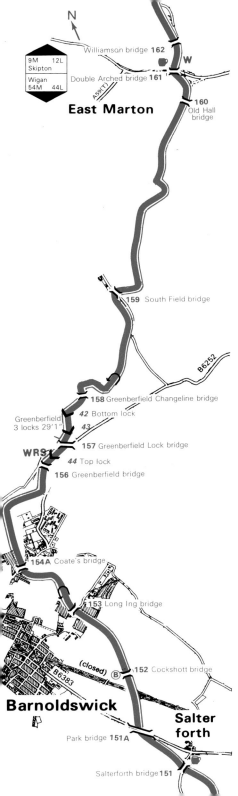

Barnoldswick

This is one of the most remote sections of the whole canal and probably the most beautiful. There is also much canal interest, for just south of bridge 153 was the junction, now disappeared, of the Rain Hall Rock Branch, essentially a linear quarry where the limestone was loaded directly from the rock face onto the boats. Walk up the road from the bridge (east) and turn right at the top where it will come into view, straddled by a tall three-arched viaduct. A mile further along one rounds a corner and is confronted by Greenberfield Top Lock (showers, camping), which introduces the beginning of the long descent towards Leeds. (The feeder from the distant Winterburn reservoir enters the canal at the top lock.) The three locks here were built in 1820 to replace the original flight (the old dry bed of the earlier route can be seen on the towpath side) and are set in beautiful uplands – for the next few miles the canal winds through scenery that is composed of countless individual hillocks, some topped by clumps of trees. Beyond are distant mountains. Around East Marton, after skirting the isolated church, the surroundings change briefly: the navigation enters a cutting, passes under a double-arched main road bridge and enters a sheltered fold housing a farm, a pub and some moorings. But a steep wooded cutting leads the canal out of this pastoral interlude and back into the rugged moorlands. There is a useful shop and café at Wilkinsons Farm by bridge 162, which can also be reached via a lane to the side of the Cross Keys.

Pennine Way The Pennine Way is a walking route covering over 250 miles of Pennine highland from Edale in the south to Kirk Yetholm in the north. Because of the nature of the route much of the Way is rough, hard walking, but it gives a superb view from the mountains. At East Marton the Pennine Way shares the canal towpath for a short distance – you will notice that the stones here abound with fossils.

Barnoldswick
Lancs. EC Tue. PO, tel, stores, garage, bank. Set back from the canal, the mainstay of this town's existence is the Rolls Royce factory, where experimental work is done on aero engines. The centre of the town is compact and dominated by the modern Holy Trinity Church completed in 1960.

BOATYARDS

Ⓑ **Doug Moore (Boatbuilders)** Lower Park Marina, Kelbrook Road, Barnoldswick (0282 815883). Ⓢ Ⓦ Ⓓ Pump-out, gas, narrowboat hire, day hire craft, overnight mooring, groceries, chandlery, gifts, books and maps, boat building, engine repairs, telephone, fresh milk.

PUBS AND RESTAURANTS

🍺✖ **Cross Keys** East Marton (0282 843485). By bridge 161. Large and handsome pub with a comfortable polished wood interior. Theakston and Webster's real ales, bar snacks and more substantial meals in the candlelit dining room. Telephone kiosk close by. There are plenty of pubs in Barnoldswick.

Gargrave

This is another outstanding stretch, in which
the navigation continues to snake
extravagantly around the splendid green and
humpy hills that fill the landscape. The six
Bank Newton Locks in their wooded setting
lower the canal into Upper Airedale, yielding
excellent views across the valley to the hills
and moors beyond. The River Aire flows in
from the north, accompanied by the railway
line to Skipton and Leeds from Morecambe,
Settle and distant Carlisle. The canal crosses
the river by a substantial stone aqueduct.
Meanwhile, yet more locks take the canal
round Gargrave, between the village and the
hills; the beauty of the area may be judged by
the fact that the Yorkshire Dales National
Park borders the navigation along here. There
is a launching slipway at Higherland Lock.

Gargrave
N. Yorks. PO, tel, stores, garage, bank, station.
A very attractive and much-visited village.
Holding an enviable position near the head of
Airedale between the canal and the river, this
place is the ideal centre for boat crews to
explore the surrounding countryside. The
River Aire cuts Gargrave in two, and the
bridge over it forms the centre of the village.
There is a charming station, and some pretty
stone cottages along the green. The church is
mostly Victorian, except for the tower, which
was built in 1521. Excellent home bakery, and
a coal merchant, by bridge 171.
Yorkshire Dales National Park Some of
England's finest walking country is contained
in this area of fine views, deep valleys, open
moorland and rugged hills. Designated as a
National Park in 1954 the Dales, covering
680sq miles, are hardly scarred by habitation.

PUBS AND RESTAURANTS

■ **Mason's Arms** Gargrave. An old
attractive local opposite the church.
Whitbread real ale and snacks.
■ **Old Swan** Main Street, Gargrave.
Imposing village centre hotel serving
Whitbread real ale and meals *lunchtime and
evenings.* Accommodation.
■✕ **Anchor Inn** By Anchor Lock, Gargrave.
(0756 749666). A large smart pub/hotel/
restaurant with comfortable low-ceilinged bars
where you can enjoy Theakston and Younger
real ales. Meals (*L & D*) and a large garden
with a superb children's play park.

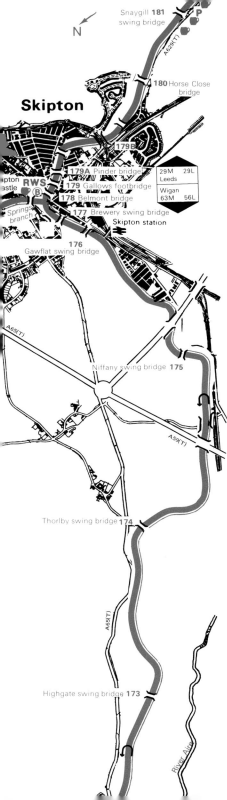

N

Snaygill **181**
swing bridge

180 Horse Close
bridge

Skipton

179B

179A Pinder bridge

RWS

179 Gallows footbridge

178 Belmont bridge

177 Brewery swing bridge

Skipton station

	29M	29L
	Leeds	
	Wigan	
	63M	56L

Springs
branch

176
Gawflat swing bridge

A65(T)

Niffany swing bridge **175**

A59(T)

Thorlby swing bridge **174**

A65(T)

Highgate swing bridge **173**

River Aire

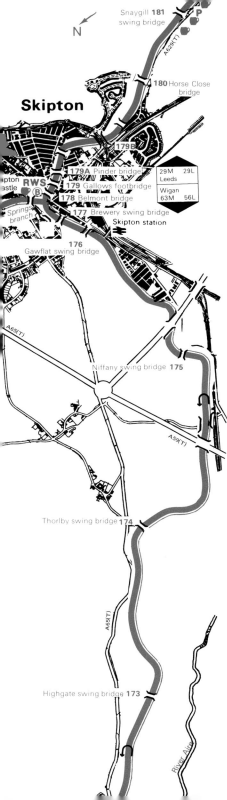

Skipton

The canal now turns south east and proceeds
down Airedale, a valley which contains it from
here right through to Leeds. Upper Airedale is
a flat, wide valley defined by tall steep hills.
The countryside is open, unploughed and very
inviting to walkers, especially with the
moorlands stretching away over the top of the
hills. In this robust landscape the navigation
hugs the hillsides just above the valley floor,
enjoying a lock-free pound that is 17 miles
long – although the navigator's relief at the
absence of locks may be tempered by the
abundance of swing bridges. Entering
Skipton, which is usually bristling with
pleasure boats, the navigator will see the
Springs Branch, a little arm packed with
moored craft, that leads off past the town
centre and soon finds itself in what is virtually
a ravine, overlooked by the castle more than
100ft above. Boats longer than 35ft will have
difficulty in turning round along the branch.
At the junction is a boatyard: next door is a
restored canal warehouse.

Navigational note
Bridges 173, 174, 175, 176 & 177 require
anti-vandal keys.

Skipton
*N. Yorks. EC Tue. MD Wed, Sat. All services
(including cinema) and excellent shops.* Skipton
is probably the most handsome town along the
whole Leeds & Liverpool Canal. It is an
excellent place for visiting from the canal, for
one can moor snugly and safely about one
minute's walk away from the centre. It still
maintains its importance as a market town,
which is referred to in its name: Saxon 'Scip-
tun' means sheep-town. The wide High Street
is very attractive, lined with mostly Georgian
houses, and headed at the northern end by the
splendid castle and the well-kept graveyard of
the parish church. There is an interesting
watermill beside the Springs Branch.
Church of the Holy Trinity Standing
opposite the castle, it is a long battlemented
church, encircled by large lawns and
flourishing gardens. It is in Perpendicular style
dating from the 14thC, though it was greatly
renovated after suffering serious damage
during the Civil War. It has a fine oak roof and
a beautifully carved Jacobean font cover.
Skipton Castle Skipton (0756 792442). A
magnificent Norman castle, with 17thC
additions, that dominates Skipton High
Street. After a three-year siege during the Civil
War, Cromwell's men allowed the restoration
of the castle, but ensured that the building
could never again be used as a stronghold.
The six massive round towers have survived
from the 14thC and other notable features are
the 50ft-long banqueting hall, a kitchen with
roasting and baking hearths, a dungeon and
the 'Shell Room', the walls of which are
decorated with sea shells. *Open daily (closed
Sun morning).* Charge.
Tourist Information Centre 8 Victoria
Square, Skipton (0756 792809).
Springs Branch
A short (770yds) but very unusual branch that
leaves the Leeds & Liverpool Canal, passes the
centre of Skipton and soon finds itself in what
is virtually a ravine, overlooked by the castle
that towers 100ft above. The branch is
navigable, and makes an interesting diversion
by boat or foot. (The towpath continues past
the arm, into Skipton Woods.) It was built by
the Earl of Thanet, the owner of Skipton
Castle, to carry limestone away from his
nearby quarry. It was extended by 240yds in
1797 from the watermill bridge through the
deep rock cutting, and 120ft-chutes were
constructed at the new terminus to drop the
rock into the boats from the horse tramway
that was laid from the quarry to the castle. The
quarry still flourishes, but the canal and
tramway have not been used since 1946.
Trains and lorries have replaced them. The
Springs Branch acted for many years as a
feeder to the Leeds & Liverpool Canal, taking
water from Eller Beck, which runs beside it. It
is now a picturesque backwater and an

excellent place to moor if your boat is less than 35ft long or you are confident that you can reverse out, as turning is restricted.

Skipton Woods Fine woods leading up the little narrow valley from the Springs Branch. For access, just keep on walking up the towpath of the branch.

Yorkshire Dales Railway Embsay Station (0756 794727). 1 mile north of Skipton off the A59/65 bypass. Bus service from Skipton. A 4-mile round-trip either steam or diesel hauled. Museum, mining centre, picnic area, shop, café. *Services every hour 11.00-16.15 Sun, Apr-Dec; Tue & Sat, Jul & Aug; plus various 'specials'.*

BOATYARDS

Ⓑ **Pennine Cruisers** The Boat Shop, 19 Coach Street, Skipton (0756 795478). At junction with Springs Branch. Ⓡ Ⓦ Ⓓ Pump-out, gas, narrowboat hire, day hire craft, overnight mooring, dry dock, chandlery, books and maps, boat building, boat sales, engine sales and repairs, toilets. *24hr* emergency breakdown service.

BOAT TRIPS

Pennine Boat Trips Skipton (0756 790829). Trips and party hire in *Cobbydale.*

PUBS AND RESTAURANTS

🍺 **Bay Horse** Canalside at bridge 182. A 'Family Inn' serving meals *lunchtime and evenings.* Tetley's real ale, garden and children's room.

✕ 🍺 **Copper Beech** Close to bridge 181. Younger real ale and meals *lunchtime and evenings* in this large modern hotel/restaurant. Garden with pond, children's room.

✕ 🍺 **Inn Between** Not far from bridge 181. (0756 795711). Modern restaurant (*L & D*) serving Tetley's real ale.

🍺 **Rose & Crown** Coach Street, Skipton. By the junction with the Springs Branch. Tetley's real ale served in this town centre pub.

🍺 **Royal Shepherd** Canal Street, Skipton. Whitbread, Castle Eden and Chester real ale available in this lively pub overlooking the Springs Branch.

✕ ❗ **Waterfront** Skipton (0756 790121). Restaurant and disco at junction of Springs Branch.

🍺 **Hole in the Wall** High Street, Skipton.

🍺 **New Ship** Canalside, up the Springs Branch.

There are at least 25 other pubs and hotels in the town.

Leeds & Liverpool Canal at Farnhill, near Skipton. *Derek Pratt.*

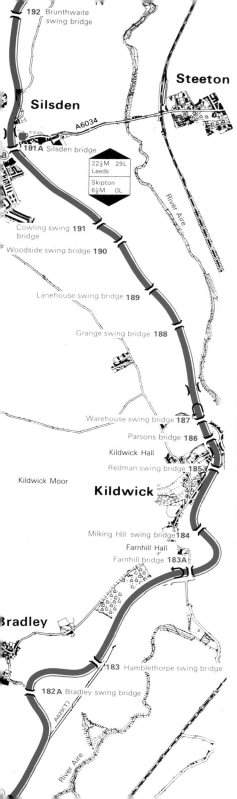

Kildwick

The canal continues along the hillside down
the valley of the River Aire, with the main road
just beside and below the navigation.
Excellent views are offered up and down this
splendid valley and the surrounding
countryside. The village of Bradley has an
attractive waterfront – the *PO stores* are
situated beyond the imposing mill building.
There is a fine wooded stretch north of
Kildwick; then one curves sharply round the
outcrop on which crouches Farnhill Hall, a
mellow stone building. The intriguing village
of Kildwick has some well-restored canalside
buildings now used as private residences.
There are good moorings here prior to quieter
country: the main road and the railway cut the
valley corner while the canal takes the longer
route round to Silsden and beyond. This
stretch of the navigation is liberally
punctuated with swing bridges – many,
thankfully, not requiring an anti-vandal key.

Silsden
W. Yorks. EC Tue. PO, tel, stores, garage, bank.
A well-contained, stone-built industrial town
spreading uphill from the canal. In addition to
its proximity to the Yorkshire Dales National
Park, it offers plenty of shops near the canal.
The canalside warehouses are attractive; there
is also an old corn mill dated 1677.
Kildwick
*W. Yorks. PO (in Farnhill, on the opposite side of
the canal), tel, stores.* An interesting and
unusual village spilling down the hillside. The
streets are extremely steep; one of them goes
under the canal through a narrow skewed
aqueduct.

BOATYARDS

ⓑ **Black Prince Holidays, Silsden Boats**
The Wharf, Silsden, near Keighley (0535
653675). Ⓡ Ⓦ Ⓓ Ⓔ Pump-out, gas,
narrowboat hire, day hire craft, overnight
mooring, slipway, books and maps.
ⓑ **Snaygill Boats** Skipton Road, Bradley, nr
Keighley (0756 795150). At bridge 182.
Ⓡ Ⓢ Ⓦ Ⓓ Ⓔ Pump-out, gas, narrowboat
hire, overnight mooring, long-term mooring,
books and maps, engine repairs, toilet,
shower.

PUBS

🍺 **Bridge Inn** Main Street, Silsden. Cosy
canalside local serving John Smith's real ale.
🍺 **Grouse Inn** Main Street, Silsden. Tetley's
real ale in a popular pub close to the canal.
🍺 **King's Arms** Bolton Road, Silsden.
Young people's pub offering Tetley's real ale.
🍺 **White Lion** Priestbank Road, Kildwick.
17thC coaching inn near the canal. Tetley's
real ale, *lunchtime* food, garden.

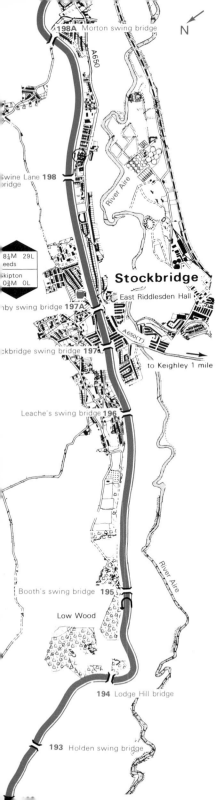

Keighley

Here the canal continues south east along the
side of the green hills that overlook Airedale.
The hills are very steep and beautifully
wooded in places. The distant rows of
chimneys, factories and terraced houses across
the valley comprise Keighley; most of its
industrial and suburban tentacles are quickly
passed by the canal, although the constant
succession of little swing bridges
intermittently impedes a boat's progress.
Some of these bridges can be rather stiff to
operate. There is an attractive mooring by
woods, to the east of bridge 195.

East Riddlesden Hall (0535 607075). *NT
property.* Just south of swing bridge 197A. A
17thC stone manor house complete with tithe
barn. Fine collection of furniture, paintings
and armour. Fishing is permitted in the ponds
in the grounds. *Open Jun-Aug 11.00-18.00
Wed-Sun; Apr & May, Sep & Oct 14.00-18.00
Wed-Sun. Closed Nov-Mar.* Charge.
Keighley
*W. Yorks. EC Tue. MD Wed, Fri, Sat. All
services.* Compared with some other industrial
centres in the area, Keighley is a clean and
pleasant town. It boasts a large new shopping
centre, much modern housing and some
handsome older stone terraces. The oldest
part is around the parish church of St Andrew,
a large perpendicular building whose main
attraction is its shady churchyard.
Cliffe Castle Spring Gardens Lane,
Keighley (0274 758231). Once the home of
the Butterfield family, it has been completely
restored and now houses the museum and art
gallery. Local exhibits illustrate the
archaeology, natural history and industrial
history of the area. There are reconstructed
craft workshops and a textile room.
Picturesque grounds where band concerts are
held. *Open 10.00-18.00 Apr-Sep, 10.00-17.00
Oct-Mar, closed Mon.* Free.
Keighley & Worth Valley Railway (0535
45214). Privately preserved by volunteers of
the Keighley & Worth Valley Railway
Preservation Society, the line runs for 5 miles
from the British Rail station at Keighley up to
Haworth, the home of the Brontë family, and
Oxenhope. British Railways closed the line in
1961, but the Society eventually succeeded in
reopening it in 1968 with a regular service of
steam trains. In the mornings, the service is
operated by diesel railbuses, but in the
afternoons magnificent steam engines puff
their way along the track. In the goods yard at
Haworth the Society has a splendid collection
of steam engines and carriages, mostly
ancient. The line was made famous by the film
The Railway Children.
Tourist Information Centre West Lane,
Howarth (0535 42329).

PUBS

● **Marquis of Granby** At swing bridge
197A. *PO and stores* the other side of the
bridge.
● **Worth Valley Inn** 1 Wesley Place, Ingrow.
Useful for visitors to the railway. A cosy little
pub serving Whitbread real ale. *Lunchtime*
food, and children allowed in then as well.
There are plenty of pubs in Keighley.

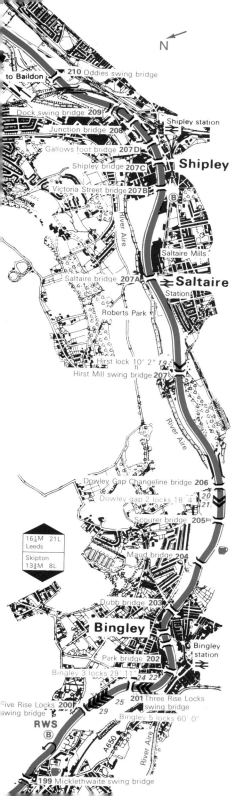

to Baildon
210 Oddies swing bridge
Dock swing bridge **209**
Junction bridge **208**
Shipley station
Gallows foot bridge **207D**
Shipley bridge **207C**
Shipley
Victoria Street bridge **207B**
River Aire
Saltaire Mills
Saltaire bridge **207A**
Saltaire
Station
Roberts Park
Hirst lock 10′ 2″ **19**
Hirst Mill swing bridge **207**
River Aire
Dowley Gap Changeline bridge **206**
Dowley gap 2 locks 18′ 4″ **20** **21**
Scourer bridge **205**
16¼M 21L
Leeds
Skipton
13¾M 8L
Maud bridge **204**
Dubb bridge **203**
Bingley
Bingley station
Park bridge **202**
Bingley 3 locks 29′ 11″ **24 22**
201 Three Rise Locks
swing bridge
Five Rise Locks
swing bridge **200**
25
29
Bingley 5 locks 60′ 0″
RWS
A650
River Aire
199 Micklethwaite swing bridge

Bingley and Shipley

The impressive Bingley Five-Rise staircase locks (see below) mark the end of the long level pound from Gargrave, and from here to Leeds there are no more views of a sweeping, uncluttered river valley. Just a few hundred yards south of the five locks are the three-rise staircase locks, which bring one steeply down into Bingley. The canal bisects this town, but one can see little of the place from the water. Leaving Bingley, trees lead to Dowley Gap and the two staircase locks. At the foot of the locks the towpath changes sides and the navigation crosses the River Aire via a stone aqueduct. Woods escort the canal along to the single Hirst Lock; from here one moves past the big mills at Saltaire and right through Shipley.

Navigational note
Bridge 199 needs a BW key. Bridge 209 needs a BW key and a windlass.

Baildon
W. Yorks. EC Tue. All services. 1½ miles north of Shipley. A very old industrial town huddled on a hilltop on the edge of Baildon Moor. Stretching from Baildon to Bingley is The Glen, a wooded valley that curves below the heights of the moor. A splendid scenic tramway carrying two tramcars connects the coach road to the higher parts of Baildon Moor. (In summer a frequent service operates, but in winter it is arranged only to suit the needs of residents at the upper level.)

Shipley
W. Yorks. EC Wed. MD Fri, Sat. All services. A dark stone town built on a generous scale and based on textile and engineering industries. There are powerful-looking mills to be seen, as well as the town hall and a suitably battlemented Salvation Army citadel. Shipley is lucky enough to be on the edge of Baildon Moor and Shipley Glen. The 3-mile-long Bradford Canal used to join the Leeds & Liverpool in Shipley, by bridge 208, but this has all been filled in for years.

Saltaire
W. Yorks. Stores, BR station. An estate village that owes its existence to the Utopian dream of Sir Titus Salt, a wealthy Victorian mill owner. He was so appalled by the working and living conditions of his workers in Bradford that he decided to build the ideal industrial settlement. This he did in 1850 on the banks of the canal and the River Aire – hence the name Saltaire. He provided every amenity including high standard housing, but no pub – for he was a great opponent of strong drink. The village has changed little since those days; everything is carefully laid out and the terraced houses are attractive in an orderly sort of way. (And there is still no pub!) There is an Italianate church near the canal, and a large park beside the river. (Rowing boats can be hired here in the summer.) Admirers of David Hockney's work should visit the art gallery.

Bingley
W. Yorks. EC Tue, MD Fri. All services. An industrial town now known nationally as a centre for thermal underwear. Standing at the south-east end of it amidst several old cottages is the large parish church of Holy Trinity, with its massive spire conspicuous from the canal.

Bingley Five-Rise Locks A very famous and impressive feature of the canal system built in 1774 in 'staircase' formation. They are all joined together rather than being separated by pounds of 'neutral' water. The top gates of the lowest lock are the bottom gates of the lock above, and so on. This means it is not possible to empty a lock unless the one below is itself empty. The rapid elevation thus resulting is quite daunting. The locks are *open 8.00–18.30* and may be used only under the supervision of the lock keeper, who lives in the interesting house at the top of the flight. The BW Sanitary Station is housed in a handsome old stable, where towing horses were once rested.

BOATYARDS

Ⓑ **Apollo Canal Carriers** Wharf Street, Shipley (0274 595914). Ⓡ Ⓦ Ⓓ Pump-out, gas, overnight mooring, engine repairs, toilets.

Ⓑ Hainsworths Boatyard Bingley (0274 565925). 200yds above the five-rise. Ⓦ Ⓓ Pump-out, gas, overnight mooring, long-term mooring, winter storage, slipway, chandlery, boat building, boat sales, repairs, emergency call out. Boat transport.

BOAT TRIPS

Apollo Canal Carriers have a water bus, plus two boats with restaurant and bar for up to 50 persons. Details from 0274 595914.

PUBS

There are plenty of pubs in Bingley and Shipley.

🍺 **Shoulder of Mutton** Otley Road, Charlestown. ¼ mile east of bridge 210. Tetley's real ale.
🍺 **Sun** Market Place, Shipley. 250yds south of bridge 207C. Tetley's real ale.
🍺 **Fishermen's** Canalside, above Dowley Gap locks.
🍺 **Brown Cow** Ireland Bridge, Bingley. ¼ mile west of bridge 202. Timothy Taylor real ale.
🍺 **Ferrands Arms** Queen Street, Bingley. 250yds south of bridge 202. Timothy Taylor real ale.
🍺 **Royal** 200yds down the hill from Micklethwaite swing bridge. Tetley's real ale.

Bingley Five Rise Locks. *Derek Pratt.*

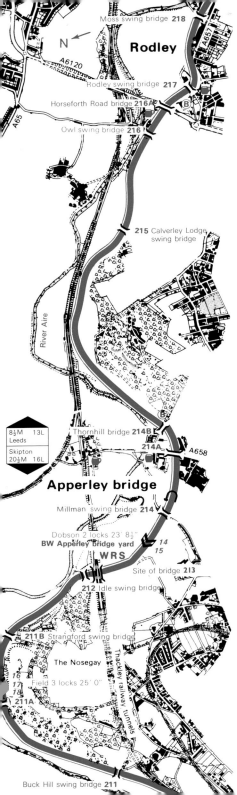

Apperley Bridge

This section sees the end of the wide open moorlands that frame the scenery further upstream: from now on, industry and housing begin to feature more as one approaches the outskirts of Leeds. The navigation, however, is thankfully sequestered from these intrusions into the landscape. Leaving Shipley, the adjacent railway line cuts through a 500-ft high hill in two mile-long tunnels. The canal goes all the way round this delightfully wooded hill, tenaciously following the Aire Valley. Halfway round the long curve are Field Locks: there is an extensive but inconspicuous sewage works nearby, which has its own railway system. Beyond the main railway bridge is a British Waterways maintenance yard at the head of Dobson's Locks. Here the British Waterways facilities for boats are housed in former canal stables. Temporarily traversing a built-up area, the navigation emerges yet again onto a wooded hillside overlooking the still rural and charming valley that contains the River Aire.

Navigational note
Bridge 214 needs a BW key. Bridge 215 is padlocked open to the canal.

Rodley
W. Yorks. PO, tel, stores. A useful village on the canal bank. There are two pubs, several shops and good temporary moorings.

BOATYARDS

🚢 **Rodley Boat Centre** Canal Wharf, Canal Road, Rodley, Leeds (0532 576132). By bridge 216A. R S W D E Pump-out, gas, narrowboat hire, day hire craft, overnight mooring, long-term mooring, winter storage, slipway, chandlery, books and maps, boat building, boat sales, engine sales and repairs.
🚢 **Switchcraft** The Boathouse, Parkin Lane, Apperley Bridge, Bradford (0274 611786). By bridge 214B. W D E Pump-out, gas, narrowboat hire, day hire craft, overnight mooring, long-term mooring, winter storage, groceries, chandlery, books and maps, canal ware, boat fitting, boat sales, engine sales and repairs, toilets, showers.
BW Apperley Bridge Dobson Locks (0274 611303). R S W.

PUBS AND RESTAURANTS

🍺 **Owl** Rodley. Pleasant and friendly pub. John Smith's real ale. Meals *lunchtime and evenings (not Sun evenings).*
🍺 **Rodley Barge** Unpretentious canalside pub by bridge 217.
🍺 **Railway** Near the canal at bridge 216A. Pleasant young people's pub serving Tetley's real ale. Garden with swings, *lunchtime* food.
🍺 **Crown & Anchor** Town Street, Rodley. Large lounge and small public bar. Tetley's real ale.
🍺✕ **George & Dragon** 200yds north east of bridge 214A (0274 612015). A Porterhouse restaurant with three bars, built around an old oak tree which still grows through the ceiling. Tetley's real ale and meals (*L & D*).

Leeds

This is a section full of contrasts; and it probably represents the most pleasant way of entering the city of Leeds. Although the area becomes more and more built up as one travels eastward, the canal remains unaffected by it, maintaining its privileged position on the wooded south side of the narrowing Aire Valley. Leaving the ruined Kirkstall Abbey on the other side of the river, the navigation passes the Mackeson brewery and borders for a while the steeply sloping edges of an extensive park. Kirkstall Power Station is reached, with its own private canal 'lay-by': until the mid 1960s, scores of barges used to come up to fuel this establishment every week; now both dock and power station are unused. Beyond, by bridge 225, is the Leeds Industrial Museum. There are six locks in the last mile down to Leeds and the junction with the Aire and Calder navigations at River Lock which, along with the preceding two locks, looks spruce and smart, due to landscaping and refurbishment. A good place to moor a boat in Leeds is Office Lock and River Lock (enquire at the car park); an arm leaves this short pound to disappear into the dark under City station – it once served the river wharves, but is now closed off. The route of the Aire & Calder to Castleford, Wakefield and Sheffield is continued on page 14.

Navigational note
Passage between Newlay 3 Locks and Forge 3 Locks is only allowed under supervision of BW staff. *Open 08.00-18.30.* Ring 0274 611303 if in doubt.

Leeds
W. Yorks. EC Wed. MD Tue, Fri, Sat. All services. See also page 14
Leeds Industrial Museum Armley Mills, access from bridge 225A (0532 637861). There have been corn and fulling mills on this site since at least 1559, with the present building dating from 1805. When built it was the most advanced in the country and it now houses a superb range of real-life exhibits demonstrating the local textile, heavy engineering, tanning and printing trades. There are working cranes, locomotives and waterwheels, and a cinema of the 1920s. The little stone bridge over the canal here dates from around 1770. *Open Tue-Sat, & Sun afternoons.* Charge.
Kirkstall Abbey The large elegant ruins of a Cistercian abbey founded in the 12thC. The remaining walls narrowly escaped demolition in the late 19thC, but are now carefully preserved surrounded by an attractive park.
Abbey House Museum (0532 755821). Just near the abbey is the splendid folk museum illustrating the life and work of the people of Yorkshire during the last 300 years. As well as exhibiting toys, costumes and pottery, it houses three streets of fully furnished 19thC shops, cottages and workshops, including those of a saddler, chemist, tanner and blacksmith. *Open Mon-Sat, & Sun afternoons.* Small charge.

BOATYARDS

ⓑ **Yorkshire Hire Cruisers** 26 Canal Wharf, Leeds (0532 456195). Ⓡ Ⓢ Ⓦ Ⓓ Ⓔ Pump-out, gas, overnight mooring, dry dock, toilets, café *(closed Mon)*.
ⓑ **Fallwood Marina** Pollard Lane, Leeds (0532 581074). By bridge 221. Ⓡ Ⓢ Ⓦ Gas, overnight mooring, long-term mooring, winter storage, slipway, crane, boat building, boat and engine sales, toilets.

PUBS AND RESTAURANTS

See also page 15
🍺 **Ancestor** Just south of bridge 223. Tetley's real ale.
🍺 **Bridge** 100yds east of bridge 222. Whitbread and Castle Eden real ales.
🍺 **Abbey** 50yds downhill from bridge 221. Whitbread real ale.
Ross Valley Mill Shop By bridge 219. Lunches and teas.

MACCLESFIELD

Maximum dimensions
Length: 70'
Beam: 7'
Headroom: 7'

Mileage
HARDINGS WOOD JUNCTION (Trent &
Mersey Canal) to
Congleton Wharf: 5¾
Bosley Top Lock: 11½
Macclesfield: 17
Bollington: 20
MARPLE JUNCTION (Peak Forest Canal):
27¼

Locks: 13

Manager
061-273 4686

Ever since the Trent & Mersey Canal had been completed in 1777, there had existed a demand for an alternative canal link between the Midlands and Manchester, and a more direct line through the manufacturing town of Macclesfield was an obvious choice of route.

However, it was not until 1825 that Thomas Telford was asked by promoters of the canal to survey a line linking the Peak Forest Canal and the Trent & Mersey Canal. The 28-mile line he suggested was the canal that was built, from Marple to just north of Kidsgrove, but Telford did not supervise the construction. (He left to go and build the Birmingham & Liverpool Junction Canal.) William Crosley was the canal's engineer. It is interesting to note that the Macclesfield Canal (which opened in 1831) was built so long after the peak period of canal construction that it was actually envisaged by some of its promoters as the route for a possible railway track and was consequently quite shallow.

The canal, which runs along the side of a tall ridge of hills west of the Pennines, bears the distinctive mark of Telford's engineering. Like his Birmingham & Liverpool Junction Canal (ie the Shropshire Union from Autherley to Nantwich), the Macclesfield is a 'cut and fill' canal, following as straight a course as possible, and featuring many tremendous cuttings and embankments. Apart from the stop lock at Hall

Green whose 1ft rise was insisted upon as a water preservation measure by the Trent & Mersey Canal Company – to whose Hall Green Branch the Macclesfield Canal connected at the stop lock – all the locks are grouped into the flight of 12 at Bosley. The canal is fed from nearby reservoirs, at Bosley and Sutton.

In spite of intense competition from neighbouring railways and the Trent & Mersey Canal, the Macclesfield carried a good trade for many years. Much of this was coal, and cotton from the big mills established along its northern reaches.

This was not greatly affected by the surrender in 1846 to what was to become the Great Central Railway Company. (The Peak Forest and Ashton canals were also bought by that railway.) The railway company ran the three canals efficiently, but as narrow canals they were all bound to decline sooner rather than later.

The Macclesfield Canal today is an extremely interesting cruising waterway, and forms part of the popular 100-mile 'Cheshire Ring' canal circuit. Look out for the original, and very large, stone milestones showing distances from Hall Green stop lock (the original end of the canal) and Marple. These were removed during the Second World War in fear of helping invading forces. They have been lovingly restored to their former glory by the Macclesfield Canal Society.

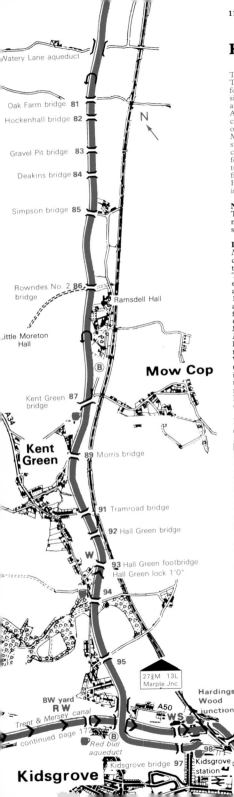

Kent Green

The junction of the Macclesfield with the Trent & Mersey Canal is a curious one, for the former leaves the Trent & Mersey on the south side, then crosses it on Red Bull Aqueduct after the T & M has fallen through two locks. After passing through the stop lock in the cutting at Hall Green, one comes out into the open countryside at Kent Green. To the east, Mow Cop crowns the tall ridge of hills that stretches parallel to the navigation for miles to come. You can take a good walk to the top, on footpaths from bridge 85 (where there is a telephone box). The canal wanders past the front lawn of the mansion that is Ramsdell Hall. Beyond this point, the canal loses itself in the countryside for several miles.

Navigational note
The Macclesfield Canal is quite shallow, and mooring is usually only possible at recognised sites.

Little Moreton Hall
NT property (0260 272018). ¾ mile west of canal (Walk north west from bridge 86, along the footpath on the left side of the hedge.) This fabulous moated house is an outstanding example of black-and-white-timbered architecture. It was built between 1559 and 1580, with carved gables and ornate windows and has scarcely changed since. It contains a fine collection of oak furniture and pewter. *Open afternoons (except Tue) Mar-Oct.*

Mow Cop
NT property. A hill nearly 1100ft above sea level, which gives a magnificent view across the Cheshire Plain, beyond Stoke and into Wales. (This looks particularly good at night.) On top of the hill is Mow Cop Castle, an imitation ruin built in 1750. It was on this spot that the Primitive Methodists held their first meeting in 1807, which lasted 14 hours.

Kent Green
Ches. PO, tel, stores.

BOATYARDS
Ⓑ **Heritage Narrowboats** Kent Green, Scholar Green, Kidsgrove (0782 785700). Ⓡ Ⓢ Ⓦ Ⓓ Ⓔ Pump-out, gas, narrowboat hire, day hire craft, long-term mooring, slipway, chandlery, books and maps, engine repairs.
Ⓑ **David Piper** Red Bull Basin, Church Lawton, Kidsgrove (0782 784754). By Red Bull Aqueduct. Ⓦ Ⓓ Pump-out, gas, overnight mooring, long-term mooring, winter storage, slipway, chandlery, books and maps, boat building, boat sales, engine sales and repairs. Information on Harecastle Tunnel opening times.

PUBS
🍺 **Rising Sun** Kent Green. Near the canal. A fine pub offering Tetley's and Marston's real ale, and excellent food.
🍺 **Three Horseshoes** Kent Green. Near canal.
🍺 **Bleeding Wolf** Hall Green. Near bridge 94. Food, except at weekends. *PO, tel, stores* nearby.
🍺 **Canal Tavern** Canalside, at Hardings Wood.
🍺 **Blue Bell** Canalside, at Hardings Wood Junction. Friendly one bar local serving Boddingtons, Whitbread and Castle Eden real ale. Bar snacks *lunchtime only.*
🍺 **Red Bull** By lock 43 on the T & M. A popular pub close to Hardings Wood Junction, serving Robinson's real ale. Food *lunchtime and evenings, but not Mon, Tue, Wed, Fri evenings out of season.* Vegetarians catered for. Canalside seating area.

Congleton

The canal continues north east. On one side,
the land falls away gradually; to the east, the
ever-present range of substantial hills reminds
one that the Pennine Chain lies just beyond.
Passing a golf course, one arrives at the
embanked wharf that overlooks Congleton:
there is an aqueduct over the road that runs
down into the town and then a beautifully
symmetrical 'roving' bridge (76). These are
known locally as 'snake bridges'. There is a
useful grocers/off-licence a short distance
south (uphill) of Congleton Wharf. Past
Congleton railway station, the canal is carried
by a high embankment – a common feature of
the Macclesfield – across a narrow valley,
affording a good view westward of the tall and
elegant railway viaduct crossing the same
valley. Meanwhile the looming fell known as
The Cloud (over 1000ft high and with
remains of ancient earthworks) is given a wide
berth as the navigation continues on its lonely
lock-free course through this very fine
landscape. There is a good walk to the top of
The Cloud along footpaths east of bridge 71.

Navigational note
There are some underwater obstructions at
Congleton Wharf, so take care if mooring
here. There are alternative moorings between
bridges 75 and 76.

Congleton
Ches. EC Wed. MD Tue, Sat. All services. A
compact, busy market town hemmed in by
hills. The Victorian Town Hall in the High
Street, looks like a cross between a 17thC
Dutch guildhall and St Mark's, Venice.
Astbury
Ches. PO, tel, stores. About 1 mile north west of
bridges 79 and 80. A pretty village set back
from the A34. Tudor and 18thC houses are
set around the green. The church is amazing:
its roomy interior and wide aisles are
complemented externally by generous
battlements along the roof and a spired tower
standing quite separate from the body of the
church.

PUBS AND RESTAURANTS
🍺 ✕ **Bull's Head Hotel** Congleton (0260
273388). Food *lunchtime and evenings.*
🍺 **Robin Hood** South west of bridge 61.
Marston's real ale in a cosy pub. Good food
lunchtime and evenings.
🍺 **Railway** Near Congleton station. Food.
🍺 **Queen's Head** Canalside at bridge 75.
Food *lunchtime and evenings,* garden with
swings, children welcome *before 20.00.* Shops
close by.
🍺 **Wharf** Near Congleton Wharf. Greenall
Whitley real ale in a very pleasant pub. Snacks,
children welcome *lunchtime and early evenings.*
🍺 ✕ **Lion & Swan** Congleton (0260
273115). Food *lunchtime and evenings.*
🍺 **Egerton Arms** Astbury.

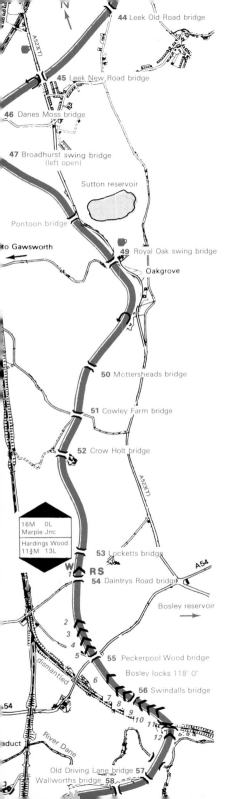

Bosley Locks

Scenically, this is another impressive stretch.
The massive hills to the right still dominate as
the canal crosses the River Dane on an
embankment and arrives at the foot of Bosley
Locks (good moorings here). These are in a
really delightful setting which is semi-wooded
and semi-pastoral, all the time overlooked by
The Cloud from the south. Beyond the locks,
the hills/mountains (some are over 1200ft
high) spill right down to the canal near
Oakgrove. The navigation follows the contour
of the land as it begins to swing round the hills
containing Macclesfield, which is now clearly
visible to the north.

Navigational note
The once notorious Royal Oak Swing Brige
has been replaced with a hydraulic bridge.
You will need a British Waterways key to
operate it; just follow the instructions on the
control box.

Sutton Reservoir
Close to the canal north of bridge 49, this
reservoir holds up to 94 million gallons of
water. There is a private sailing club: and the
public are welcome to ramble and picnic here.
Oakgrove A delightful spot with a nearby pub
and a superb backcloth of tall, green hills
which are ideal for energetic walks. The lane
west of the bridge leads to Gawsworth. Sutton
reservoir is just north.
Gawsworth
Ches. 2 miles west of Oakgrove. A refreshingly
unspoilt village with several small lakes and a
lovely 13thC church, approached by a long
avenue of elm trees. Facing the church is the
old rectory, a half-timbered house built by
Rector Baguley in 1470. Close to the church is
Gawsworth Hall, a beautiful 16thC black-
and-white manor house. The park encloses a
medieval jousting ground. *Open Wed, Sat, Sun
& G. Fri afternoons, Mar-Oct.*
Maggoty's Wood In this pleasant wood just
outside the village is the grave of the eccentric
fiddler and playwright, Maggoty Johnson.
After being totally rejected by London critics
he returned to Gawsworth where he died in
1773, having ordered that he should be buried
far from the vulgar gentry who did not
appreciate his genius.
Bosley Locks
Effectively the only locks on all the 27 miles of
the Macclesfield Canal, these 12 splendid
stone locks are relatively deep, raising the
canal level by fully 118ft to well over 500ft
above the sea. Each lock has a pair of mitre
top gates instead of only a single one – indeed
Bosley Locks are very rare among narrow
locks in this respect. They are a good example
of Telford's practice of grouping locks
together in flights; here are 12 in 1 mile.
Bosley Reservoir
1 mile east of Bosley Locks, along the A54. A
canal reservoir with a wide variety of land and
water birds, which holds 402 million gallons of
water. An excellent rambling and picnic area.
The fishing rights are exercised by an angling
club.

PUBS
◗ **Star** North of bridge 45. Marston's real ale,
in a quiet, popular local. Snacks, garden.
◗ **Royal Oak** Oakgrove. Horse brasses,
meals and Boddingtons real ale in a rural pub.

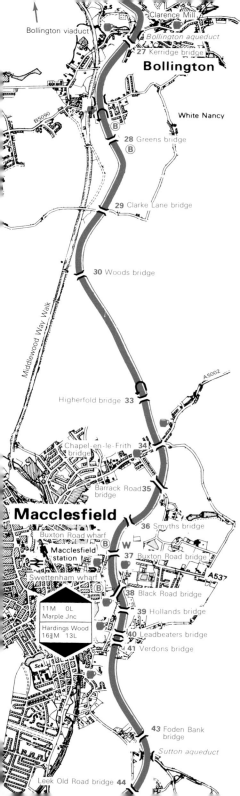

Map labels: Bollington viaduct, Clarence Mill, Bollington aqueduct, 27 Kerridge bridge, Bollington, White Nancy, B5090, 28 Greens bridge, 29 Clarke Lane bridge, 30 Woods bridge, Middlewood Way Walk, A5002, Higherfold bridge 33, Chapel-en-le-Frith bridge 34, Barrack Road 35 bridge, Macclesfield, 36 Smyths bridge, Buxton Road wharf, Macclesfield station, 37 Buxton Road bridge, Swettenham wharf, 38 Black Road bridge, 39 Hollands bridge, 11M 0L Marple Jnc, Hardings Wood 16¾M 13L, 40 Leadbeaters bridge, 41 Verdons bridge, A537, 43 Foden Bank bridge, Sutton aqueduct, Leek Old Road bridge 44

Macclesfield

Leaving the green and hilly countryside, the navigation enters the outskirts of Macclesfield, passing a coal yard at bridge 41. A very wide stretch is overshadowed by a vast and beautifully restored flour mill which marks the site of the original Macclesfield Canal Company. The town itself is down the hill; the best place to moor is south of bridge 37, which is also handy for the shops (including bottled gas supplies). Meanwhile the canal continues northwards near a closed railway line to Bollington, passing the Adelphi Mill, once a silk mill and now converted into offices and a pub. The Macclesfield and Vale Royal Groundwork Trust Office (*open 14.00–16.30 Tue-Sun*) is also here. A 60ft-high embankment and two aqueducts then carry the navigation across the valley towards the huge Clarence Mill, a textile mill now converted into small manufacturing units.

Bollington
Ches. EC Wed. PO, tel, stores, garage, bank.
One gets a good view of this stone-built town from the huge canal embankment that cuts across it. Hills crowd round the town, which is only a mile from the boundary of the Peak District National Park. The white tower on the ridge south of the town is called White Nancy. One popular story is that it was built to commemorate the battle of Waterloo by a member of the Gaskell family and took its name from one of the ladies of the family called Nancy.

Macclesfield
Ches. EC Wed. MD Tue, Fri, Sat. All services.
An interesting combination of a thriving silk manufacturing town and an old market town with its cobbled streets and picturesque medieval market place. There are several interesting classical buildings, making the most of the local stone. In the 18thC it was one of the leading silk producing centres and is still important for its textile and pharmaceutical industries. An interesting feature of the town is the Unitarian Chapel in King Edward Street, approached through a narrow passage and guarded by a lovely wrought-iron gate: it is dated 1689 and is 'for William and Mary's subjects dissenting from the Church of England'.
St Michael's Church Market Place. Very little remains of the original structure founded in 1278 by Queen Eleanor but it still contains many fine monuments.
Paradise Mill Park Lane, Macclesfield (0625 618228). Built between 1820-60, this handloom silk-weaving mill finally closed down in 1981. Here you can see Jacquard handlooms in action, authentic room settings and an exhibition of a whole wealth of material connected with one of Macclesfield's major industries. *Open 13.00-17.00 Tue-Sun* Charge (*joint ticket for this and the museum results in a saving*).
Silk Museum Roe Street, Macclesfield (0625 613210). The first museum in the country devoted entirely to the study of the silk industry: audio visuals, costume, textiles, room settings and even parachutes. Visit also The Heritage Centre in the old 1813 Sunday School building. Tea room, shop. *Open 11.00-17.00 Tue-Sat, 13.00-17.00 Sun.* Charge (see above).
West Park Museum Prestbury Road, Macclesfield (0625 619831). Located on the edge of a park which has the largest bowling green in the country. Founded in 1898 by the Brocklehurst family, the museum contains fine and decorative art material, local history, Egyptian antiquities and, notably, some paintings by Charles Tunnicliffe, the bird artist who trained in Macclesfield. *Open 14.00-17.00 Tue-Sun.* Free.
The Middlewood Way A 40-mile footpath and cycleway along the course of the old Macclesfield, Bollington and Marple Railway, which opened in 1869. It was converted for recreational use in 1985. Information and leaflets from Macclesfield Leisure Services on 0625 500100.
Tourist Information Centre Town Hall, Market Place, Macclesfield (0625 21955).

BOATYARDS

ⓑ **Anglo-Welsh** Bollington Wharf, Grimshaw Lane, Bollington (0625 572464). Ⓡ Ⓦ Ⓓ Pump-out, gas, narrowboat hire, day hire craft, books and maps, boat sales, engine repairs, toilets.

ⓑ **Kerridge Dry Dock** Bollington. Between bridges 28 and 29 (0625 574287). Ⓦ Ⓓ Pump-out, long-term mooring, winter storage, boat building, boat sales, engine sales and repairs.

ⓑ **Peak Forest Cruisers** The Wharf, Buxton Road, Macclesfield (0625 424172). Narrowboat hire, long-term mooring.

ⓑ **Macclesfield Marina** Swettenham Wharf, Brook Street, Macclesfield (0625 420042). Ⓡ Ⓢ Ⓦ Ⓓ Ⓔ Gas, overnight mooring, long-term mooring, winter storage, slipway, chandlery, gantry, books and maps, boat sales, engine sales and repairs, toilets. *Closed Wed.*

BOAT TRIPS

The White Nancy Cruising Restaurant Operate a restaurant boat from Bollington Wharf. Book well in advance on 0663 763936.

PUBS

Macclesfield and Bollington have been described as one of the seven wonders of the real ale enthusiast's waterways, with 86 such pubs within striking distance of the canal.

🍺 **Waggon & Horses** 200yds beyond Adelphi Mill. Boddingtons real ale.

🍺 **Dog & Partridge** West of Bollington Aqueduct. A sociable village pub with an open fire offering Robinson's real ale and food *12.00–19.00.*

🍺 **Barge Inn** In part of the old Adelphi Mill, opposite Anglo-Welsh. Boddingtons real ale, food *lunchtime and evenings*, children welcome.

🍺 **Lord Clyde** West of Clarke Lane Bridge. Small country pub in a listed building. Greenall Whitley real ale.

🍺 **Three Crowns** East of bridge 34. Victorian stone terrace pub with a garden. Robinson's real ale.

🍺 **Britannia** West of bridge 34. Unspoilt terraced pub serving Greenall Whitley real ale.

🍺 **Puss in Boots** Canalside at bridge 37. Boddingtons real ale, open fire, garden.

🍺 **Navigation** South of bridge 38. Victorian local built for the original canal navvies. Tetley's real ale, *closed lunchtime Mon-Fri.*

🍺 **Dolphin Inn** West of bridge 40. Robinson's real ale in a friendly local with an open fire. Food at *lunchtime.*

🍺 **Bee Hive** South west of bridge 41. Cosy Boddingtons real ale local.

'Snake Bridge', Congleton, on the Macclesfield Canal. *Derek Pratt.*

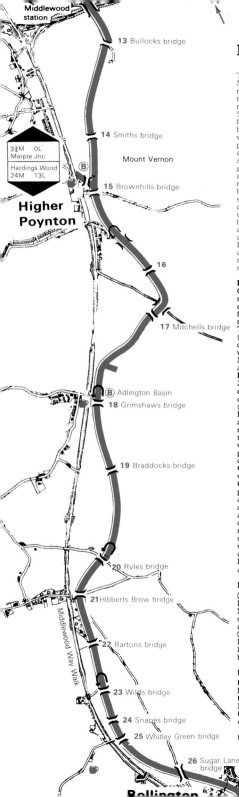

13 Bullocks bridge

14 Smiths bridge

Mount Vernon

B

3¾M   0L
Hardings Wood
24M   13L

15 Brownhills bridge

Higher Poynton

16

17 Mitchells bridge

B Adlington Basin
18 Grimshaws bridge

19 Braddocks bridge

20 Ryles bridge

21 Hibberts Brow bridge

Middlewood Way Walk

22 Bartons bridge

23 Wilds bridge

24 Snapes bridge

25 Whitley Green bridge

26 Sugar Lane bridge

Bollington

Middlewood station

Higher Poynton

This lonely stretch is typical of the Macclesfield Canal and in its beautifully quiet, rural isolation it is representative of much of the charm that most canals possess. Winding northwards along the summit level at over 500ft above the sea, the navigation generally follows the contours of this upland country, but crosses several valleys on embankments with fine aqueducts. There are few centres of population, only the odd pub here or there, and the countryside is entirely unspoilt. Around Higher Poynton (*PO, tel, stores, garage*) the canal becomes wider, the result of ancient subsidence from a coalmine, which necessitated the continual raising of the canal banks and bridges (to hold the water in the sinking canal). Be sure to adhere to the main channel here. An old branch near bridge 15 used to lead to the mine; now it is used by a boatyard. A mile north of here, one crosses yet another massive embankment and a tall aqueduct (over a railway) on the way into High Lane. The towpath is in excellent condition, and the Middlewood Way follows the course of the old railway. There are good moorings between bridges 19 and 20.

Higher Poynton
Ches. PO, tel, stores, garage. Considered by some to be the most pleasant moorings on the canal, where the wide water supports large families of ducks, geese and swans. There is a recreation field adjacent, and a handy pub.
The Anson Museum Anson Road, Poynton (0477 34845 or 0625 874426). A working display of early internal combustion engines, with emphasis on those made in the Manchester area. *Open Sun only 11.00-17.00 May-Oct.*
Lyme Park *NT property* (0663 62023). 2 miles east of Higher Poynton. Pedestrian entrance at West Parkgate, ¼ mile south east of bridge 17 or footpath from bridge 15. (Vehicular access from Disley, on the Peak Forest Canal, see page 124.) In the centre of an extensive park containing deer, is a magnificent Elizabethan house that belonged to the Legh family from the 14thC until 1947 when it was handed over to the nation in payment of death duties. It has a fine interior containing many works of art and four Chippendale chairs claimed to be covered with material from a cloak worn by King Charles I at his execution. Adventure playground for the children. *House open afternoons, except Mon & Fri, gardens open daily.*
Adlington Hall (0625 827595). 2 miles west of bridge 21. An attractive manor house with a mixture of architectural styles: a Georgian south front and an Elizabethan black-and-white-timbered wing. The banqueting hall contains a 17thC Bernard Smith organ. Pleasant gardens. *Open summer Sun & B. Hols, also Wed & Sat in Aug.*

BOATYARDS
B **Constellation Cruises** Lyme Road, Higher Poynton, Stockport (0625 873471). Near bridge 15. W (charge) D Gas, 25ft slipway, long-term mooring, chandlery, books and maps, boat building, boat sales.
B **Lyme View Marina** Adlington Basin, Poynton (0625 874638). R S W D Gas, long-term mooring, winter storage, slipway, boat sales.

PUBS
Boar's Head Higher Poynton. Down the hill from bridge 15. Boddingtons real ale.
Miners Arms Near bridge 18. Boddingtons real ale.
Windmill 250yds west of bridge 25. Large open-plan pub in a former cotton mill, built in 1675. Marston's and Boddingtons real ale, food *lunchtime and evenings,* garden, open fire.

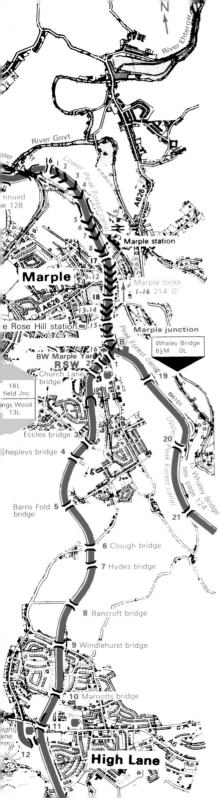

Marple Junction

The canal proceeds northwards in a cutting through High Lane, passing the junction with the short High Lane Arm – now used as a club mooring site – and a children's playpark. There are moorings between the arm and bridge 11, with shops close by. Beyond the town is a restored mill; then open country intervenes, offering views westward of Stockport and the southern outskirts of Manchester. On the offside, between bridge 8 and 7 is a deer farm. The deer can often be seen feeding by the (electrified) fence. There is a useful shop, the Doodfield Stores, down the hill from bridge 6. At bridge 3 Goyt Mill appears, heralding the start of Marple, a busy boating centre much enjoyed by the citizens of Manchester. Goyt Mill is yet another mill which has been thankfully restored, and now houses workshops. There are shops, a café and a launderette nearby. The area of the junction with the Peak Forest Canal is delightful: an old turnover bridge, mellow wharf buildings and the nearby flight of Marple Locks are framed by the distant mountainous country across the Goyt Valley. The canal here is 500ft above sea level – the highest useable pound on the English canal system.

Marple
Gt Manchester. All services. A typical residential town, serving as a dormitory base for Stockport and Manchester. Elements of the old village can still be seen, buried amongst the suburbia, but much the most attractive part is by the canal. The rugged Ludworth Moor is not far away, where 'Robin Hood's Picking Rods' still stand, the supposed remains of a Celtic Druid's temple.

Marple Locks
The flight of deep, narrow locks is superbly sited, at the top flanked by terraced houses and a play park; midway, fine gardens and restored stone cottages back on, and towards the bottom the passage is tree-lined. The friendly lock keeper lives by lock 9 opposite a superb canal warehouse which has now been carefully restored. The top lock is the second deepest narrow lock in the country.

High Lane
Gt Manchester. PO, tel, stores, garage, station, fish & chips. More a spread than a village; good moorings and useful for stores. High Lane is effectively at the south-east corner of the Manchester conurbation, and is quite indistinguishable from its neighbours. The very long Disley railway tunnel passes deep underneath the place.

BOATYARDS

Ⓑ **Top Lock Marine** At Marple Junction (061-427 5712). Pump-out, day boat hire, long-term mooring, boat sales, emergency engine repairs.
British Waterways Marple Yard Marple Junction (061-427 1079). Ⓡ Ⓢ Ⓦ Overnight mooring.

BOAT TRIPS

Top Lock Marine 5 Lime Kiln Lane, Marple (061-427 5712). 12-seater restaurant boat for private charter and day boat hire.

PUBS AND RESTAURANTS

⚓✗ **Ring O'Bells** Marple (061-427 2300). By bridge 2. Robinson's real ale, good food *lunchtime and evenings* and excellent children's menu. Garden. Telephone kiosk outside.
⚓ **Bull's Head** High Lane. At bridge 11. A lovely comfy, cosy, friendly, locals' pub with an open fire, settles and bookshelves. Boddingtons real ale and excellent *lunchtime* food in generous quantities. Canalside terrace.
⚓ **Dog & Partridge** 200yds from bridge 11. Real ale, food, garden. Children welcome.

PEAK FOREST AND ASHTON

Maximum dimensions

Length: 70'
Beam: 7'
Headroom: 6'

Manager
061-273 4686

Mileage

ASHTON CANAL
Duckinfield Junction to
Ducie Street Junction: 6½

Locks: 18

PEAK FOREST CANAL
Whaley Bridge to
Marple Junction: 6½
Dukinfield Junction: 14½

Locks: 16

THE ASHTON CANAL

This navigation was authorised in 1792 and opened shortly afterwards, as an isolated narrow canal from the centre of Manchester to Ashton-under-Lyne. It is short, at only 6½ miles, but several substantial branches were built, with a total length twice that of the main line.

From the beginning, the Ashton was a strong rival of the Rochdale Canal – with which it connects in Manchester. The two canals were constructed simultaneously, partly to tap the big coal producing area around Oldham (north east of Manchester): in addition the Ashton opened a new trade route from Manchester to the textile mills of Ashton, while the Rochdale served as a broad canal link over the Pennines between the Mersey and the rivers of Yorkshire. Before long, the Ashton Canal was joined by the Peak Forest and Huddersfield canals: both provided useful trade and the latter provided a secondary through route across the Pennines. And in 1831 completion of the narrow Macclesfield Canal gave the Ashton the added bonus of becoming part of a through route from Manchester to the Potteries.

The 1830s saw the peak of the Ashton Canal's prosperity. After this it was seriously threatened by railway competition, and the canal company sold out to the forerunner of the Great Central Railway Company in 1846. This company continued successfully to maintain and operate the canal for many years, but traffic declined in the present century and the branches began to decay.

By 1962 it was unnavigable – however a determined effort by the Peak Forest Canal Society, the IWA, local councils and the BWB resulted in its reopening in 1974.

THE PEAK FOREST CANAL

This canal runs from the Ashton Canal at Ashton through Marple to Whaley Bridge and Buxworth. Its name is misleading, for Peak Forest is only a small village 2½ miles east of Doveholes, and the canal never went to Peak Forest. Its history is similar to, and tied up with, its neighbour the Ashton Canal; authorised by Act of Parliament in 1794, it was aimed at providing an outlet for the great limestone deposits at Doveholes, a few miles south east of Whaley Bridge. However, since Doveholes

is over 1000ft above sea level, the canal was terminated in a basin at Buxworth, and the line was continued up to the quarries by a 6½-mile tramroad.

Construction of the canal and tramway and their four short tunnels was carried out by navvies directed by Benjamin Outram, a notable Derbyshire engineer and one of the founders of the famous Butterley Ironworks. The canal was completed in 1800, except for the flight of locks at Marple, which were not built until four years later. A second, temporary, tramway bridged the gap in the meantime.

Buxworth soon became a bustling interchange point where the horse-drawn wagons bringing the stone down from Doveholes tipped their load either into canal boats or into lime-kilns, for burning into lime. This traffic, and the boats bringing coal *up* the canal for firing the kilns at Buxworth, accounted for the greatest proportion of the canal company's revenue.

Like the Ashton Canal, the Peak Forest was greatly boosted by the opening of the Macclesfield Canal to Marple top lock in 1831. This made it (with the Ashton) part of a new through route from Manchester to the Potteries. In 1831 too, the Cromford & High Peak Railway was opened, joining up Whaley Bridge with the Cromford Canal on the far side of the Peak District.

By the early 1840s the Peak Forest Canal was suffering from keen competition on trade between Manchester, the Midlands and London. The competition came not only from the long-established Trent & Mersey Canal Company but also from two new railways. All the companies tried to undercut each other; the Peak Forest came off badly, so in 1846 the company leased the navigation in perpetuity to the Sheffield, Ashton-under-Lyne & Manchester Railway, which later became the Great Central. The canal declined slowly up to the present century. In 1922 the Buxworth traffic finished, while (through) traffic on the 'lower' Peak Forest Canal – from Marple Junction northwards – gradually disappeared by the last war.

Along with the Ashton, full navigation was restored in 1974, with the Buxworth line currently being restored.

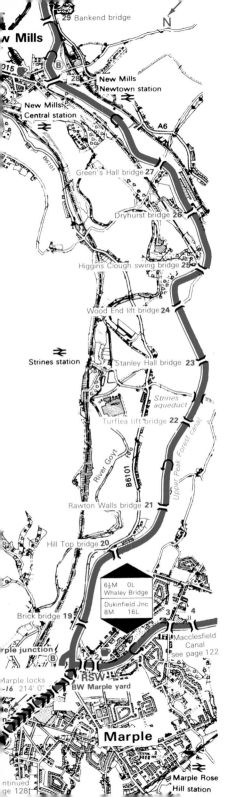

New Mills

As one passes from the Macclesfield Canal to the Upper Peak Forest Canal one enters at once dramatic, mountainous scenery. To the north and east, the land falls away sharply, with the Marple flight of locks emphasising the drop. The Upper Peak Forest Canal leads off to the south east; and it rapidly becomes apparent that this is a navigation set in a robust, handsome landscape. Clinging desperately to a wooded mountainside overlooking the steep, wide Goyt Valley, it winds its precarious way to New Mills. The trains that traverse the opposite side of the valley look like tiny models on the distant, massive mountains. There are good moorings at bridge 24, where a public footpath gives easy access to Strines. Near Disley, another railway pops out of the long Disley Tunnel, way below the canal; while yet another line appears above and beside the canal, from High Lane. Thus around New Mills the valley contains three fully operational and very picturesque railways. One of the pleasant features of this terrain is the easy co-existence of woods, fields and a canal on the one hand, and a certain amount of industrial urbanisation on the other. As you approach New Mills you will notice the smell of sweets in the air – Matlows, the makers of 'Swizzles', have their factory here. From here to Whaley Bridge the cut is very shallow the slow progress gives time to appreciate the surroundings fully.

Navigational notes
1 You will need a Leeds & Liverpool type padlock key for the locks on this and the Ashton Canals. These can be obtained from the Canal Manager's Office, BW, Vesta Street, Manchester M4 6DS (061-273 4686). 2 Bridge 24 is windlass operated.

New Mills
Derbs. PO, tel, stores, garage, banks, launderette, stations. A mostly stone-built town on the Cheshire/Derbyshire border: its industries include textile printing, engineering and engraving. One can still see the ruins of the extensive canal stables just east of bridge 28.
Disley
Ches. PO, tel, stores, garage, station. On the south bank of the canal. The centre of the village is quite pretty, slightly spoilt by the A6 traffic. The village is up the hill, south west of bridge 26. The attractive church stands among trees above the little village square. It was greatly renovated in the last century, but the ancient tower with the griffin leering down at passers-by dates from the 16thC. Vehicular and pedestrian access to Lyme Park (see page 121) is from the A6 near Disley, 1½ miles south west of bridge 26.
Strines
Gt Manchester. PO, tel, stores, station. A useful place for supplies.

BOATYARDS
Ⓑ **New Mills Marina** Hibbert Street, New Mills (0663 745000). Ⓡ Ⓢ Ⓦ Ⓓ Pump-out, gas, overnight mooring, long-term mooring, winter storage, boat sales and repairs, chandlery, gifts, provisions, toilets and showers.
British Waterways Marple Yard at Marple Junction, on the Macclesfield Canal. (061-427 1079). Ⓡ Ⓢ Ⓦ Overnight mooring.
Ⓑ **Top Lock Marine** At Marple Junction (061-427 5712). Pump-out, day boat hire, long-term mooring, boat sales, emergency engine repairs.

BOAT TRIPS
Top Lock Marine 5 Lime Kiln Lane, Marple (061-427 5712). 12-seater restaurant trip boat for private charter.

PUBS AND RESTAURANTS

🛥✕ **The Beehive** 67 Albion Road, New
Mills (0663 742087). Opposite New Mills
Marina. A welcoming stone-built pub run by
canal enthusiasts. A variety of good real ale is
always available, together with home-cooked
bar meals. Booking advisable for the
restaurant.

🛥✕ **Ram's Head Hotel** Disley (0663
762019). Smart hotel with full restaurant
(*evenings only*).

🛥✕ **Dandy Cock** Disley (0663 763712). Bar
lunches.

🛥✕ **Ring O'Bells** Marple (061-427 2300).
Near the junction. (On the Macclesfield
Canal). Good food *lunchtime and evenings*, fine
children's menu and Robinson's real ale.
Garden. Telephone kiosk outside.

The Peak Forest Canal at Marple. *Derek Pratt.*

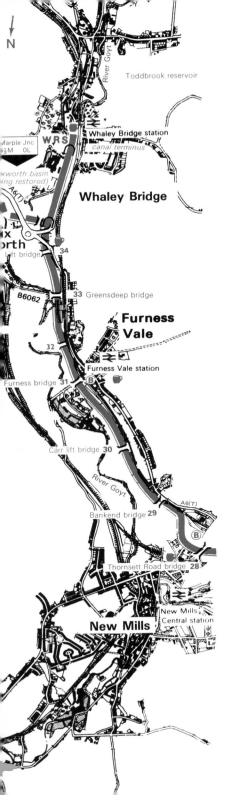

Whaley Bridge

The canal continues south east along the
mountainside towards Whaley Bridge. It is an
enchanting stretch, passing plenty of woods,
pastures and grazing horses. The A6 road and
the railway are always close to the navigation,
but they detract not at all from its isolation.
There are charming stations at New Mills,
Furness Vale and Whaley Bridge: from these
one may take a magnificent railway trip past
two canal-feeding reservoirs and over the hills
to the summit, 1200ft above sea level, then
down to the old Roman town of Buxton, now
unfortunately the end of the line. As the canal
approaches Whaley Bridge, and the River
Goyt comes closer, there is a swing bridge and
two lift bridges to contend with – they can be
hard work. South of bridge 34 the canal splits:
the original main line, at present closed
beyond the bridge, turns east across the Goyt
on an aqueduct to Buxworth (its name
changed from the supposedly less desirable
Bugsworth) with its basin complex. The
former Whaley Bridge Branch continues for a
short distance south to Whaley Bridge, where
it terminates in a small basin, with a boatyard,
at the north end of the town. There is a
building at the basin of great interest to
industrial archaeologists: it covers a dock and
was built in 1832 at this, the junction of the
Peak Forest Canal and the Cromford & High
Peak Railway. Here, transhipment between
canal boat and railway wagon could take place
under cover. The former railway's Whaley
Bridge inclined plane (now a footpath) rises to
the south of this historic building. There are
controversial plans to build a by-pass along
the valley. It will have a devastating effect if
ever completed.

Coombs Reservoir 1½ miles south of
Whaley Bridge. An 84-acre canal reservoir
with public access from the three highways
round it. It is used extensively as a sailing club
and a centre for angling.
Toddbrook Reservoir Just south of Whaley
Bridge. A very pleasant area for picnicking and
walking. Private sailing club; fishing rights on
this BW reservoir are exercised by an angling
club.
Whaley Bridge
*Derbs. EC Wed. PO, tel, stores, garage, station,
launderette, fish & chips, banks.* Built on a
steep hill at the end of the canal, with good
views across the Goyt valley, this is now a
quiet and pleasant place, a new by-pass
having removed much of the traffic. The
beautiful nearby hills are, however, more
noteworthy than the town.
Cromford & High Peak Railway In the
early 1820s a physical connection was planned
between the Peak Forest Canal at Whaley
Bridge and the Cromford Canal, way over to
the south east on the other side of the Peak
District, using a junction canal. However a
canal would have been impracticable through
such mountainous terrain, and so a railway
was constructed. Known as the Cromford &
High Peak Railway, it was opened throughout
in 1831, 33 miles long. With a summit level
over 1200ft above the sea, this extraordinary
standard-gauge goods line was interesting
chiefly for its numerous slopes and inclined
planes, up which the wagons were hauled by
either stationary or tenacious locomotive
steam engines. (The steepest gradient on the
line was 1 in 7.) The C & HPR closed in 1967;
much of the route is now being turned into a
public footpath and bridleway. Around
Whaley Bridge one may still see the remains of
the short inclined plane (now a footpath)
which brought the goods down the hill, then
through the town to the wharf at the terminus
of the Peak Forest Canal.
Buxworth
Derbs. PO, tel, stores. The main feature in
Buxworth is the old terminal basin system.
This used to be a tremendously busy complex,
and is of great interest to industrial
archaeologists. The canal line to Buxworth
(once Bugsworth) was built to bring the canal
as near as possible to the great limestone

quarries at Doveholes, a plate tramway being constructed in 1799 via Chapel Milton to complete the connection. Known as the Peak Forest Tramway, this little line, 6½ miles long, brought the stone down the hills to Buxworth, where it was transhipped into waiting canal boats. Throughout the history of the line, the wagons on the tramway were drawn exclusively by horse-power – except for a 500yd inclined plane in Chapel-en-le-Frith, where the trucks were attached to a continuous rope so that the descending trucks pulled empty ones up the 1 in 7½ slope. The tramway was closed by 1926, and the sidings and basins at Buxworth have been disused and overgrown since that time. However the Inland Waterways Preservation Society and BW are working towards a complete restoration of the complex. See the noticeboard by the bridge for the latest information.
Furness Vale
Derbs. PO, tel, stores, garage, station. A main road (A6) village, useful for supplies.

BOATYARDS

Ⓑ **Furness Vale Marina** At bridge 31 (0663 742971). Ⓦ Ⓓ Pump-out, long-term mooring, dry dock, painting, repairs. Toilet.
Ⓑ **New Mills Marina** Hibbert Street, New Mills (0663 745000). Ⓡ Ⓢ Ⓦ Ⓓ Pump-out, gas, overnight mooring, long-term mooring, winter storage, boat sales and repairs, chandlery, gifts, provisions, toilets and showers.

BOAT TRIPS

Judith Mary Unicorn Marine, The Wharf, Canal Street, Whaley Bridge (0663 734737). Lovely 70ft-narrowboat available for private charter.
African Dream available for day hire from Furness Vale. Ring 0663 733411.

PUBS AND RESTAURANTS

🍺✗ **Jodrell Arms** Whaley Bridge (0663 732164). Wilson's real ale, meals *lunchtime and evenings.*
🍺✗ **Railway** Whaley Bridge (0663 732245). Robinson's real ale, meals *lunchtime and evenings. Children welcome.*
🍺 **Navigation** Whaley Bridge, near the canal terminus. Boddingtons real ale.
🍺 **Navigation** Buxworth, by the canal terminus. Superbly situated pub overlooking the old basins. Ruddles and Webster's real ale, food *lunchtime and evenings.* Very comfortable bars, one with a canal theme. B & B.
🍺 **Dog & Partridge** Near the junction to Buxworth Basin. Real ale, food, children welcome.
🍺 **Soldier Dick** Furness Vale.
🍺 **Crossings** By the level crossing up from bridge 31. Robinson's real ale and food *lunchtime and evenings.*

Rose Hill 'tunnel', Lower Peak Forest Canal. *Derek Pratt.*

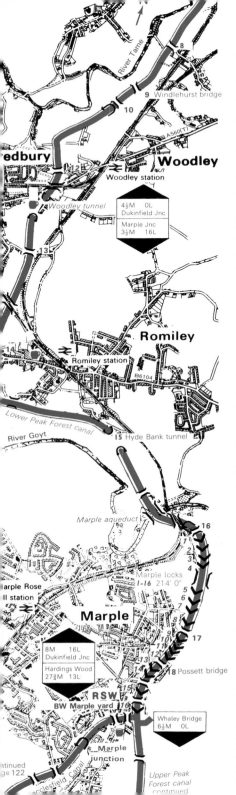

Marple Aqueduct

At Marple Junction the 16 narrow (standard 7ft beam) Marple Locks carry the Peak Forest Canal down 214ft past the Macclesfield Canal towards Manchester. The southernmost 5 miles of the Lower Peak Forest Canal (ie from Marple Junction northwards) are very beautiful. The locks themselves, which are spaced out over 1 mile, have an unrivalled setting in an excellent combination of built-up area, parkland, tall trees and steep hillside; the River Goyt is hidden down in the wooded valley to the east. Look out for the interesting Possett Bridge, where there is a small tunnel for the towpath (and horse) and an even smaller one for the boatman, leading down to the lock. At the foot of the locks, where the River Goyt is crossed, one is treated to the double joys of a major canal aqueduct with an even bigger railway viaduct alongside. West of here a long narrow stretch was once Rose Hill Tunnel, long since opened out. The canal then traverses a wooded hillside before diving into Hyde Bank Tunnel, 308yds long. The towpath is diverted over the hill, past a farm. There is a swimming pool close to the canal at bridge 14. On the other side, a couple of minor aqueducts lead the canal northwards, away from the Goyt Valley and past Romiley, Bredbury and Woodley. Here is a narrow 176yd-long tunnel, this time with the towpath continued through it. Beyond these not unattractive outer suburbs of Manchester, the canal runs again along a hillside in unspoilt countryside, overlooking the tiny River Tame. There are plenty of trees and the occasional textile mill to add interest to the rural scenery. One should relish this length of the canal – it is the last one sees of the countryside before entering the vast conurbation of Manchester. The towpath is well used between Woodley and Ashton, and is marked with wooden signposts giving mileages.

Navigational notes
1 There is no mooring on the Marple flight since water levels in the pounds can fall dramatically when the locks are in use.
2 Hyde Bank Tunnel, although appearing wide, does not have sufficient clearance for two boats to pass. Hold back until it is clear.

Romiley
Gt Manchester. All services. A useful place for supplies.

Marple
Gt Manchester. All services. Once a famous hat-making centre, the town is most interesting by the canal. There are shops just downhill from bridge 17.

Marple Aqueduct
Deservedly scheduled as an ancient monument this three-arched aqueduct over the River Goyt is a very fine structure, in an exquisite setting almost 100ft above the river. Designed by Benjamin Outram its construction utilises circular pierced shoulders above each arch to reduce the weight of the rubble filling whilst providing a decorative feature. Contrast and interest are further added by the use of two different colours of gritstone in the parapets and ledges.

Marple Locks
The 16 locks at Marple were not built until 1804, four years after the rest of the navigation was opened. The 1-mile gap thus left was bridged by a tramway, while the Canal Company sought the cash to pay for the construction of a flight of locks. This was obviously a most unsatisfactory state of affairs, since the limestone from Doveholes had to be shifted from wagon to boat at Buxworth Basin, from boat to wagon at Marple Junction, and back into boat again at the bottom of the tramway. Not surprisingly, a container system was developed – using iron boxes with a 2-ton payload – to ease the triple transhipment. However, this was no long-term solution, and when the necessary £27,000 was forthcoming the company authorised construction of the flight of locks. Today they stand comparison with any flight on the network: note especially Samuel Oldknow's superb warehouse, by lock

9 opposite the lock keeper's house, now
tastefully converted to offices.

BOATYARDS
British Waterways Marple Yard At Marple
Junction, on the Macclesfield Canal (061-427
1079). [R] [S] [W] Overnight mooring.

PUBS AND RESTAURANTS
🛥 **Navigation** Woodley. At north end of
tunnel. Robinson's real ale, garden.
🛥 **Spread Eagle** Hatherlow, Romiley.
🛥 **Railway** Romiley.
✗ **Bridge Café** 164 Stockport Road,
Romiley (061-430 5937). Moor north of
bridge 14. A friendly and welcoming café
decorated in canal style, offering reasonably
priced, authentic, home-made food including
vegetarian dishes. Fresh vegetables, Scotch
salmon, hams and turkeys roasted on the
premises. *Open 11.30-15.00 Mon-Fri;* gourmet
evenings *every second Sat in month* - book for
this and bring your own wine. Swimming pool
adjacent and shops and services close by.
🛥 **Duke of York** 250yds east of bridge 14.
Food, garden.
🛥 **Navigation** By lock 13. Useful for 'lock
wheelers' (no mooring on flight!). Chinese
take-away close by.

The bridge at Dukinfield Junction. *Derek Pratt.*

Hyde

The canal continues northward through a
landscape which becomes less rural, but in
some ways more interesting. At bridge 7 the
towpath changes sides; the building nearby is
the headquarters of the Peak Forest Canal
Society. Bridge 6 is a pretty roving bridge,
grown wider over the years. Beyond is a wharf
with some well-restored buildings and good
moorings on either side. To the north the
industrial tentacles of Hyde – Greater
Manchester – ensnare the canal traveller.
Beyond Hyde the canal traverses a great
expanse of landscaped wasteland. There used
to be two short branches along here; they are
both untraceable now. The approach to
Dukinfield Junction (Portland Basin) is now
very pleasant. The towpath is nice and tidy,
with plenty of grass, trees and seats. Below
and to the west there is a fine farmhouse, with
horses in the paddock. A Llangollen-type lift
bridge, an aqueduct over the River Tame and
a stone roving bridge provide canal interest.
The warehouse which faces you across the
junction has been restored as a canal heritage
centre and museum. Heading off to the south
west, the Ashton Canal takes you into
Manchester proper: to the north west is a half
a mile restored section of the Huddersfield
Narrow Canal, including three locks. Should
you decide to explore this section by boat,
there is nowhere to turn above the top lock....
If you pass this way during *July*, you may see
the colourful Ashton Canals Festival, which
has been running successfully for over 10 years
now. Portland Basin is a recommended
mooring place for those on the Cheshire Ring.

Heritage Centre and Museum Portland
Basin, Ashton-under- Lyne. The museum
tells the rich story of Tameside's social and
industrial history by drawing on seven very
different facets of local life. Water wheel and
many other things of interest. *Open Tue-Sat &
Sun afternoons.* Admission free.

BOATYARDS

Ⓑ **Warble Narrowboats** Warble Wharf,
Broadway, Hyde (061-367 9205). Ⓡ Ⓦ Ⓓ
Pump-out, gas, day hire boat, overnight
mooring, winter storage, crane, chandlery,
books and maps, boat building, boat sales,
engine repairs.

PUBS

🍺 **Globe** By bridge 2. Food.
🍺 **Cheshire Ring Hotel** A few yards east of
bridge 6. *Shops and station nearby.*

Droylsden

From start to finish, the Ashton Canal passes through a densely built-up area in which the canal is conspicuous as an avenue of escape from the oppressive townscape that flanks it. Its clear water, its excellent towpath, its functional but dignified old bridges and the peace that surrounds it make it a haven for local schoolchildren, anglers, walkers and idlers, and for anyone else who enjoys an environment that is quite separate from and unrelated to ordinary daily life. The rare pleasure, afforded only by an English canal, of stepping out of the noise and bustle of everyday life in a city suburb, into the peaceful and unpretentious atmosphere of the 18thC is once again, with gradual restoration work, becoming available to all. Leaving Dukinfield Junction – where substantial old canal warehouses and docks face the Peak Forest Canal – one turns west towards Manchester. Electrified suburban railway lines jostle the canal, which enters a cutting and passes Guide Bridge. There are pubs, shops and a railway station nearby, but it can be difficult to scramble up the bank out of the cutting. Droylsden is memorable for the wonderful smell of a marmalade factory – here the 18 locks begin the descent to the Rochdale Canal. Shops and pubs are all close to the junction; there is also a sanitary station. One can see the remains of several old canal arms along the Ashton Canal: one of the more important ones was the 5-mile Stockport Branch, leaving from Clayton Junction just below lock 11.

Navigational notes
1 A British Waterways Leeds & Liverpool type anti-vandal key is needed for all the locks and moveable bridges on the Ashton, and for the first lift bridge on the Lower Peak Forest. Be very careful where you moor in this area, and do not offer anyone a ride in your boat.
2 Bridge 21 is *very* low.

BOATYARDS
British Waterways Fairfield Junction (061-273 4686). S W Toilet.

PUBS
 Bridge Inn Canalside at Lock 11. Basic two-room pub offering Chester's real ale and food at *lunchtime*. Children usually allowed in (ask). Garden.
 Church Inn Canalside at Lock 11.
 Strawberry Duck Canalside at Lock 13. Traditional two-room pub which welcomes children. Wilson's and Holt real ale and *lunchtime* food.
 Friendship Canalside by Lock 15. Busy popular local serving Chester's real ale and *lunchtime* food. Garden, children welcome.
 Church Hotel Ashton Road, Droylsden. Victoriana in the lounge, and a sparsely decorated vault. Chester's real ale, *lunchtime* food and garden. Children welcome *mid-day*.

Manchester

The canal now falls through the remaining
seven locks into Manchester. The
surroundings are brightened by the well-
cared-for Beswick flight, but eventually
become industrial until the canal is totally
hemmed in by the back walls of tall factories –
originally built there because of the canal's
very presence – for ½ mile above the bottom
three locks. The necessary but tiresome chore
of unlocking and locking the paddle gear tends
to slow progress. The Rochdale Canal, which
is still privately owned, used to stretch for 33
miles over the Pennines from Manchester to
Sowerby Bridge – where it joined the terminus
of the Calder & Hebble Navigation (see page
23). It has been closed to navigation, and in
Manchester much of the canal has been
reduced to a shallow, landscaped water
channel. However, the bottom mile of the
canal is navigable, from the junction with the
Ashton Canal at Ducie Street down to
Castlefield and the junction with the
Bridgewater Canal. This remaining mile of the
Rochdale Canal is thus a vital link between the
Bridgewater and Ashton canals in the 100-
mile 'Cheshire Ring'. Large-scale
redevelopments are underway at Paradise
Wharf and Piccadilly Village. Permanent and
temporary moorings have been provided here
– handy if you wish to visit the 'Jolly Angler'
pub – and concerts on a canalside stage.
Persons wishing to navigate the nine wide
locks to the Bridgewater Canal should apply to
the Head Office of the Rochdale Canal
Company, 75 Dale Street, Manchester (061-
236 2456) for a separate licence, if they do not
already have one. The locks can accommodate
vessels up to 74ft long and 14ft wide, drawing
up to 4ft, with a height above water level of up
to 9ft. The Rochdale passage is described in
full on page 38, in the Bridgewater section.
There are good moorings, and a sanitary
station, at the BW Office by locks 1 and 2 on
the Ashton Canal.

Navigational note
Beswick Locks are closed overnight, and *re-
open at 08.00.*

Manchester
See page 38.
Salford
See page 40.

BOATYARDS

British Waterways Section Office Vesta
Street, Ancoats (061-273 4686). R W

PUBS AND RESTAURANTS

🍺 **Navigation** Near lock 6, Ashton Canal.
🍺 **Jolly Angler** Ducie Street, Manchester,
near the junction. Small pub used by the
Ashton Canal Society and Mike Harding,
offering Hydes' real ale, *lunchtime* meals and
snacks *at all times.* Irish folk music sessions.
Children welcome.
✕ ❢ **La Péniche Café-Bar** Paradise Wharf,
Ducie Street (061-273 5553). A floating
French-style bar offering Brittany pancakes,
galettes and crêpes. *L & D (not Sat L or Sun
D).*
🍺 **Pollard Inn** Pollard Street, Manchester.
Basic friendly pub serving Lees real ale and
snacks *at all times.*
🍺 **Mitchell Arms** Corner of Every Street and
Ashton New Road, Manchester. Well
renovated pub where children are welcome.
Banks's real ale and snacks *at all times.*

SHEFFIELD & SOUTH YORKSHIRE

Maximum dimensions

Sykehouse to Rotherham
Length: 230'
Beam: 20'
Headroom: 10' over 16' width
Rotherham to Sheffield
Length: 61' 6"
Beam: 15' 6"
Headroom: 11'
Bramwith to Keadby
Length: 62'
Beam: 17'
Headroom: 11' over 16' width

Manager

(0636) 704481

Mileage

AIRE AND CALDER
Junction with New Junction Canal to:
Bramwith Junction: 5½ miles, 1 lock
Doncaster Lock: 12 miles, 2 locks
Swinton Junction: 21½ miles, 7 locks
Rotherham: 27½ miles, 10 locks
SHEFFIELD Basin: 33½ miles, 25 locks
BRAMWITH Junction to:
Thorne: 5 miles, 2 locks
Crowle Wharf: 11¼ miles, 2 locks
KEADBY, Junction with River Trent: 14¾ miles, 3 locks

Four separate waterway developments combine to make up the Sheffield & South Yorkshire Navigations. Prior to their improvement, trade with the industrial heartland of South Yorkshire was by horse and cart to Bawtry and then by the natural line of the River Idle into the Trent and so into the Humber estuary. The River Don was largely given over to powering water wheels along its upper length – a right jealously guarded by the mill owners – whilst its lower reaches split into two channels west of Thorne and drained into the Trent. In 1627 Cornelius Vermuyden was employed to drain Hatfield Chase and the Isle of Axholme. His scheme involved blocking one of the River Don's outlets into the Trent, thereby forcing all its waters into the tidal River Aire. This was unsuccessful, and resulted in the flooding of adjacent land and villages, and made what had been an already difficult river navigation into a hazardous one. To alleviate the problem, a new channel, the Dutch River, was cut east from the River Don into the Ouse. This improved drainage, but not navigation. For rather more than 150 years traders on the lower Don had to contend with this state of affairs, although access to the River Aire remained possible until the end of the 17thC, when a moveable bridge was fixed closed during repairs.

Upstream, the river between Doncaster and Mexborough had, by 1729, been considerably improved, with complete navigation to Tinsley, four miles from Sheffield, a reality by 1751. Over the next 50 years all goods to and from Sheffield for shipment by water travelled by road between a river wharf at Tinsley and the city. It was not until 1815 that an Act of Parliament was obtained to build a canal, climbing 12 locks, into the city centre. The Sheffield Canal was opened on February 22nd 1819, built at a cost of £104,719. For the first time the city was linked directly to the sea, via the Trent and Humber.

The Trent link had in fact been made 17 years earlier, with the construction of the Stainforth & Keadby Canal, which by-passed the tidal reaches of the old Dutch River.

As with so many canals, after a short period of prosperity, the company fell victim to railway competition, and was taken over by The Doncaster & Goole Railway. The navigation declined until 1888, when, after pressure from Sheffield industrialists, the Sheffield & South Yorkshire Navigation Company was formed, and improvements made. The straddle warehouse built over Sheffield Basin dates from this period, as did the negotiations with the Aire & Calder Navigation to link Sheffield directly to the port of Goole and the more northerly coalfields. These negotiations resulted in the opening of the New Junction Canal on January 2nd 1905, the last canal to be constructed in the country. Subsequent improvements mainly involved enlarging the locks below Rotherham to keep pace with the changing traffic. These modifications ended in 1983, when the navigation was upgraded to the 700-tonne Eurobarge standard. Unfortunately, with no established traffic, the annual tonnage of goods carried is now just a fraction of the record one million tonnes achieved in 1951, and the navigation's future now seems to be in the area of leisure and recreation.

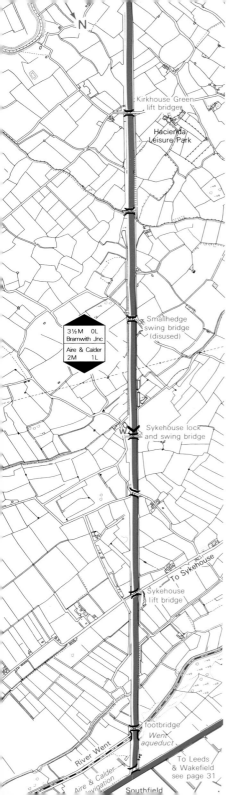

New Junction

The New Junction Canal provides a link between the Aire & Calder and the Sheffield & South Yorkshire navigations. The canal is 5½ miles long and completely straight all the way, the monotony being broken only by a series of swing and lift bridges, all of which are manned. There are aqueducts at each end of the long corridor formed by the navigation, the first carrying the canal over the River Went. The large cooling towers of Thorpe Marsh Power Station to the south can be seen on entering the New Junction and dominate the landscape for many miles. Although the countryside here is flat, it is not without character. Moorings are available to the north of Sykehouse Bridge and from here the village of Sykehouse and its two pubs may be reached, approximately ¾ mile to the west of the canal. Further moorings are available to the north of Kirkhouse Green Bridge. Boaters could be forgiven for thinking that their eyes are deceiving them at this point as palm trees and pagodas come into sight on the horizon. This is, in fact, the Hacienda Leisure Park, a theme park in miniature which offers entertainment for the children as well as eating places for the family.

Navigational note
All locks and moveable bridges are operated by keepers along the New Junction. Times are more restrictive than on the adjoining Aire & Calder navigation and at present there is no boater operation facility. During winter working – *October to March* - there are no duty keepers over the weekend. Special passage may be requested; for this and details of opening hours contact the Waterway Manager on 0636 704481.

Sykehouse
S. Yorks. Tel, stores, garage. A linear settlement which sprawls extensively to either side of the canal. Two pubs and a shop will be found to the west where there is some attractive new housing, much of which has been thoughtfully constructed of old brick. The Holy Trinity Church has an attractive brick tower which was added to the original stone structure in 1724. The stone was subsequently replaced by a Victorian brick edifice.
Hacienda Leisure Park Kirkhouse Green (0405 85648). 200yds west of Kirkhouse Green Bridge. A miniature theme park with several eating venues. Admission charge.

PUBS

◼ **Old George Inn** Sykehouse. Once the home of the local cricket team, the adjoining field now contains an extensive adventure playground which has made this a popular pub with families from the surrounding towns and villages. The *summer* months attract visitors from far and wide who come to enjoy the swimming pool, boules and short mat bowls. There is also a regular quiz night on *Thursdays*. The building dates back some five hundred years, the pub having been formed from what was once a terrace of cottages consisting over the years of a shop, a dame's school, a farrier, a butcher's and a slaughter-house. The original wheel for hoisting the animals aloft for slaughter still hangs in the restaurant. One room in the pub has its ceiling covered with old coins, all stuck there with the froth off the beer. Tetley's real ale is served here and food is available *lunchtime and evenings Mon-Sun* both in the bar and the restaurant. A free child's meal is available with every steak.
◼ **Three Horseshoes** Sykehouse. A quiet pub on the outskirts of the village. Bar food. *Closed lunchtime out of season.*

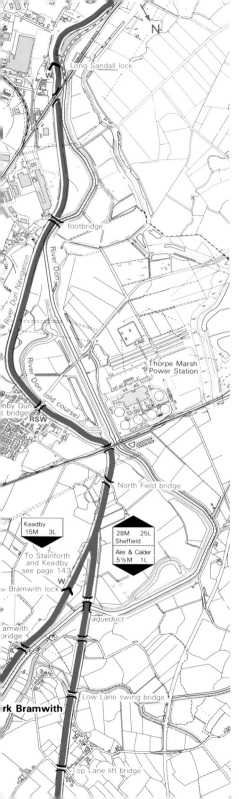

Barnby Dun

This stretch of the waterway starts with another bridge lifting effortlessly as the boater approaches. Beyond is Low Lane swing bridge, carrying the road leading into Kirk Bramwith, with its interesting Norman church. Then the Don aqueduct appears. It presents a rather foreboding feature as it is contained by large guillotine gates at either end. Passing boats, although protected by a barrier on one side, have no more than a girder fixed at water level on the other side, to prevent their descent into the river below. Once over the aqueduct the canal is joined by the Stainforth & Keadby section of the navigation meeting at a very fine angle from the left. Its junction is masked by trees growing on the narrow spit of land formed between the two canals. Immediately under the next railway bridge oil barges berth to deliver fuel oil to Thorpe Marsh power station, whilst ¼ mile ahead Barnby Dun Lift Bridge comes into view. Passing the village the navigation bends round to the south west and the first of many industrial complexes looms on the left bank – in this case the Pilkington glass works. By way of compensation there is a tiny, though delightful, hotch potch of a church, nestling beside a farmyard. An impressive line-up of BMW motorcars is parked next to the glass factory, awaiting loading onto road transporters and distribution throughout the country; then Long Sandall Lock with its tower-shaped Control Cabin looking down on manicured lawns and neat flower beds.

Navigational notes

1 All locks to Rotherham operate mechanically and are controlled by lock keepers during normal working hours. Obey the traffic light signals.
2 Long Sandall is the first of the series of locks leading to Rotherham that can be boater operated outside normal working hours. Two 'Castell' keys, available from the Waterway Manager's office at Swinton and the lock keepers at Long Sandall and Sir Frank Price Locks, against a refundable deposit, open two lockside control panels. These allow the boater to operate the hydraulic paddle gear and the lock gates by pressing a series of buttons. Those anxious about operating these controls should consult the lock keeper during duty hours.

Barnby Dun

S. Yorks. PO, tel, stores, garage. An attractive village laid out along one side of the canal on slightly rising ground facing the stark cooling towers of Thorpe Marsh Power Station on the opposite bank. Once a picturesque mix of old cottages, more recent infilling threatens to overpower the original village and turn it into a Doncaster suburb. It is reported that the once boggy marshland around the village yielded a surprising find: the vertebrae of a whale. While the shop beside the lift bridge keeps irregular hours, a walk further along the street that almost parallels the canal will be rewarded by a butcher, an excellent farm shop selling fresh local produce, two pubs and a restaurant. The church is over 600 years old and worth a visit.

PUBS AND RESTAURANTS

◗ Star East of the canal, a typical brewery-owned pub serving bar food *lunchtime Mon-Sat.*
◗ White Hart Theakston and John Smith's real ales are dispensed in this cosy welcoming pub. The bar and seating area are liberally decorated with antiques, particularly china, while the portions of food are generous in the extreme. The landlady holds the Gordon's Gin Landlady of the Year Award 1989 and for sheer attentiveness it would be hard to better her.
◗✕ Gateway Restaurant opposite White Hart (0302 882849). A licensed restaurant offering a varied, reasonably priced menu. Vegetarians catered for. *L & D Tue-Sun.*

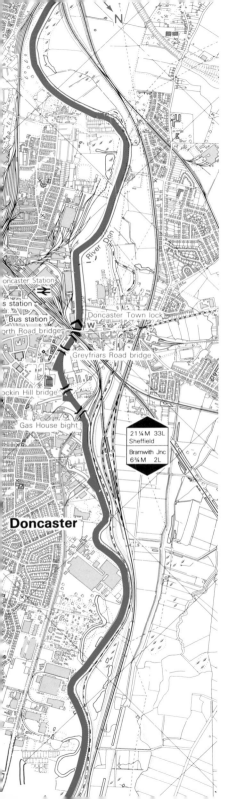

Doncaster

There is little of interest between Long Sandall
Lock and first glimpsing the 170ft pinnacled
tower of St George's church in the centre of
Doncaster; a town that Dickens visited in 1857
and described as being thronged with 'horse-
mad, betting-mad, drunken-mad, vice-mad
crowds'. Some say it is quieter now. To the left
a ribbon of industry continues to accompany
the canal towards the town. The Case
International tractor works, sprawling around
the outside sweep of a wide bend, is followed
by the ICI fibres factory, while all the time the
River Don hugs the right-hand bank, obscured
by flood embankments. Then the navigation is
in Doncaster, widening out opposite the
church and beside the disused coal staithe.
Ahead through Greyfriars Bridge is a real
jumble of transport systems as road crosses
railway, which in turn crosses the canal, all at
the same point. The bottom gates of Doncaster
Town Lock can also be discerned once the
boater's eyes become accustomed to the
gloom. Above the lock the navigation joins the
Don for the first time and the town is soon left
far behind as the waterway traces a path
through green fields.

Navigational notes
1 At Doncaster Town Lock the boater is
entering a river navigation which together with
a series of artificial cuts continues through to
Tinsley, on the outskirts of Sheffield. Many of
the locks are accompanied by large weirs, so
keep a sharp look out for signs which direct
you safely into the locks.
2 Once the river level rises 2ft above normal
(gauging sticks are fixed at the top of all locks)
pleasure craft may well experience difficulty
due to the current, floating debris and the pull
at weirs. Seek the advice of the lock keeper
before proceeding.

The towpath
There is no towpath from Gas House Bight
through to the top of Doncaster Town Lock.

Doncaster
*S. Yorks. EC Thur. MD Tue, Fri, Sat. All
services.* Once the site of a Roman station –
Danum – the town became an important
industrial centre in the 19thC; the home of a
large railway and carriage works and ringed by
a girdle of mining villages. Exploited for
almost a century the pits of the South
Yorkshire Coalfield yielded open-cast coal to
the west, whilst to the east of a dividing ridge
of magnesium limestone, deep mines were
sunk. In the early part of the 19thC when the
town was largely an agricultural community
straddling the Great North Road, its high
street was regarded as the finest along the
route between London and Edinburgh. Alas,
most of the buildings of the last fifty years pay
little regard to the original character of the
High Street. One consistent link with the past
is, however, provided by the annual St Leger
horse race, first run in 1776, and pre-dating
the Derby by two years.
Parish Church of St George Built to a
design by Gilbert Scott in 1858 on an almost
Cathedral scale, it replaced a medieval church
burnt down in 1853. A very fine example of
Victorian Neo-Gothic.
Mansion House High Street, Doncaster
(0302 734011). An impressive civic building
designed by James Paine and finished in 1748.
Open by appointment.
Museum and Art Gallery Chequer Road,
Doncaster (0302 734287). Opened in 1964, it
contains relics from the Roman station, early
town documents, costumes, paintings,
ceramics and silver. *Open Sat-Thur.*
Cusworth Hall Museum Cusworth Park,
Doncaster (0302 782342). The house (rebuilt
and then altered by James Paine in the 1750s)
contains a museum which illustrates South
Yorkshire's history, industry and social life.
Small waterways exhibit. *Open Sat-Thur.*

PUBS AND RESTAURANTS
There are plenty of pubs and restaurants in
Doncaster, though none beside the navigation.

Conisbrough

Passing beneath two iron-girdered railway bridges the waterway now enters a pleasant tree-lined valley, only briefly intruded upon by the noise of motorway traffic crossing overhead on the slender Don viaduct. At Sprotbrough Lock a short canalised section provides excellent moorings and access to the village. This unexpectedly handsome stretch of the navigation continues with the valley sharply defined by steep sides covered with delightful woods. Quarrying for the honey-coloured magnesium limestone has long been a feature of the area, leaving the surrounding foliage powdered with a yellow dust. A loading wharf on the right, close to the quarry floor, indicates that the waterway is still used to transport the limestone. Ahead towers the tremendous Conisbrough Railway Viaduct, built in Staffordshire blue bricks and now sadly disused except by pedestrians. Then Conisbrough Castle, with its fine drum tower and spurs, comes into view, dominating the skyline for some miles to come. The castle is well worth a visit but, in common with much along this stretch of the waterway, access by boat is at present far from easy. Beyond Conisbrough the valley starts to flatten out leaving the woods behind, as the river winds its way towards Mexborough Cut. This area was once alive with colliery workings, but now the pit heaps have been bulldozed and landscaping is under way.

The towpath
Technically the towpath follows the right-hand bank throughout this stretch. However, sections above Conisbrough are in a poor state of repair, and to cross the River Dearne walkers must deviate ½ mile to the north west and use the road bridge (BW has plans to make improvements).

Sprotbrough
S. Yorks. PO, tel, stores. An attractive village running up from the north bank of the Don and a useful source of provisions, even on *Sundays.* Sir Walter Scott is reputed to have written part of *Ivanhoe* here. The church, dating back to at least the 12thC, has much to offer and is well-supported by an excellent guide. There is a 17thC stone chair, or 'frith stool', in the chancel, together with Elizabethan carvings on the pew ends.

Conisbrough
S. Yorks. All services. The town is dominated by the castle which contrasts dramatically with the industrial surroundings.
Conisbrough Castle (0709 863329). A Norman castle – circa 1185 – with a circular keep once capped by a conical wooden roof, standing high above the River Don. It is the oldest and best preserved of its kind in the country, being originally founded by Earl de Warenne. The surviving work is by Hameline Plantagenet – half brother of Henry II. *Open daily.* Charge.

BOAT TRIPS
Alan Oliver (Cruises) (0302 856513). Waterbus service from above Sprotbrough Lock on *Sun and B. Hols* aboard ex-Clyde ferry *Wyre Lady.*

PUBS AND RESTAURANTS
🍺 **Boat Inn** Sprotbrough. On north bank above the lock. Since 1652 this much-beamed building has regularly alternated between farmhouse and pub. After lying derelict for 20 years, it was renovated to the present high standard and now serves John Smith's real ale. An attractive dining room offers a varied menu and snacks are available at the bar. Vegetarians catered for. *No food on Sun.*
🍺 **Ivanhoe** Sprotbrough. ½ mile from the river at the top of the village. Samuel Smith real ale, together with bar meals. Lively, comfortable pub overlooking the cricket pitch. *No food Mon evenings.*
✕ ❢ **Eidelweiss Restaurant** Sprotbrough (0302 853923). In the centre of the village and serving mainly Continental food. Vegetarians catered for by prior notice. *D, closed Mon.*

Swinton Junction

The first section of Mexborough Cut, one of the last of the artificial 'cuts' to be built, is both wide and featureless. Gone are the collieries and pit heaps that lined this stretch and once produced so much of South Yorkshire's coal. Gradual reinstatement is taking place, and as this area seeks a new identity, it is to be hoped that this broad corridor of dereliction will become gradually greener. The fruits of EC land reclamation grants are already in evidence between here and Sheffield, in the form of both landscaping and tree planting, as the concept of waterways as linear parks comes one step nearer to reality. Bordering Mexborough the gardens of private houses make good use of the canal. Once keels plied this waterway, often able to sail up the river as far as Mexborough. An abundance of low bridges above the town made further use of sails impractical so they were left here and a horse, with attendant 'Marine', was hired from the extensive stables to complete the journey. There was also a blacksmith – Bingley's – beside the navigation, largely devoted to shoeing the horses. The Barnsley British Co-operative Society's flour mill received regular water-borne deliveries of grain. At Swinton Junction, where the Dearne & Dove Canal used to climb the four locks off the mainline towards Barnsley, the lock has been renamed Waddington Lock in recognition of the contribution that E. V. Waddington's barges have made to the navigation. Today they throng the junction, using the empty pounds of the branch canal as a dry dock, and often making the approach to the lock difficult.

The towpath
At Double Bridges the towpath crosses on the first bridge, descends immediately onto the A6022 and follows the road south until it crosses the derelict arm of the Dearne & Dove Canal. Here it turns left and picks up the towpath again on the right bank of the mainline.

Swinton Junction
Here the Dearne & Dove Canal left the mainline and provided a route to Barnsley and thence via the Barnsley Canal to Wakefield. Together they made up the southern loop for the so-called Yorkshire ring. Both waterways have long since fallen into disrepair but ambitious plans are afoot to open up these navigations. Once a busy waterway junction and boat building centre, it still forms an interesting canal settlement with three pubs virtually side by side.

Mexborough
S. Yorks. EC Thur. MD Mon, Fri, Sat. All services. The town's development appears to have taken place in stages, progressing away from the waterway; an effect accentuated by the routing of the by-pass between canal and town centre. Close to Mexborough Cut the houses are in the main both attractive and secluded, almost hiding the tiny church of Norman and early English origin, dedicated to St John the Baptist. Gravestones describe how in 1864 the River Don flood left 250 inhabitants dead. In the town itself the High Street is now pedestrianised. The diversity of Victorian façades suggests an earlier prosperity. There are both covered and open-air markets.

PUBS
Reresby Arms ¼ mile north east of Pastures road bridge. Garden.
Miners South west of Pastures road bridge. Lively pub with entertainment most *evenings*. Bar food *lunchtime*.
Ferryboat Close to the canal at Mexborough Top Lock. An outside seating area, bar snacks available.
George & Dragon Near to the Ferryboat with garden and children's play area. Snacks.
Ship Swinton Junction. Comfortably furnished pub.
Red House Swinton Junction.
Towpath Swinton Junction. Beer garden.

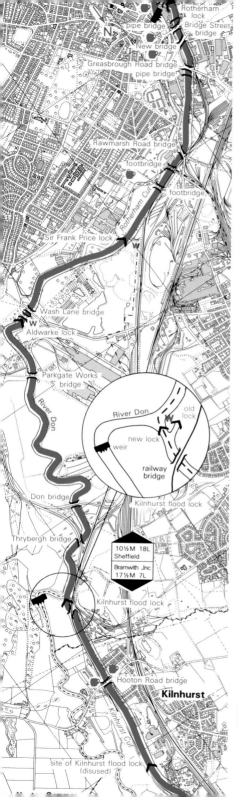

Kilnhurst

To the left Hooton Common, criss-crossed
with hedges and trees, rises to a more distant
skyline, offering some relief from the
industrial landscape. Once a tar works and a
colliery lined the right bank, the former
receiving the bulk of its deliveries by barge
from local town gas works before natural gas
made these plants redundant. At Hooton
Road Bridge there is a comfortable mooring, a
grocer's and post office, together with two
pubs; then the remaining short length of
Kilnhurst Cut brings the boater to Kilnhurst
Flood Lock and back onto the river. At this
point the towpath has to cross the waterway
onto the left bank. Without the benefit of a
bridge, barge horses were obliged to use flat-
decked chain ferries. The navigation now
twists and turns between high and often tree-
lined banks, passing gaunt modern factory
complexes, largely engaged in specialist steel
manufacture. All discharges from these works
are now carefully monitored for purity and to
this end brightly coloured booms surround
each outfall, containing their emissions for
regular testing by the National Rivers
Authority. Within recent memory the Don
was fast becoming one of the most polluted
rivers in Europe, but stringent control
measures have reversed this trend and fishing
on this stretch of water is regaining popularity.
It is now the River Rother, joining the Don
above Rotherham, that is the major source of
contamination. At Aldwarke Lock a short
channel by-passes the weir and a new concrete
flyover has now taken over from Wash Lane
bridge. Built in 1834, this listed structure
bears the marks of much abuse from both
barges and road traffic alike. There is a
proposal to form a new channel – leaving the
old one for offset moorings – to the south side
of the bridge, so marooning it forever. Half a
mile upstream the boater passes the wharf of
Sheffield Haulage and Storage which, until
1983, would have marked the entrance into
Rotherham Cut. When the Eastwood Locks
were combined on the upper site the river was
re-aligned along the old canal bed, explaining
the deep 'bight' in the left bank, previously a
sharp bend in the navigation. The new lock,
opened on 1st June, 1983, by the then
Chairman of BWB and called 'Sir Frank Price'
lock in his honour, completed the
modernisation to the 700-tonne barge
standard of the Sheffield & South Yorkshire
Navigation.

Eastwood
S. Yorks. PO, tel, stores. A suburb of
Rotherham, with an excellent variety of corner
shops dotted throughout the streets. Access is
over River Don via a bridge above Eastwood
Lock, which also offers overnight moorings.
Kilnhurst
S. Yorks. PO, tel, stores. A nondescript village
merging into the conurbation linking
Mexborough with Rotherham. Once the site
of an ironworks and, more recently, a colliery
which is now closed down. It was also known
for the production of earthenware pottery.

PUBS

🍺 **Ship Inn** East end of Hooton Road Bridge,
Kilnhurst. Cosy pub serving Whitbread real
ale and bar food. Garden.
🍺 **Commercial** West end of Hooton Road
Bridge, Kilnhurst. Bar food and games room.
🍺 **Donfield Tavern** Eldon Road,
Rotherham. Cross the Don on the bridge
above Eastwood Lock, walk beside the playing
fields and the pub is on the left on Eldon
Road. The landlord claims to serve the
cheapest beers, including Castle Eden real ale,
in Rotherham. A basic, though very friendly,
local.

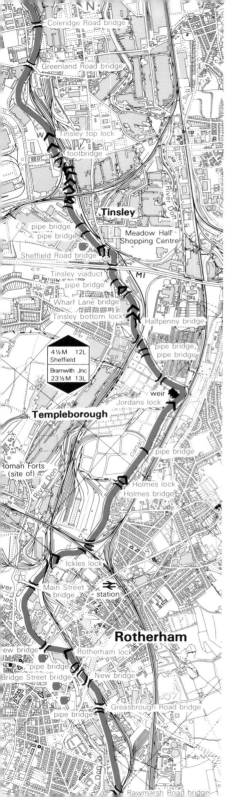

Rotherham

Approaching Rotherham the canal seems
intent on burrowing underground as it snakes
its way into the heart of the town, passing the
BW depot on the site of a former bus garage.
Eventually, as a supermarket car park looms
on the left, the waterway appears to have
reached a dead end hemmed in by a wall of
huge limestone blocks. At the last moment an
exit reveals itself in the top left-hand corner
and the boater turns into the tiny chamber of
Rotherham lock – retaining the original keel
length of 61ft 6in. Gone now are the keepers
perched in lofty cabins and the lockside
consoles giving access to push button controls.
Through to Sheffield the navigation remains
virtually unchanged since its original
construction as it briefly joins the Don only to
leave it again, separated by a thin ribbon of
trees. Three further locks, almost equally
spaced, bring the canal back into the river on a
wide sweeping bend across the head of a large
weir, and the two combine for exactly a mile
before the river forks right under Halfpenny
bridge, finally leaving the navigation. Ahead
the canal enters the bottom lock of the Tinsley
flight which begins its ascent under the
shadow of the massive steel viaduct carrying
the M1 across the valley. A total of 11 locks
lifts the navigation to the summit level through
tranquil wide pounds and open views, with the
bright-green domed roofs of the Meadowhall
Shopping Centre dominating the outlook to
the north.

The towpath

In order to avoid a perilous crossing (over a
leat adjacent to Jordan's Lock) walkers are
advised to follow the footpath deviating to the
right beside the pipe bridge. This passes
between the railway and two houses and
crosses a field parallel to the canal, which it
rejoins above Jordan's Lock.

Rotherham

S. Yorks. EC Thur. MD Mon, Sat. All services. A
surprisingly attractive town set amidst the
industrial heartland of South Yorkshire. The
buildings, although dating from a variety of
periods, integrate well to form a coherent town
centre, suggesting a community conscious of its
heritage and unwilling to be seduced by
insensitive developers. A part of the medieval
town plan remains while the old town hall, in its
new guise of arcade, presents a delightful
renovation. Rotherham's modern growth dates
from 1746 when Samuel Walker, a former
schoolmaster, established its first ironworks.
Coal mining developed, as well as the
production of brass, steel, rope and glass, yet it
is probably for the production of quality steels,
in the form of fine-edge tools, that the town is
best known. In more ancient times it was an
important seat of learning, the College of Jesus
being founded in 1482 by Archbishop Thomas
and surviving until the dissolution. The
pinnacled tower of All Saints church dates from
1409, and the remainder was almost entirely
constructed during the same century. Its
position, whilst maintaining an intimate contact
with the town, is nevertheless imposing.
Standing on the remaining four arches of a
bridge that once spanned the River Don, the
Chapel of Our Lady was built in 1482 and again
fell victim to the dissolution, after which it
variously became an almshouse, a prison and a
tobacconist's. It was finally restored and
reconsecrated in 1924 and forms an attractive
feature in the lower part of the town.
Museum and Art Gallery Clifton Park,
Rotherham (0709 382121). A collection
containing Roman remains from
Templeborough, gemstones and examples of
Rockingham and other local pottery. Loan
exhibitions of paintings. *Open 10.00-17.00
Mon-Thur & Sat, 14.15-16.45 Sun. Free.*
✕ **Meadowhall Shopping Centre** Tinsley.
Immense indoor shopping mall accessible
from above Lock 9 on the Tinsley flight.

PUBS AND RESTAURANTS

A wide selection near the canal in the centre of
Rotherham.

Sheffield Basin

At Greenland Road Bridge the towpath crosses to the south side of the canal and the industrial buildings begin to form a long corridor which leads to Sheffield Basin. As recently as 1987 the water in this stretch of the canal was renowned for its vivid yellow colour, the result of iron, contained in the water, being pumped out of the underground workings of Nunnery Colliery. This source of pollution has now been eliminated and already the wildlife is beginning to recover. Fishermen can be seen along the banks, as can clumps of michaelmas daisies, toadflax and valerian. Beyond Greenland Road Bridge the landscape is dominated by stadiums built to accommodate the Universiade, or World Student Games, in 1991. Access to the Don Valley Stadium, shops, pubs and cafes, can be found by leaving the towpath at the Darnall Road Aqueduct. Built in 1819 and known locally as 'T'Acky Dock', the aqueduct spanned the Attercliffe to Worksop turnpike. Passing under the railway bridge the canal widens briefly to form a broad pool, once popular with the local children for swimming! Staniforth Road Bridge again provides access to pubs, cafés, restaurants and shops on Attercliffe Road. This bridge also marks the beginning of factory buildings which made use of the canal, transporting coal, iron, bone, horn, steel and tools along the waterway. At Bacon Lane Bridge there is evidence of boats having been crow-barred through. Built in 1819 this bridge was also known as 'Needle's Eye' due to the problems it posed at high water. Approaching Bernard Road Bridge it is possible to peep into the rolling-mills and see the workers handling strips of red-hot steel with tongs. To the south rises the tall chimney of the refuse incineration plant. Sheffield City Council has been far-sighted enough to make use of the heat generated by the plant to provide hot water for nearby offices and works. Just before Cadman Road Bridge are several grindstones now capping the factory wall, which were once used in the manufacture of tools and cutlery. As the basin draws near, Sheffield is now well in sight. This area was once surrounded by blast furnaces, old Blast Lane being cut in two by the canal. The basin itself is dominated by the impressive Straddle Warehouse, added in 1895 by the South Yorkshire Navigation Company and built on columns over the water. Immediately behind this stands the Grain Warehouse with its bucket elevator for lifting grain. Beyond this is the original Terminal Warehouse of 1819 standing an imposing seven storeys high. Now derelict, it is hard to believe that this area was once the hub of transport, being surrounded by railway goods yards and carrying trains of the Manchester, Sheffield and Lincolnshire Railway across the vast complex of high-level lines. It is hoped to redevelop the basin whilst retaining the many fine listed buildings which are essential to its character and a reminder of the canal's heyday. An IWA plaque is available from the boatyard to all intrepid boaters who reach the basin.

Navigational note
Although it is possible to moor at several points along this stretch of the towpath, it is advisable to use moorings available in the vicinity of the basin for overnight stops.

The towpath
The towpath throughout this section is in good repair, having been recently reinstated under various work experience schemes. Many of the bridges carry signs directing towpath users to local services.

Sheffield
S. Yorks. EC Thur. MD Tue, Fri, Sat. All services. Sheffield is England's fourth largest city and owes its world-famous reputation to the manufacture of steel, cutlery and silverware. The unique landscape upon which Sheffield was built contributed to its importance during the Industrial Revolution.

Five river valleys facilitated the operation of
water wheels, and hills rich in iron ore made
Sheffield a natural pioneer of the steel
industry. Today Sheffield remains one of the
few cities which has managed to retain a sense
of individuality amidst new development. Sensitive
planning has succeeded in merging new
shopping complexes with the existing mix of
Georgian and Victorian architecture.
Pedestrianisation schemes have added to the
sense of light and space in the city centre
which incorporates many interesting and
unusual shops as well as seven markets. Tudor
Square brings together the internationally
famous Crucible Theatre with the Lyceum
Theatre, now restored to its former Victorian
splendour. Also nearby are the award-winning
Ruskin Gallery and Graves Art Gallery.
Town Hall Pinstone Street (0742 734793).
Built in 1897 the Town Hall has a clock tower,
193ft high, crowned with a statue of Vulcan,
Roman god of the forge. Public tours for pre-
booked parties.
Cutlers' Hall Church Street (0742 728456).
Built in 1832, the Cutlers' Hall houses the
Cutlers' Company collection of silver. Tours
for parties.
City Museum Weston Park (0742 768588).
The museum contains the largest collection of
Sheffield plate in the world and has a unique
section devoted to cutlery. *Open 10.00-17.00
Tue-Sat, 11.00-17.00 Sun.* Free.
Cathedral Church of St Peter & St Paul
Opposite the Cutlers' Hall in Church Street.
A largely 15thC Cathedral with an interesting
extension incorporating a new glass and steel
porch. Visitors will enjoy the stained-glass
windows depicting local history and the
Chaucer window in the Chapter house.
Sheffield Industrial Museum Kelham
Island off Alma Street (0742 722106). The
museum takes the visitor through Sheffield's
industrial past with a chance to see craftsmen
at work in the 'Little Mesters' workshops.
Occasionally the River Don Engine (a 12,000
bhp engineering wonder) is in steam. *Open
10.00-17.00 Wed-Sat, 11.00-17.00 Sun.*
Admission charge.
Abbeydale Industrial Hamlet Abbeydale
Road South (0742 367731). Four miles south
west of the city centre. A superb example of
industrial archaeology which displays a
restored community, built around a water-
powered scythe and steel works. *Open 10.00-
17.00 Wed-Sat, 11.00-17.00 Sun.* Admission
charge. Bus 24 from Pinstone Street.
Shepherd Wheel Whiteley Woods,
Hangingwater Road (0742 367731). Four
miles south west of the City Centre. A water-
powered grinding shop dating from the 16thC
and now in working order in the heart of the
woods. *Open 10.00-12.30, 13.30-17.00 Wed-
Sat.* Free. Bus 33 from Pinstone Street.
Bishop's House Meersbrook Park, Norton
Lees Lane (0742 557701). A timber-framed
Yeoman's house of 15thC origins with 16thC
and 17thC additions. Other displays include

Sheffield in Tudor and Stuart times. *Open
10.00-16.30 Sat, 11.00-16.30 Sun.* Admission
charge. Bus 34, 38, 39 from Bus Station.
South Yorkshire Steam Railway Barrow
Road, Meadowbank (0709 531266).
Although in the early stages, there are
currently 11 industrial steam locomotives to
be seen. *Open 11.00-16.00 Sat & Sun.* Free.

ART GALLERIES

Graves Central Library Building, Surrey
Street (0742 734781). A fine collection of
English watercolours, French paintings and
Old Masters. *Open 10.00-18.00 Mon-Sat.*
Free.
Mappin Weston Park (0742 726281).
Victorian paintings including Pre-Raphaelites.
English 18th-19thC paintings including
Constable and Turner. *Open 10.00-17.00 Tue-
Sat.* Free.
Ruskin Norfolk Street (0742 735299). A fine
collection of minerals, paintings and
illuminated manuscripts collected by John
Ruskin for the people of Sheffield. *Open
10.00-18.00 Mon-Fri, 10.00-17.00 Sat.* Free.

BOATYARDS

Ⓑ **Sheffield Canal Co.** Sheffield Basin, or
just outside, depending on development plans
for the basin (0742 727233). Ⓡ Ⓢ Ⓦ Ⓓ
Gas, pump-out, slipway, chandlery, boat
building, repairs, engines, showers, toilets.

BOAT TRIPS

Princess Mary 59 passengers. *Every Sat &
Sun from Easter-Sep.* Departing Sheffield
Basin. Available for charter. Details 0742
727233.

PUBS

There are many pubs and restaurants in
Sheffield. The following are simply a selection
of those nearest to the navigation.
🍺 **Cocked Hat** 300yds west of the canal at
the Darnall Road Aqueduct. A comfortable
Marston's real ale pub with an interesting
collection of old bottles. Popular with the
locals and handy for the Don Valley Stadium.
Bar snacks *lunchtime only.* Garden.
🍺 **Cutlers Arms** A down-to-earth local,
opposite the Cocked Hat. Particularly popular
with the football fans.
🍺 **Alexandra** 500yds west of the basin. A
basic city pub serving Stones real ale. Snacks
available *Mon-Fri lunchtime, Sat sandwiches
only.* Children welcome. Music *Tue evening.*
B&B.
🍺 **Market Tavern** West of the basin towards
the city centre, behind the open market. A
popular pub dispensing Whitbread real ale.
Food.
🍺 **Lady's Bridge** West of the basin just
beyond the Lady's Bridge over the River Don.
Next door to the Whitbread Exchange
Brewery. Whitbread real ale.

Stainforth

The lock at Kirk Bramwith acts as a gateway into a navigation which evokes an intimacy more typical of the narrow canals. Peaceful moorings are to be found here and an attractive screen of trees masks a pleasant picnic and barbecue area. Access to Kirk Bramwith with its pretty church can be gained at the swing bridge. The approach to Stainforth presents what is probably the most attractive part of the town as a series of pretty cottages line the banks. Just beyond the bridge, to the right, is a pub with moorings for patrons and access to the town. A dry dock once existed alongside the pub, together with a blacksmith and barge repair shop, all signs that Stainforth was once an important trading centre. Leaving Stainforth the remains of the old river lock can be seen beyond the entrance to the basin now used by the Thorne Cruising Club. The lock once allowed passage of craft into the tidal Don. However, the chamber was filled in when the river banks were raised for flood protection. In the distance to the north can be seen the ruins of an old brick windmill, now minus its cap, and the lofty yet delicate tower of the church at Fishlake. Dedicated to St Cuthbert the church is said to be the last resting place of Cuthbert's body before its burial at Durham. Although the River Don prevents any direct access to the village from this point on the canal, walkers may take the minor road from Stainforth bridge. Finally the river veers away to the north as the navigation passes under the M18 viaduct. Some of the first steam-powered vessels were built nearby at Waterside in the boatyard of a Mr Pearson. The river has now been diverted away from the stone wharf where vessels once dealing in whaling and rope making could be seen. Stanilands marina, immediately beyond the railway bridge, provides both safe moorings and a range of services, the town centre being only ¼ mile away. Beyond Thorne bridge there are further moorings, available to visitors, at the Blue Water Marina.

Stainforth
S. Yorks. All services. Open air market Fri evening. An unprepossessing town.

Thorne
S. Yorks. EC Thur. MD Tue, Fri, Sat. All services. A small market town with an attractive pedestrian precinct, Finkle Street, which offers a wide variety of shops. Thorne once depended on rope making, sacking and weaving with a canal traffic of coal, pig-iron and stone. The town was in fact dependent on the river and the canal for its water supply, the only boreholes supplying Darley's brewery and the workhouse. St Nicholas' church is a variety of architectural styles, due to large-scale renovations in the 14thC.

BOATYARDS

Ⓑ **Stanilands** Lock Lane, Thorne (0405 813150). ⓇⓌⒹ Chandlery, gas, slipway, dry dock, moorings, boat building, repairs, refits, engines, boat sales. Clubhouse and bar serving snack meals at *weekends.*

Ⓑ **Thorne Boat Services** Thorne (0405 814197). Ⓓ Gas, chandlery, outboards.

Ⓑ **Blue Water Marina** Thorne (0405 813165). ⓇⓈⓌⒹ Pump-out, gas, repairs, engines, servicing, boat sales, boat building, moorings, slipway, toilets, showers. Clubhouse *open Fri, Sat, Sun and Public Holidays.* Food. Visitors welcome.

PUBS

🍺 **New Inn** Stainforth. Canalside pub with moorings. Bar snacks *lunchtime and evenings. No food Wed and Sun evenings.*

🍺 **Canal Tavern** Thorne. North of Thorne Bridge. A lively pub with a beer garden. Snacks available *lunchtime only.* Music and quiz nights. Pool, darts, TV, mooring for patrons.

🍺 **Rising Sun** Thorne. South of Thorne Bridge. An attractive Darley real ale pub. Children welcome. Bar meals *lunchtime and evenings.*

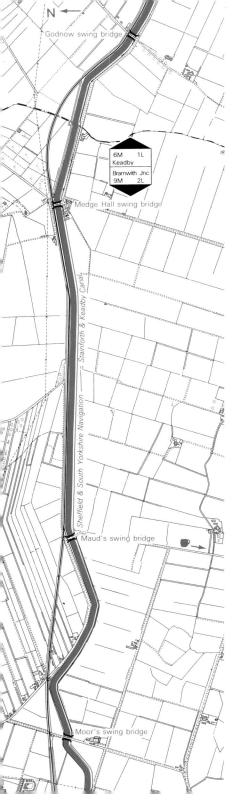

N ←

Godnow swing bridge

6M 1L
Keadby

Bramwith Jnc
9M 2L

Medge Hall swing bridge

Stainforth & Keadby Canal

Sheffield & South Yorkshire Navigation

Maud's swing bridge

Moor's swing bridge

Medge Hall

Leaving Thorne the landscape again opens up and a rich, fertile plain borders the navigation. Boaters will no doubt enjoy operating the Wykewell Lift Bridge, which together with the road barriers and flashing red lights, is controlled by pressing the appropriate buttons in the grey box, located on the left bank. At Moor's swing bridge (still to be converted for boater operation) a line of farms can be seen to the north of the canal. Here there is still evidence of the old 'strip' system of farming, where each dwelling is backed by a long narrow strip of land. These units of land would vary in size according to the type of soil and the lie of the land. The one-acre strip (220yds long by 22yds wide) was a rarity in most parts of the country, farms generally possessing strips much smaller than this. Much of the land along the length of the navigation from Stainforth to Keadby was prone to seasonal flooding and consequently benefited greatly from the drainage schemes established during the 17thC. The drainage ditches which run parallel to the canal prove a popular hunting ground for the herons which abound in this area. The heron displays endless patience and will stand poised, ready to strike with lightning reflex at frogs, fish and water voles. In spite of its great size, take-off seems effortless and once airborne the head is drawn back and the legs trailed behind in a slow but majestic flight. Grebe too can be seen along the more overgrown sections of the waterway, where their floating nests are anchored to the reeds. Only a hundred years ago these birds had been all but exterminated in England due to fashionable Victorian ladies wishing to display, not just the odd feather, but occasionally the entire plumage, in their hats. It is comforting to note that there is now a healthy population of more than 4000 adult birds in the country. At Maud's Bridge, again boater operated, instructions for its operation are to be found on the white box on the left bank. Now the railway adds some excitement by joining the canal running close along the north bank to Medge Hall where it moves briefly away only to rejoin the line of the navigation at Godnow bridge. Both these bridges are manned at present although boater operation of the latter is possible at weekends.

PUBS

🍺 **Black Bull** High Levels, nr Thorne. Follow the unclassified road for ½ mile south of Maud's Swing Bridge to its junction with the A18. A comfortable pub serving Stones real ale. Food available *lunchtime and evenings* both at the bar and from a full à la carte menu in the restaurant *Mon-Sun*. Vegetarians catered for. Children are welcomed and there is a large garden. Dances *Sat evenings*.

Crowle Bridge

From Crowle Bridge the nearby village of
Ealand can be reached. A mile further to the
north is Crowle itself, with a selection of shops
and pubs and an interesting church. In 1747
the body of a woman was found nearby in the
peat moor, buried upright at a depth of six feet.
From the sandals on the feet it appeared that
the body had been there for several centuries
but was remarkably well preserved. Just beyond
Crowle Station there is evidence of the site of
the old Axholme Joint railway bridge,
demolished in 1972. The bridge must have
proved an impressive landmark, consisting of
four brick archways and a circular brick
abutment upon which the railway pivoted
through 90 degrees, thus allowing the passage
of the tall sailed keels. Ahead lies the long
straight to Keadby. It is not without
excitement, however, as immediately beyond
Yazon Swing Bridge there is a remarkable
railway bridge, skewed across the canal only a
couple of feet above the water. Built in 1915
the bridge is supposedly one of only three of its
kind in Europe. In order to allow the passage of
boats, winches slide the bridge deck sideways,
so clearing the navigation and by a further
series of wire cables and pulleys, winch the
deck back into place. The entire operation is
controlled from the nearby signal box. Once
beyond the bridge the canal passes the now
redundant Keadby Power Station which
dominates the north bank. Ahead is Keadby
Swing Bridge and Lock, allowing entry into the
tidal Trent. There are two pubs and a post
office nearby and a boatyard offering basic
services. Moorings are available immediately
before the swing bridge.

Ealand
Humberside. PO, tel, stores. A small settlement
next to the canal. There are some pretty
cottages in the village. Also a station.

Crowle
Humberside. All services. A straggling village
one mile north of the canal. There are some
attractive Georgian houses in the vicinity of
the church. The Market Square retains some
of its character and is dominated by the
elaborate Victorian facade of the old ballroom,
now used for discos. The church, dedicated to
St Cuthbert, is a handsome structure with a
lofty square tower. During the restoration of
the tower in 1840 a carved stone, some 7ft in
length, was found over the doorway. It is
believed to date from *c.*AD 650 and now
stands at the back of the church. There is a
rare clerestory and the porch displays some
impressive 12thC carvings.

Keadby
Humberside. PO, stores. A dull settlement which
has declined since the Stainforth & Keadby
Canal ceased to carry commercial traffic. The
only real activity is provided by craft entering
the tidal Trent, and the commercial vessels
unloading at the river wharf.

BOATYARDS

ⓑ **Keadby Marine** Canalside, Keadby (0724
782302). Ⓡ Ⓢ Ⓦ Ⓓ Overnight mooring, long-
term mooring nearby, engine sales. Marine
engineering, toilets.

PUBS AND RESTAURANTS

🍺 **New** Trent Wharf Road, Ealand. A
roadside pub selling John Smith's real ale.
🍺✕ **Market Tavern** Market Place, Crowle.
Originally the old Victorian ballroom, now a
venue for local discos.
🍺 **Cross Keys** Market Place, Crowle. Rebuilt
in 1832 the pub has an attractive brick façade.
John Smith's real ale and bar snacks.
🍺✕White Hart Market Place, Crowle. The
oldest inn in the Isle of Axholme, serving John
Smith's real ale.
🍺 **George & Dragon** Crowle. Basic pub
serving John Smith's and Stones real ale.
🍺 **Riverside Inn** Keadby. A down-to-earth
pub. Younger and Wilson's real ale.
🍺 **Friendly Fox** Keadby. Wards real ale is
served in this welcoming family pub. Food is
available in both the bar and restaurant.
Vegetarians catered for. Play area.

Stainforth & Keadby Canal at Crowle. *Derek Pratt.*

RIVER TRENT

Maximum dimensions

Shardlow to Meadow Lane Lock,
Nottingham
Length: 81'
Beam: 14' 6"
Headroom: 8'
Meadow Lane Lock to Gainsborough
Length: 165'
Beam: 18' 6"
Headroom: 13'

Manager

(0509) 212729 *Derwent Mouth to Beeston, and
the Nottingham Canal*
(0636) 70481 *Trent Bridge northwards*

Mileage

DERWENT MOUTH to
Cranfleet Lock: 2¾
Beeston Lock: 7
Meadow Lane Lock, Nottingham: 12
Gunthorpe Bridge: 22
Fiskerton: 29¾
Newark Castle: 35½
Cromwell Lock: 40½
Dunham Bridge: 53
TORKSEY Junction: 57
Littleborough: 60½
GAINSBOROUGH Bridge: 67
WEST STOCKWITH: 71¼
KEADBY Junction: 84¼
TRENT FALLS: 93¾

Locks: 12

The River Trent is a historic highway running for about 100 miles from the Midlands to the Humber ports and the North Sea. It has long been of prime economic and social importance to the areas through which it flows.

It is thought that as long ago as the Bronze Age the Trent was part of the trade route from the Continent to the metal-working industry in Ireland. The discovery of two dug-out canoes in the river bed near Nottingham, dating from about 1000BC and complete with bronze weapons, indicates that the Trent was probably being navigated at this time.

The Romans recognised the value of the river as a route to the centre of England from the sea. In about AD120, in the time of Emperor Hadrian, they built the Foss Dyke canal to link the Trent Valley with Lindum Colonia (now Lincoln), the River Witham and the Wash. The Trent later acted as an easy route for the Danish invaders, who got past the guardian Knights of Torksey and penetrated as far as Nottingham. They wintered at Torksey in AD872 and, under King Swein Forkbeard, at Gainsborough in 1013.

In about AD924 Edward the Elder expelled the Danes from Nottingham and built the first bridge there. The second bridge at Nottingham was built in 1156 (some 20 years earlier than Old London Bridge) and lasted 714 years. Its remains can still be seen. The third bridge was built in 1871 and forms the basic structure of today's Trent Bridge. The traditional role of the Trent as a dividing line between one region of the country and another (many people still consider it to be a useful division between north and south England) is strengthened by the existence even today of only seven road bridges in the 80 miles between Nottingham and the sea.

Although the first Act of Parliament to improve the Trent as a navigation was passed in 1699, the first important one was in 1783. This Act authorised the construction of a towpath, thus allowing for the first time the passage of sail-less barges. Ten years later the Trent Navigation Company's Engineer drew up a comprehensive scheme to build locks and weirs, to increase the depth in certain reaches and build a number of training walls to narrow and thus deepen the channel. Some of these works were carried out, but the scheme was far from complete by 1906, when the Royal Commission on Inland Waterways adopted it as the official future plan. The Act of 1906 authorised for the first time locks at Stoke Bardolph, Gunthorpe, Hazleford and Cromwell; but, owing to the shortage of available money caused by the Great War, the works were not completed until 1926. Trade soon increased fourfold.

At its peak in the 19thC and early 20thC, the Trent formed the main artery of trade for the East Midlands, being connected with the Sheffield & South Yorkshire navigations, the Chesterfield Canal, the Foss Dyke, the Grantham Canal, the Erewash Canal, the River Soar Navigation and the Trent & Mersey Canal. Although it remains so connected today to all but the Grantham Canal, the large trade between these waterways had dwindled away with railway competition, and in particular as a result of railway ownership of most of those connecting waterways. Today most of the commercial carrying is from the Humber ports to Gainsborough, as well as hundreds of thousands of tons of gravel from Carlton, below Newark. But there is not very much trade now on the non-tidal section, even to Nottingham.

The Trent remains a useful through route for pleasure craft, easy of navigation and with many interesting connections. Although it is notable for the numerous large power stations sited along its banks, the Trent is not otherwise an industrial waterway and has many attractive reaches. British Waterways has improved facilities for pleasure craft with landing stages at the locks, extra moorings and easier lock operating systems.

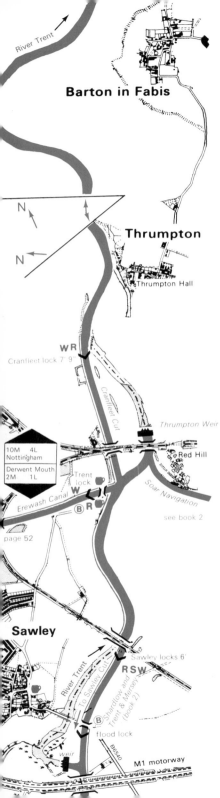

Thrumpton

Downstream from Derwent Mouth (see Book 2), the navigation goes through Sawley Cut, avoiding the weir to the north, by the M1 bridge. Near the head of the Cut is a flood lock, which under most conditions is open. Beyond this lock and the main road bridge is a wide stretch of waterway, where both banks are crowded with moored boats. Just at the tail of Sawley Locks (a pair – one manual, one mechanised with a keeper, 0602 735234) is a large railway bridge over the river; this line carries oil and coal trains to Castle Donington and Willington power stations. To the east the cooling towers of the huge Ratcliffe Power Station are clearly visible, but they are discreetly tucked away behind Red Hill and their intrusion into the landscape is thus minimised. Trent Lock marks the junction of the Erewash Canal with the River Trent, while at the wooded Red Hill is the mouth of the River Soar. It is important not to get lost here, for there is a large weir just downstream of the railway bridges. Boats aiming for Nottingham should bear left at the big sailing club house, entering Cranfleet Cut. They will pass a pair of protective flood gates, another railway bridge (the line disappearing into the decorative tunnel through Red Hill), another long line of moored motor cruisers (many belonging to the Nottingham Yacht Club) and an attractive white accommodation bridge. At the end of the Cut is Cranfleet Lock; from here one may enjoy a view of the woods hiding Thrumpton Park. The old lockhouse at Cranfleet is now the headquarters of the Nottingham Yacht Club. Steep wooded slopes rise behind Thrumpton, while the towers of the power station still overlook the whole scene. Below Thrumpton, the river winds through flat land, passing the village of Barton in Fabis.

Barton in Fabis
Notts. Tel. A small and isolated village, composed mainly of modern housing and set well back from the river. The 14thC church seems unbalanced in several respects; it has a great variety of styles. The building has, however, considerable charm; it is light, and attractively irregular. It contains several monuments to the Sacheverell family.
Thrumpton
Notts. PO, tel. This little village beside the Trent is, like so many other places on the river, a dead end. Motorists only go there if they have good reason to. Hence Thrumpton is a quiet and unspoilt farming village, with new development only up at the far end. Although the impressive Hall is hidden away at the west end of the village, its large uncompromising gateway serves to remind the villagers what they are there for. The tiny church, with its narrow nave and a tower, was built in the 13thC but restored in 1872 by the well-known architect G. E. Street, at the expense of Lady Byron. The single street winds past it down to the river – there used to be a ferry here.
Thrumpton Hall Basically a James I mansion built around a much older manor house. The Hall is famous for its oak staircase, which dates from the time of Charles II. The ground floor rooms are well used, and elegantly decorated; the grounds are delightful, encompassing a backwater off the River Trent. The house is private.
Trent Lock
A busy and unusual boating centre at the southern terminus of the Erewash Canal (see page 52). There is a boatyard and two pubs here.
Sawley
Notts. PO, tel, stores, garage. The tall church spire attracts one across the river to Sawley, and in this respect the promise is fulfilled, for the medieval church is very beautiful and is approached by a formal avenue of lime trees leading to the 600-year-old doorway. But otherwise Sawley is an uninteresting main road village on the outskirts of Long Eaton.
Sawley Cut
In addition to a large marina and a well-patronised BW mooring site, the Derby Motor

Boat Club have a base on the Sawley Cut. All
kinds of boats are represented here: canal
boats, river boats and even sea-going vessels.
It is certainly no place to be passing through
on a summer Sunday late-afternoon, for there
will be scores of craft queueing up to pass
through the locks after spending the weekend
downstream. There are windlasses for sale at
Sawley Lock, as well as the more conventional
facilities.

BOATYARDS

Ⓑ **Sawley Bridge Marina** Above Sawley
Locks (0602 734278). Ⓦ Ⓟ Ⓓ Pump-out,
gas, day hire boats, extensive moorings, 2
slipways, 18 ton crane, chandlery, boat sales,
engine sales, café, toilet, showers. Maintains a
watch on marine VHF.
Ⓑ **Davison Boat Builders** Trent Lock,
Long Eaton (0602 734643). On the Erewash
Canal, just above the lock. Boat building and
fitting out, dry dock, moorings.

PUBS AND RESTAURANTS

🍺✗ **Steamboat Inn** Trent Lock, on the
Erewash Canal (0602 732606). Built by the
canal company in 1791, when it was called the
Erewash Navigation Inn, it is now a busy and
popular venue. The bars have been
handsomely restored and decorated with
suitably nautical objects. Real ale. Bar and
restaurant meals *lunchtime and evenings*.
Garden, playground, children welcome.
🍺 **Navigation Inn** Trent Lock. Large
popular pub with a garden. Home real ale and
lunchtime food.
🍺 **Nag's Head** Sawley, north of the Flood
Lock. Marston's real ale and excellent
lunchtime food.
🍺 **Tiger** Tamworth Road, Long Eaton.
North of B6540 bridge. Refurbished
Marston's real ale pub. *Lunchtime* food.
🍺 **Barge** 200yds east of B6540 bridge.
Shipstone's real ale and *lunchtime* meals.

The Nottingham Canal, by the Waterways Museum. *David Perrott.*

Lenton Chain

The river winds on towards Nottingham,
passing the picturesque Barton Island (keep to
the west of it), the old gravel pits of the
Attenborough Nature Reserve and many
sailing boats; this is clearly a popular stretch of
the river. To the south runs a ridge of hills on
which stands Clifton Hall. At the boatyard one
should keep to the north side of the river to
avoid the weir and enter Beeston Lock. This
introduces the Beeston Canal or Beeston Cut,
which bypasses an unnavigable section of the
River Trent. The canal passes first a housing
estate and then the industrial estate of Boots,
followed by Players' Horizon Factory,
designed by Arup Associates. East of the A52
bridge, the canal passes Lenton Chain. This
marks the end of the short Beeston Canal, for
at this point the Nottingham Canal used to
flow in from the north. The junction was
called Lenton Chain because the Trent
Navigation Company used to lock their
Beeston Canal (with a chain across it) from
Saturday evening until Monday – without fail.
The major part of the Nottingham Canal,
from Lenton to the Erewash Canal at Langley
Mill (see page 55) is now closed, but the rest
of it forms the main line of through navigation
from the Beeston Canal back to the River
Trent at Meadow Lane Lock. The
Nottingham Canal leads the traveller towards
the town centre.

Navigational note
All the locks on the River Trent, apart from
Cromwell Lock, can be self-operated.

Beeston Lock
Nottingham (0602 254946). A splendidly
kept lock where facilities are available for
boats. The pretty cottages and the little
backwater off the canal are a hint of its past
importance; until some years ago there used to
be a lock down into the river here, at right
angles to the present lock. The river channel
used to be navigable – by shallow-draft vessels
– from here down to Trent Bridge, the
Beeston Canal being cut to connect with the
Nottingham Canal and to afford access into
the middle of the town. But now the river is
unnavigable as a through route and the canal
is the only way.
Attenborough Nature Reserve Worked out
gravel pits, once derelict and unsightly, are
now providing an interesting habitat for plant
and animal life. A comprehensive nature trail
has been laid, and a wooden observation hide
erected.

BOATYARDS

Ⓑ **Beeston Marina** Riverside, Beeston (0602
223168). Ⓦ Ⓟ Ⓓ Gas, overnight mooring,
long-term mooring, winter storage, slipway,
crane, dry dock, groceries, chandlery, books
and maps, boat building, boat sales, engine
sales and repairs, toilets, coffee shop, pub.

PUBS

◖ **Johnsons Arms** Abbey Street,
Nottingham, west of Lenton Chain. Friendly
Shipstone's real ale pub serving *lunchtime* food.
◖ **Boat** Priory Road, Nottingham, west of
Lenton Chain. Home real ale in a single-bar
pub.
◖ **Jolly Anglers** Meadow Road, Beeston.
North of Beeston Lock. Large pub with two
comfortable lounges. Home real ale and
lunchtime and evenings food.
◖ **Boat & Horses** Trent Road, Beeston.
North of Beeston Lock. Once a change-over
station for barge horses. Fine traditional pub
seving Home real ale.

Nottingham

East of Lenton Chain, the Nottingham Canal
continues towards Nottingham Castle, which
is clearly visible on its rocky cliff near the
centre of the city. A large new marina, new
houses and a Sainsbury's superstore cheer up
what was once a gloomy aspect. Beyond the
shallow Castle Lock is the Waterways
Museum, situated in the old Fellows, Morton
& Clayton warehouse. Notice the covered
loading bay with a boat and butty inside. Stop
here if you can; the moorings opposite are
excellent, and the new pub and restaurant
adjacent to the museum are very handy. Now
buildings close in as the canal makes a sharp
turn at what was once a junction, and
progresses in a cutting, tidied up and grassed
towards Meadow Lane Lock (0602 862498)
and the River Trent. Upstream the river is
navigable for a short distance above Trent
Bridge, but the main navigation is to the west.
Near Meadow Lane Lock is the Notts County
football ground, while on the opposite side of
the river is the Trent Bridge cricket ground,
with Nottingham Forest football stadium next
to it. Below the latter is the entrance to the
now derelict Grantham Canal. Downstream
from the railway bridge, the wide river soon
leaves Nottingham behind and enters pleasant
countryside. On the north bank are many
boating centres and the Colwick racecourse.
On the south side, an exploration of the
landscaped area will reveal the magnificent
rowing course at Holme Pierrepont.
Downstream are Holme Locks and sluices
(0602 811197). The locks are on the south
side – there is a small one for pleasure boats
next to the very big one.

Grantham Canal
A long-disused but delightful canal from
Trent Bridge, Nottingham, to Grantham. The
canal was built purely to serve the agricultural
communities of eastern Nottinghamshire, so it
pursues a remarkably circuitous course
through pleasant farmland, including the Vale
of Belvoir (pronounced 'beever'). Belvoir
Castle, seat of the Duke of Rutland, is only
about a mile from the canal at one point, and a
tramway was constructed to connect them in
order to carry coal up to the castle, using
wagons drawn by horses. Traces can still be
seen of this, one of Nottinghamshire's earliest
railways. The Grantham Canal still feeds
water down from secluded reservoirs at
Knipton and Denton to the Trent. There are
well advanced plans for its complete
restoration and re-connection to the River
Trent. Details from 1 Willesden Green, Felley
Mill, Nuthall, Nottingham NG16 1QF.

Nottingham
Notts. All services. The city's prosperity derives
largely from the coal field to the north, and the
long-established lace industry. John Player &
Son make all their cigarettes here and Raleigh
Industries turn out bicycles for the world. The
city centre is busy and not unattractive – there
is an imposing town hall in Slab Square – but
little of the architecture is of note. Modern
developments are encouraging, however,
notably the superb Playhouse Theatre and the
appearance of the Nottingham Festival in
1970, which revived in this country the gentle
art of jousting. The Festival is now an annual
event, taking place in the splendid Wollaton
Park on the west side of the town. A big hot-air
balloon race starting in the park is one of its
most spectacular features.
Nottingham Castle Nottingham (0602
483504). William the Conqueror's castle,
which was notorious as the base of Robin
Hood's unfortunate enemies while King
Richard I was away crusading, has been
destroyed and rebuilt many times during its
tumultuous history. (It was a Yorkist
stronghold in the Wars of the Roses and it was
here that Charles I raised his standard in 1642,
starting the Civil War.) Though the original
secret caves beneath the castle still exist and
can be visited by appointment, the present
building dates only from 1674. It now houses
the city's museum and art gallery which

include a fine display of English pottery and textiles, and special collections of the works of Bonington and Sandby, artists from the Nottingham area. *Open daily.*

Nottingham Goose Fair The Goose Fair is now a conventional funfair, but on a gigantic scale. It features traditional entertainments like boxing bouts (challengers invited to fight the 'house champ'), as well as the usual mechanical fairground delights. The fair's original site was in the town centre, but now it is out on the Forest Recreation Ground, a mile to the north east (served by buses). The fair takes place in the *first week of Oct* and it is advisable to get there before the Saturday, when the prices are doubled.

Waterways Museum (0602 598835). Below Castle Lock in the Fellows, Morton & Clayton warehouse. An excellent museum assembled around a working boat and butty moored in the covered loading dock. Local waterways history and some beautiful models. A fine crane stands on the wharf, the scene of a tragic accident on the 28 September 1818, when 21 barrels of gunpowder were accidentally ignited by a boatman. Eight men and two boys were killed in the explosion, which destroyed the warehouse and threw one body over 100yds into Tinkers Leen. Nottingham & Beeston Canal Trail book available. *Open daily and Sun afternoons. Closed Mon & Tue in winter.* Free.

BOATYARDS

Ⓑ **Nottingham Castle Marina** Nottingham (0602 412672). Ⓡ Ⓢ Ⓦ Ⓓ Ⓔ Pump-out, gas, day boat hire, overnight mooring, long-term

mooring, winter storage, slipway, chandlery, books and maps, boat sales, engine sales and repairs, toilets.

PUBS

🍺 **TBI** Trent Bridge. Large pub near the cricket ground. Ind Coope (Burton) real ale.

🍺 **Sportsman** Trent Bridge. Ind Coope (Burton) real ale in a pub popular with football supporters.

🍺 **Aviary** Trent Bridge. Young people's pub serving Castle Eden real ale.

🍺 **Norfolk Hotel** London Road, Nottingham. Home real ale in a friendly local.

🍺 **Narrowboat** Castle Boulevard, Nottingham. Friendly pub with canal theme close to the Waterways Museum. Shipstone's real ale, Bulmers real cider and *lunchtime* food.

🍺 **Navigation** Canalside by the moorings. Banks's real ale in a refurbished pub.

🍺 **Queen's Hotel** Carrington Street, Nottingham. Shipstone's real ale and accommodation.

🍺 **Loggerheads** Cliff Road, Nottingham. Fine old pub, where caves at the rear were once used for cock fighting. Home real ale and snacks at *lunchtime.*

🍺 **Trip to Jerusalem** Set into the cliff face below Nottingham Castle, this is allegedly the oldest pub in England. Sam Smith, Marston's and Bass real ales, *lunchtime* food.

🍺 **FMC** Nottingham. Next door to the Waterways Museum in the old Fellows, Morton & Clayton warehouse, this pub has its own real ale brewed around the back, plus Castle Eden real ale and real draught cider. Restaurant for *lunchtime* meals adjoining.

The River Trent. *Derek Pratt.*

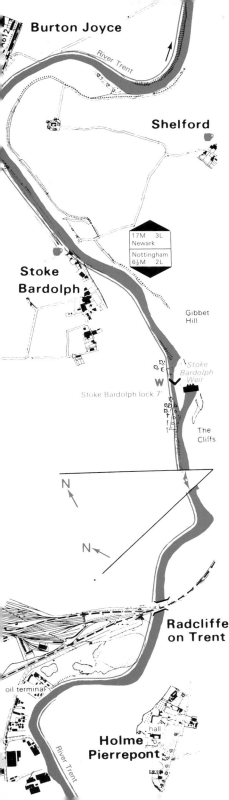

Stoke Bardolph

This section serves to establish the Trent's
attractive rural character as it continues to
sweep along through Nottinghamshire.
Passing under a railway bridge (the
Nottingham–Grantham line), one sees a very
steep escarpment of tree-covered hills,
effectively cliffs, rising out of the water.
Radcliffe on Trent is concealed in the woods
by the bend, but access is difficult. It is better
to move on, down to the delightfully secluded
Stoke Bardolph Lock (0602 878563), where
there is a water point. The lock island is
covered with trees. Below the lock, the river
bends northwards and crosses over to the
other side of the valley, leaving behind the
woods and cliffs. At Stoke Bardolph there is a
sailing club, an attractive riverside pub and a
ferry (a white rowing boat). At Burton Joyce
the river rebounds from the side of the valley
and turns east again. The water meadows that
accompany the river serve to keep at bay any
inroads by modern housing.

Shelford
Notts. PO, tel, stores. A flood bank protects this
quiet and isolated village from the waters of
the Trent. The old church has a wide
Perpendicular tower which commands the
Trent valley. There is a pub, but there is no
obvious mooring place for boats to be left on
the river. Shelford Manor is 1½ miles north
east of the village. (See next page.)
Burton Joyce
Notts. All services. A long village extending
along the very busy A612. There is a railway
station by the river (Nottingham–Lincoln
line). The cricketer Alfred Shaw – the
'Emperor of Bowlers' – was born here.
Stoke Bardolph
Notts. Tel. Most of the village, which is of little
interest, is away from the river. But the focal
point is the riverside pub – the sailing club is
based here and it can be a busy spot. This pub
is one of several on the river in
Nottinghamshire which, by their very
presence (invariably on the site of a ferry),
have caused the development of a tiny isolated
colony of houses. They are a magnet for local
day-trippers and anglers.
Radcliffe on Trent
Notts. Access to Radcliffe from the river is
extremely difficult, even from the chic
residential caravan site at the foot of the cliffs.
In fact this caravan site reflects the smart,
suburban atmosphere of Radcliffe.
Holme Pierrepont
Notts. An isolated village east of the Holme
Locks, this is an ancient, strange and virtually
private place, with no surfaced public roads at
all. The hall, once the home of the
Pierreponts, is an extensive stuccoed building
with the little 17thC church next to it gently
decaying. Inside the church is a remarkably
fine monument carved from Italian alabaster
commemorating Sir Henry Pierrepont, a
champion of Henry Tudor. Well to the west of
the village is the international rowing course,
parallel and close to, but quite separate from
the river. This award-winning recreational
centre, completed in the summer of 1972, was
built from a string of worked-out gravel pits. A
lot of wild birds frequent this area, including
yellow wagtails, sand martins, little winged
plover, common terns, and great-crested
grebes.

PUBS
▶ **Earl of Chesterfield** Shelford. Remote
pub serving Bass real ale straight from the
barrel.
▶ **Ferry Boat Inn** Stoke Bardolph riverside.
Good temporary mooring (ask permission) at
this popular venue by the ferry. Shipstone's
real ale and food *lunchtime and evenings.*
▶ **Manvers Arms** Radcliffe. Real ale and
food.

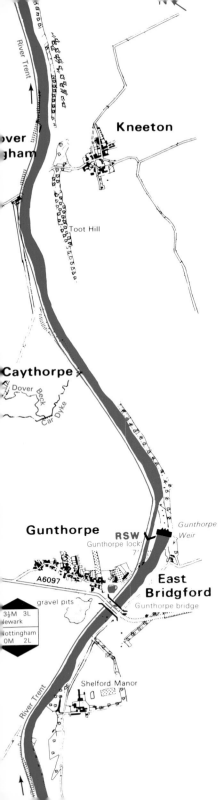

Gunthorpe

This is a stretch in which the presence of big old riverside pubs has far more effect on the river scene than do the villages that they represent. Passing Shelford Manor, one arrives at the sleek arches of Gunthorpe Bridge – the only road bridge over the river in the 24 miles between Nottingham and Newark. To the east of the bridge are the grand houses up on the hills of East Bridgford. Boats heading downstream should keep left to enter the mechanised Gunthorpe Lock (0602 663821) and avoid the foaming weir. What looks like a small boatyard just above the weir is in fact just a private mooring site. The next 5 or 6 miles below Gunthorpe are probably the most beautiful and certainly the most dramatic on the whole river. On the east side, the wooded cliffs rise almost sheer from the flat valley floor to a height of 200ft, allowing here or there the presence of a strip of fertile land on which cattle graze. Only at two places does a track manage to creep down the perilous slope to the river; otherwise, access is impossible. On the west side, by contrast, the ground is flat for miles, across to the other side of the valley.

Hoveringham
Notts. PO, tel, stores, garage. A village intimately linked with the gravel extraction industry.

East Bridgford
Notts. PO, tel, stores, garage. Accessible via a pleasant shady lane up the hill from the river, this village has many comfortable Georgian houses. The church is pleasantly light and has several monuments of the Hacker family. Rector Oglethorpe, one time incumbent of this parish, crowned Queen Elizabeth I.

Margidunum 1½ miles south east of East Bridgford is the site of Margidunum, a Roman town on the Fosse Way (the straightest road in England). Margidunum was probably located here to guard the ford at East Bridgford, which in Roman times was one of the very few easy crossings on the Trent.

Gunthorpe
Notts. PO, tel, stores, garage. Gunthorpe has been an important river crossing point for over 2000 years. The bridge built in 1875 was replaced by the present one in 1927. Prior to this, a ferry operated here. The riverside near the bridge and the pubs is a pleasant situation, backed by the hills of East Bridgford, although often crowded with motorists and trippers. Speed boats buzz about on certain days when British Waterways relax the speed limit bylaw for particular clubs. The vast mechanised lock, surrounded by trees, seems to lend a tone of sobering functionalism.

Shelford Manor Near the river just west of Gunthorpe Bridge. The old manor was burnt down in 1645 after 2000 Roundheads attacked this Royalist stronghold. They forced an entrance and massacred 140 of the 200 men inside. The manor was rebuilt in 1676. *Not open to the public.*

PUBS
🍺 **The Reindeer** Hoveringham. A very pleasant pub.

🍺 **Marquis of Granby** Hoveringham. Small village pub with a choice of Ruddles and Marston's real ale.

🍺 **Anchor Inn** Gunthorpe. Riverside.

🍺 **Black Horse** Caythorpe, 1 mile north of Gunthorpe Bridge. Reputedly once a haunt of Dick Turpin. Shipstone's real ale, food *lunchtime and evenings.*

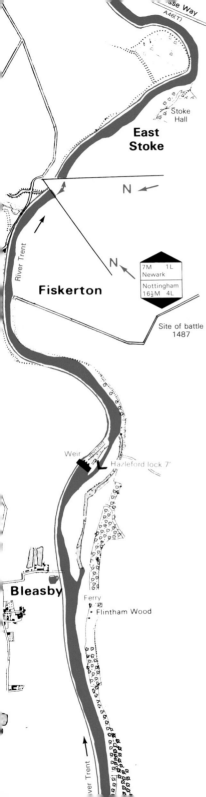

Fiskerton

The river continues along its superb isolated course, with the forested cliffs of the Trent Hills striding along the river's east bank, while on the other side the flat plain of the valley rolls away through green fields and quiet Nottinghamshire villages. Unseen up on the plateau to the east is the big Syerston Airfield, now little used. A solitary hut on the east bank houses a ferryman, who plies across the river at weekends for the fishermen. The Star & Garter pub is on the left bank near an island in the river; boats should keep west of the island to reach Hazelford Lock (0636 830312). Beyond this lock, the steep Trent Hills dwindle away and the river leaves the woods (near the battlefield of East Stoke) for Fiskerton. There is a splendid wharf here – one of the few good places on the whole of this river navigation where it is easy to tie up. Downstream of Fiskerton, the river sweeps round past the parkland at Stoke Hall. The site of a 4-acre Roman fort is on the nearby Fosse Way.

East Stoke
Notts. Tel. The village is nearly a mile from the river, and mooring is difficult. The dark and gloomy lane by the church and hall seems to brood on Stoke's violent past: in 1487 the concluding battle in the Wars of the Roses was fought here. Two years after the Battle of Bosworth Field (fought on a site near the Ashby Canal), where Henry Tudor defeated King Richard III and was proclaimed King Henry VII, the Earl of Lincoln set up Lambert Simnel – a 10-year-old lad – as the Earl of Warwick and proclaimed him King Edward VI. (The real Earl of Warwick was in fact locked up in the Tower of London.) With a 9000-strong army, comprising mainly German and Irish mercenaries, the rebels engaged the Crown's army at Stoke Field as the Earl of Oxford led Henry's 12,000 men away from Nottingham. The battle was short but sharp. After three hours most of the rebel leaders were dead and their army in total disarray. This effectively terminated the Wars of the Roses, although the last Yorkist claim to the throne was not extinguished until the real Earl of Warwick was executed in 1499. The appropriately named Red Gutter in Stoke is a reminder of the battle, although there is no physical trace.

Fiskerton
Notts. PO, tel, stores, station. A charming riverside village with excellent access for boats. Although the normal river level is well below the wharf, all the buildings along the splendid front are carefully protected from possible flood by stone walling or a bank of earth. The wharf is definitely the most interesting part of Fiskerton.

Southwell
Notts. 3 miles north west of Fiskerton, this very attractive country town is well worth visiting in order to see its Minster. The Minster was founded at the beginning of the 12thC by the Archbishop of York, and is held by many to be one of the most beautiful Norman ecclesiastical buildings in England. Its scale is vast for Southwell, but it is set well back from the houses and is in a slight dip, so it does not overawe the town centre, in spite of the two western towers and the massive central tower. Chief among the treasures inside the building are the naturalistic stone carvings in the late 13thC chapter house, and the wooden carvings of the choir stalls.

PUBS
🍺 **Bromley Arms** Fiskerton Wharf. An attractive riverside pub serving Kimberley real ale.
🍺 **Star & Garter** Hazelford Ferry, Bleasby. A huge, heavily gabled riverside pub opposite the Trent Hills and the head of the mile-long lock island. Home real ale, and meals by arrangement. Gnome-filled garden and model village.
🍺 **Waggon & Horses** Bleasby. ½ mile north of Hazelford Ferry, this fine village pub offers Home real ale.

Newark Castle. *Derek Pratt.*

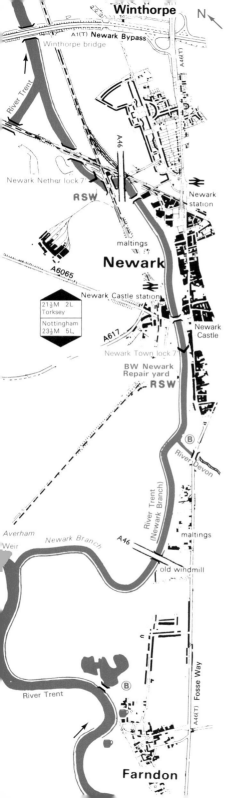

Newark-on-Trent

Farndon is a pleasant riverside village, with
sailing clubs on either side and a small ferry.
The boat population is further increased by
the use of some old gravel pits just north of
Farndon as a mooring site for pleasure boats.
For a mile or two, the flat landscape is
dominated by the great Staythorpe Power
Station, which is beside the river and is visible
for miles; this common feature of the gentle
river landscape will by now be familiar to those
cruising on the Trent. Navigators must be
especially careful to avoid the large Averham
Weir which takes the main channel of the
Trent to Kelham and round the north side of
Newark. Boats heading downstream should
keep right, steering by the 240ft spire of
Newark church. The waterway immediately
becomes narrower east of this weir. This is the
Newark Branch which takes boats straight into
the middle of the town. On the way into
Newark, the navigation passes an old
windmill, a boatyard at the mouth of the River
Devon (pronounced 'Deevon'), some
extensive old maltings, and a gently decaying
warehouse with the words 'Trent Navigation
Company' in faded lettering on the side.
Opposite is the British Waterways Repair
Yard, and just beyond it is Newark Town
Lock (0636 702226). The remains of the old
lock are alongside, half of which is now used as
a mooring for pleasure boats while the rest is a
covered dry dock. The townscape at this point
is dominated by the north-west wall of the
ruined Newark Castle. Hard by is a splendid
old seven-arched stone bridge. The size of the
arches limits the width of boats which can use
the navigation, but this bridge is listed as an
ancient monument and so cannot be altered to
accommodate bigger vessels. Just through the
bridge is Town Wharf, which is the best
temporary mooring site in Newark. Beyond
here the navigation passes the oldest and most
interesting industrial buildings in Newark – an
old ironworks, a maltings, a brewery and a
glueworks giving off a smell of old leather. A
weir follows this to the left, then a right bend
under a railway bridge, and one arrives at
Newark Nether Lock (0636 703830) with a
smart new lock keeper's cottage nearby. East
of the lock, the navigation rejoins the main
channel of the River Trent and proceeds
north-eastward under the graceful modern
road bridge carrying the Newark bypass.

Winthorpe
Notts. Tel. Access from the river is not easy.
Winthorpe is an attractive village. Bypassed by
the A1, it is free from all through traffic and the
abundance of mature trees gives it a peaceful
air. The pub is inviting and the church, in an
ostentatious Victorian style, was entirely built
between 1886 and 1888, at the sole cost of its
patron, the Reverend Edward Hadley.

Newark
Notts. EC Thur. MD Wed, Sat. Two stations.
Newark is magnificent, easily the most
interesting and attractive town on the Trent,
and it is very appealing from the navigation.
Situated at the junction of two old highways,
the Great North Road and the Fosse Way, the
town is of great historical significance. During
the Civil War it was a Royalist stronghold
which was besieged three times by the
Roundheads between March 1645 and May
1646. The defensive earthworks or 'sconces'
constructed by the Royalists are still visible.
Today Newark, like everywhere else, is large,
busy and surrounded by industry and modern
housing. But the town centre is intact and still
full of charm.
Market Place It is worth making a point of
visiting Newark on market day to view the
scene in the colourful old market. In opposite
corners of the square once stood two ancient
pubs: one of them, the White Hart now resited
elsewhere in the town, was built in the 15thC
and is the oldest example of domestic
architecture in the town; the other is the
Clinton Arms where W. E. Gladstone made
his first speech in 1832. He later became
Prime Minister.

Church of St Mary Magdalene The enormous spire is all that one can see of this elegant church from the market place, for the buildings on one side of the square hide the body of the structure. Inside, the church is made light and spacious by soaring columns and a magnificent 15thC east window in the chancel. The building was begun in 1160 and completed about 1500. It is rich in carving, both within and without, but one of the church's most interesting features is a brass made in Flanders to commemorate Alan Fleming, a merchant who died in 1375. The monument is made up of 16 pieces of metal and measures 9ft 4in by 5ft 7in – one of the biggest of its type in England.

Newark Castle Only a shell remains, the one intact wall overlooking the river. The first known castle on this site was constructed around 1129, probably for Alexander, Bishop of Lincoln. The present building was started in 1173, with various additions and alterations in the 14th, 15th and 16thC – notably the fine oriel windows. King John died here in October 1216, soon after his traumatic experience in the Wash. The castle was naturally a great bastion during the Civil War sieges and battles that focused on Newark. When the Roundheads eventually took the town in 1646, they dismantled the castle. The ruins and the grounds are *open daily*.

Newark Museum & Art Gallery Appleton Gate, Newark (0636 702358). A historical collection of local items, which includes several Civil War relics, a lead Roman coffin (and its original contents) and W. E. Gladstone's advertisement board ('Gladstone and the Conservative Cause') which he used at elections. During the early part of his career, Gladstone spent 14 years as MP for Newark. Half of the museum is in a schoolroom which is much as it was when built by Archbishop Magnus in 1529. *Open daily except Thur & Sun morning.*

Governor's House Market Place. A late 16th or early 17thC half-timbered house where successive Governors of Newark lived during the Civil War. It is thought that the quarrel between Charles I and Prince Rupert in 1645 took place here. It resulted in Rupert losing his position as Army General and Governor of Newark. It is obvious from the size and style of the house that it was built for someone of distinction, and further evidence of this is the line of cobble paving running from the house across the square to the south porch of the church. *Closed Sun.*

Tourist Information Centre The Offington, Beast Market Hill, Castlegate, Newark (0636 78962).

Farndon
Notts. PO, tel, stores. A local ferry still transports the fishermen to the far side of the river in this attractive village. The pub makes it a popular spot in summer as do the sailing boats. The extensive renovation of the 14thC church in 1891 revealed a stone coffin containing a Saxon bronze sword.

BOAT TRIPS

Newark Line Departs from just below Newark Town Lock (0636 707939).
Lock and Castle Line Pleasure and charter trips from Newark Town Wharf *each weekend Easter-Oct* plus *weekdays during peak periods.* Drinks and snacks available. Lock and Castle Line River Trips, Lock Entry Cottage, Castle Gate, Newark (0636 707939).

BOATYARDS

Ⓑ **British Waterways Newark Repair Yard** Above Newark Town Lock (0636 704106). Ⓡ Ⓢ
Ⓑ **Newark Marina** Farndon Road, Newark (0636 704022). Ⓦ Gas, overnight mooring, long-term mooring, winter storage, chandlery, crane, books and maps, boat sales, outboard sales, engine repairs.
Ⓑ **Farndon Harbour** Farndon, nr Newark (0636 705483). Ⓡ Ⓢ Ⓦ Ⓓ Ⓔ Pump-out, gas, overnight mooring, long-term mooring, slipway, crane, dry dock, chandlery, books and maps, boat building, boat sales, engine repairs, toilets, showers.

PUBS AND RESTAURANTS

🍺✕ **Admiral Nelson** Winthorpe. Good food and well-kept ale make this a popular pub, particularly during the summer. Real ales include Ruddles, Marston's and a guest beer. An interesting menu is served in the bar and restaurant, both catering for vegetarians. (*No food Mon*). Sunday evening is a special fish supper. Children welcome. Outside seating area. Barbecues and discos during the *summer months.*
🍺 **Castle Barge** Newark Town Wharf. Floating pub in a 94ft former Spiller's grain barge. The lower deck provides an atmospheric bar with lots of polished wood and an interesting display of pictures. However, many prefer to sit outside in the summer and enjoy the river. Mansfield real ale. Extended opening hours. Reasonably priced bar snacks available *lunchtime every day.*
🍺 **Crown and Mitre** Castlegate, Newark. Town pub with a good choice of real ale, including Wards, John Smith's, Courage, Darley and a guest beer. Food is available *lunchtime only.*
🍺 **Lazy Otter** Northend, Farndon. Popular riverside pub serving Ind Coope (Burton), Tetley's and Bateman real ale. Bar food (including vegetarian) *lunchtime and evenings (not Sun evenings).*
✕ **New Ferry Restaurant** Northend, Farndon (0636 76578). A Mediterranean-style restaurant with an exciting (although pricey) fish menu. Lunch *11.00-14.00.* Dinner *19.00-22.00.* More reasonably priced bar snacks available *Tue-Sat lunchtime only. Closed Mon.*
🍺 **Rose and Crown** Main Street, Farndon. Local pub dispensing John Smith's, Courage and a guest real ale. Bar snacks available *lunchtime and evenings.* Children welcome.

Newark, River Trent. *Derek Pratt.*

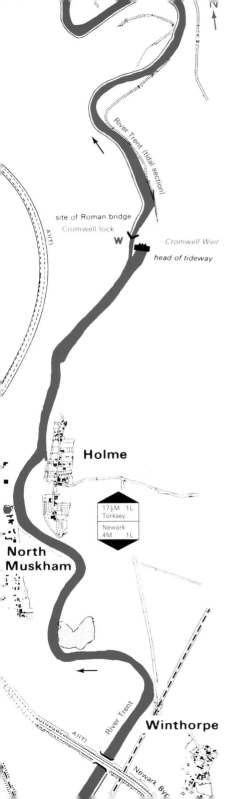

Cromwell Lock

From Newark, the Trent follows a generally
northerly course towards the Humber, which is
still over 50 miles away owing to the very
sweeping and tortuous line of the river. The
villages of North Muskham and Holme face
each other across the water and used to be
connected by ferry. A mile or more below
Holme is Cromwell Lock and Weir. Cromwell
has always been a significant place on the river;
the Romans built a bridge across at this point.
The lock here marks the beginning of the tidal
section of the Trent, so navigation north of it
requires a very different approach.

Navigational note
Cromwell Weir is the largest on the Trent. It is
buoyed and has a safety boom. All boats
should keep to the west side of the river. The
lock too is truly enormous, it is mechanised,
and there is a lock keeper on duty every day
06.00-12.00, 12.30-20.00 (0636 821213).

Navigating the tidal Trent
A suitable boat is essential: proper navigation
lights (compulsory on all the navigable Trent)
and safety equipment (including an anchor
and cable) is compulsory. Navigation notes
are available from the British Waterways, Mill
Lane, Mill Gate, Newark (0636 704481).
Deep-draughted boats should beware of
shoals at low water and should avoid the inside
of bends. The river banks are unsuitable for
mooring and there are few wharves.
Navigators who are more used to canals and
non-tidal rivers will be more likely to treat the
tidal Trent as a link route with the Fossdyke &
Witham Navigation, the Chesterfield Canal,
the Sheffield & South Yorkshire Canal or the
Humber estuary. They should plan their trip
with an eye to the tide-table. The best
approach is either to use a Hull tide-table
(available from local boatyards, fishing shops
and newsagents) bearing in mind that the
Trent floods for only about 2¼ hours and ebbs
for the remainder of the 12-hour period or, if
in doubt, to ask the British Waterways lock
keepers at the various junctions along the
river. The relevant telephone numbers are
listed below:
Cromwell Lock: 0636 821213
Torksey Lock: 042 771 202
West Stockwith Lock: 0427 890204
Keadby Lock: 0724 782205
Plan your journey so that the tide is running
with you, and note the lock operating times.

The towpath
Between the A1(T) bridge and Cromwell lock
the right to follow the towpath is currently the
subject of a legal dispute.

Holme
Notts. Tel. Separated from the river by a flood
bank and a line of trees. Holme is really more
of a large farming hamlet than a village. The
church is a delightfully irregular shape; it has a
tiny stub of a spire, and a 15thC porch that
resembles an Elizabethan gatehouse. In fact
the porch has an upper room. During the
Great Plague a woman called Nanny Scott
took refuge in it, but when she emerged to get
more food after a prolonged stay she found
that she and one man were the only people
alive in the whole village, so she returned to
the room and spent the rest of her life there.
There is no proper landing place on the river
for this village.
North Muskham
Notts. PO, tel, stores. A small, quiet village right
on the river bank. The church was built mainly
in the 15thC, and has large clerestory
windows. The village used to be in the same
parish as Holme, because previously the two
villages were on the same side of the river.
However, in Elizabethan times the river
changed its course and since then it has
separated them. No proper landing.

PUBS
■ **Muskham Ferry** North Muskham. A
riverside pub with mooring for patrons.
Fronted by a garden and children's play area.

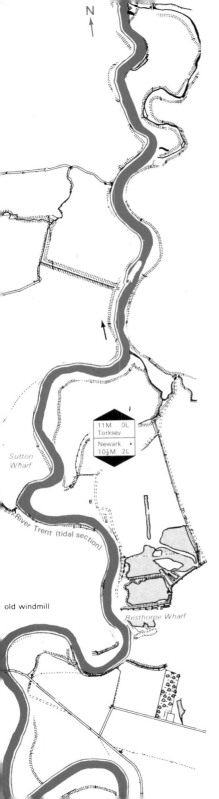

Sutton on Trent

This is a typical stretch of the upper section of the tidal Trent. The river meanders along its northward course, flanked by flood banks and with no bridges. The land is largely grazed as permanent pasture nurtured by the high summer water table maintained by the winter flood (now of course contained). Evidence of an ancient landscape is glimpsed, often on the inside of a sweeping bend, in the form of isolated stretches of hedgerow. These are rich in an abundance of species including ash, willow, wild roses and hawthorn: a picture of white blossom in springtime. Apart from these tantalising views there is little to see save for the occasional barge. Elsewhere the land yields a vast quantity of glacial gravel quarried for building and road construction. A relatively interesting place is Carlton Wharf, where there are still working barges to be seen, but the moorings here are not for pleasure boats. The village of Sutton on Trent is near this wharf; so is a large converted windmill. On the east bank is Besthorpe Wharf, which is used for feeding gravel from the adjacent pits into the river barges. These two wharves handle several hundred thousand tons of gravel every year. The Trent valley can rightly be called the powerhouse of England; electricity generating stations operating within sight of the river currently produce more than a quarter of all electricity consumed in England and Wales. This area is ideally located for the siting of power stations with its plentiful supply of water for steam production, as well as for cooling the spent steam once it has passed through the generating turbines. A large reserve of coal to fire the boilers is also available from the nearby East Midlands coalfield. Most of the power stations have been built since 1950, and their huge cooling towers stand out as prominent features on an otherwise largely agricultural landscape. Approximately half of all the electricity in the Trent valley is transmitted, via the Supergrid of overhead power-lines, to London, which as a large consumer is nevertheless poorly sited for large scale power production. Whilst waste cooling water is returned to the river the vast output of fly ash has been used to fill nearby spent gravel pits. In an imaginative scheme it has also, in conjunction with soil from sugar beet washings, been used to reclaim worked-out clay pits at a Peterborough brick works. These have then been returned to agricultural use. In most cases mooring along the tidal Trent is not recommended.

The towpath
Under the 1792 Trent River Navigation Act hauling rights were granted in return for an annual rent. Since the 1930s craft using the river have been self-propelled and these rights have not been exercised. Custom and practice has led to paths following the flood banks rather than the water margins. BW's legal rights are for maintenance access only, whilst they also have an obligation to maintain and erect the numerous 'clapper' gates as necessary. On the tidal stretch of the Trent it is often possible to follow a path on either flood bank; therefore the 'towpath' indicated on the map represents only the most straightforward, continuous route to follow.

Sutton on Trent
Notts. PO, tel, stores, bank. This pretty village is close to Carlton Wharf. Although a relatively under-developed community it manages to support a bank, a butcher's shop and a book shop, each occupying one room of a former cottage. Sadly neither these amenities nor the pub are easily accessible to the boater due to the lack of moorings. The almost oriental white cap of a converted windmill, typical of this area, can be seen from the river.

Dunham Bridge

Passing the nearby villages of High Marnham,
Low Marnham and South Clifton, the river
reaches the big cooling towers of High
Marnham Power Station. There is a
footbridge carrying a pipe across the river
here; just north of it is the iron railway viaduct
that carries the line supplying the power
station. High Marnham was at one time two
hamlets: Ferry Marnham and Church
Marnham. The old hall which stood between
them was demolished in 1800. It was the
property of the Cartwright family who held
many claims to fame. Dr Edmund Cartwright
invented the power loom which revolutionised
the weaving industry. One of his brothers was
the engineer responsible for the construction
of the 'Ramper Road' leading into Newark
over raised arches. Another was an admiral in
Lord Nelson's navy. Near the railway viaduct
is the isolated church of St George, situated
equidistant between North and South Clifton
in order to serve both parishes. North Clifton
once had the use of a ferry which was free to its
inhabitants. 1½ miles further, the river
describes a sharp S-bend as it passes a
welcome little ridge of hills, pleasantly
wooded. But the ridge fades away as one
reaches Dunham Toll Bridge (the present
structure replacing one built in 1832) and the
iron aqueduct that precedes it. Once a market
town, Dunham was notorious for its flooding.
The Trent frequently caused buildings to be
awash with up to ten feet of water. As a
consequence most of the inhabitants were
boat owners in order to maintain
communications during the floods. The
countryside resumes its flat and rather
featureless aspect, while the river now forms
the border between Nottinghamshire and
Lincolnshire (as far downstream as West
Stockwith). From Stapleford to Dunham the
river is a birdwatcher's paradise of water
meadows, pools and marshes. Mooring along
the tidal Trent is not recommended.

PUBS
🍺 **Bridge Inn** Dunham. West of toll bridge.
Food available *lunchtime and evenings.*
🍺 **Brownlow Arms** High Marnham. A
comfortable, elegantly furnished pub offering
a varied choice of real ale; M & B
(Springfield), Bass, Marston's and Bateman.
Food is available *lunchtime and evenings.*
Children will enjoy the safe outside play area.
Popular in the summer.

Torksey

At Laneham the traveller will enjoy a little
relief from the Trent's isolation. Here there is
a church and a few houses on a slight rise near
the river. A farmhouse on the river bank was
built on the site of the old manor. The cellars
in the building are reputed to date back even
further than this to the time when the land
belonged to the palace of the Archbishops of
York. To the north of the village, yet another
power station – Cottam – appears as the river
turns back on itself to the south before
swinging northwards again at the junction of
the Fossdyke Navigation (marked by a new
pumping station). The lock up into the
Fossdyke is just through the road bridge,
mooring is below the bridge, and a pub, petrol
station and shop are all near the lock. Torksey
offers a haven for the boater navigating the
tidal Trent with 72-hour landing stage
moorings, water, toilets and showers, together
with barbecue area and telephone. There is
also a good restaurant in the village – but
further information on Torksey can be found
on page 58. Nearing the railway viaduct at
Torksey, one sees the gaunt ruin of Torksey
castle standing beside the river. As at Newark,
the façade that faces the Trent is the most
complete part of the building, for the rest has
vanished. (The castle has been abandoned
since the 16thC). For the first 15ft or so from
the ground, the castle is built of stone – above
this it is dark red brick. The railway viaduct at
Torksey is disused, although, curiously
enough, the line on either side is much used;
from the west, coal trains supply Cottam
power station, while from the east oil trains
bring fuel from Immingham to an oil terminal
on the river. From here it is taken away by
lorries, mostly to the numerous air bases
around Lincolnshire. In most cases mooring
on the tidal Trent is not recommended.

Laneham
Notts. PO, tel, stores. Originally Lanum, the
parish is divided into two areas; Church
Laneham, also known as Laneham Ferry, and
Laneham itself, the two being little more than
half a mile apart. The church of St Peter is well
worth a visit. Its wonderful Norman doorway,
heavily decorated with chevron, herringbone
and sunflower patterns, still contains the
original Norman door, hanging on the very
hinges on which it was mounted in the 11thC.
The tower was once used as a watch tower
over the Trent ferry. The ringing chamber of
the tower contains 25 'wedding rings' or
'cheeses'. These date back to the period
between 1813 and 1840 when it became the
custom for couples married at the church to
pay the ringers a sage cheese or five shillings
each for the privilege of having their initials
placed in a ring.

PUBS AND RESTAURANTS
● **White Swan** Torksey. South of the lock.
Friendly family pub which is *open all day*.
Stones and Bass real ale. Food *lunchtime and
evenings* (vegetarians catered for). Outside play
area and family rooms.
✗ **Wheelhouse Restaurant** Torksey lock.
●✗ **Hume Arms** Main Street, Torksey. A
large hotel and restaurant with extensive
outside seating. Plush interior with hot and
cold carvery.
● **Ferry Boat Inn** Church Laneham.
Temporary moorings below the caravan park
give access to this friendly pub which is just a
short walk up from the river. Bass real ale is
served at the bar along with bar snacks and
take-away food, *lunchtime and evenings*. There
is a children's room together with outside
seating. Quiz nights are held *every Tue* and
bingo *Mon and Fri*.
●✗ **Butcher's** Laneham. A short walk into
the village from the Ferry Boat Inn. Village
local serving Marston's and a guest real ale.
Food *lunchtime and evenings,* (vegetarians
catered for). Health studio.
✗ **Old Cottage Restaurant** Laneham.
Dating back to 1854 the Old Cottage offers
evening meals *from 19.30* and Sunday lunch
from 12.30. B & B.

Littleborough

From Cottam, the river continues to wind
northwards towards Gainsborough. This is
not as dull a stretch as those further south. A
windmill marks the exaggeratedly named
Trent Port, which is in fact the wharf for the
small village of Marton. Speedboats operate
from here, but owners of any larger boats will
once again find it difficult to land. Marton was
important in Saxon times because of its
position near the ford where a Roman road
(now the A1500) crossed the Trent. This ford
marked the western boundary of the ancient
kingdom of Lindsey. Many historians believe
that Saint Paulinus baptised some of the first
Saxon Christians here in 627. The church of
St Margaret has evolved around an early
Saxon church, side aisles being added to the
original structure. The tapering Anglo-Saxon
tower still reveals some fine herringbone
masonry. In 1904 it was discovered that the
entire structure was unsafe having been built
on foundations only two feet deep made of
sand and pebbles. The next place of interest is
Littleborough, a tiny riverside settlement.
Fortunately boats may moor temporarily at
the floating jetty. Below Littleborough is a
beautiful reach, with steep wooded hills rising
from the water's edge on the Lincolnshire
side. The attractive timbered building set in
the parkland is called Burton Chateau. A little
further downstream, another clump of trees
on the east bank at Knaith conceals a former
nunnery and chapel, but mooring is only just
possible here. On towards Gainsborough, the
cooling towers of West Burton Power Station
stand out prominently in the flat landscape on
the west side of the river.

Knaith
Lincs. Temporary mooring just possible.
Among the trees is the hall and an interesting
old church, with its Jacobean pulpit. Both
were part of a nunnery dissolved in 1539. The
hall was the birthplace of Thomas Sutton,
who founded Charterhouse School and
Hospital.

Littleborough
Notts. An attractive hamlet with reasonably
good access from the river. The little church
stands on a slight rise; it is a delightfully simple
Norman structure and incorporates much
herringbone masonry. It is assumed from
various finds, including the perfectly
preserved body of a woman dug up in the
graveyard, that this was the site of the Roman
camp, Segelocum. The paved ford dating
from the time of Emperor Hadrian became
visible during a drought in 1933. King
Harold's army crossed this ford on their way
to Hastings in 1066.

to West Stockwith, Kneadby and the Humber

Gainsborough

Gainsborough Central station

A631

M OL
Stockwith Gainsborough Arches

ksey
M OL

mills

Gainsborough Lea Road station

River Trent (tidal sectio

Gainsborough

The river moves away from the wooded slopes, passes the power station (the northernmost on the river) and heads for Gainsborough, which is clearly indicated by a group of tall flour mills. Below the railway bridge, the river bends sharply before reaching the flour mills, the bridge at Gainsborough and the busy wharves, where it is possible to tie up (seek permission first). The town is set entirely on one side of the river, and is worth visiting.

Navigational notes
1 Below Gainsborough Arches the River Trent ceases to be under the jurisdiction of BW and is controlled by the Humber Navigation bylaws. These are administered by Associated British Ports from whom a copy may be obtained by ringing 0482 2717.
2 VHF marine band radio has become an important aid when navigating tidal commercial waterways. It allows the boater to know the whereabouts of other traffic and to maintain contact with lock keepers who listen out on channels 16 and 74, and work on channel 74. See note on page 159 for telephone contact.
3 BW request that boaters give lock keepers along the tidal river 24 hours notice of passage. Always seek advice from lock keepers and respect their skill and experience.
4 Charts are available for the whole course of the tidal Trent and further advice may be obtained from the Trent Boating Association on 0602 262055.
5 The Aegir, or tidal bore, a tidal wave of between one foot and five feet in height, and breaking at the sides, may be encountered between Keadby and Torksey. It is normally only seen on spring tides of over 25ft (Hull), and arrives at the same time as the flood, although there can be a variation of half an hour each way.
If you are on the river, keep a watch for it, and meet it head on, facing straight downstream and in the middle of the river.
If you are anchored, use twice the normal length of warp.
If you are moored, tie up to a barge or other large craft, which will itself rise and fall with the wave.

The towpath
It is possible to follow the remainder of the Trent by walking along its flood banks, on either side.

Gainsborough
Lincs. EC Wed, MD Tue, Sat. All services, two stations. Gainsborough is best seen from the river, where the old wharves and warehouses serve as a reminder of the town's significance as a port in the 18th and 19thC. Possibly Britain's furthest inland port, it now handles vessels of 850 tonnes deadweight, carrying animal feedstuffs, grain, fertilisers and scrap. Elsewhere industrial sprawl and Victorian red-brick housing tends to obscure the qualities of the old market town. There are several Victorian churches, but All Saints retains its Perpendicular tower. Gainsborough was a frequent battleground during the Civil War and George Eliot described it as St Ogg's in *The Mill on the Floss.*
The Old Hall Parnell Street, Gainsborough (0427 612669). An attractive manor house of the 15th and 16thC in the centre of the town: it contains a medieval kitchen and Great Hall. Here Henry VIII met Catherine Parr, later his sixth wife, who was the daughter-in-law of the house. The Pilgrim Fathers also met here. Now a folk museum. *Open weekday afternoons all year; Sun Easter-Oct only.*

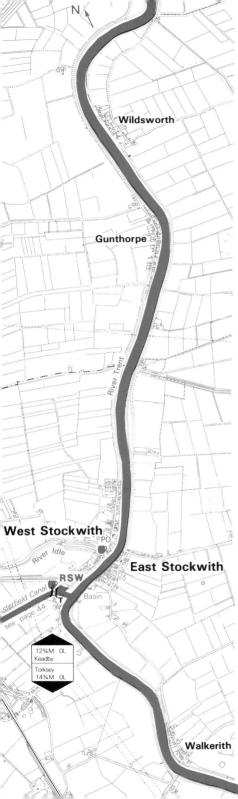

N

Wildsworth

Gunthorpe

River Trent

West Stockwith

PO

River Idle

RSW

T

Basin

East Stockwith

cterfield Canal

see page 44

12¾M   0L
Keadby

Torksey
14¾M   0L

Walkerith

West Stockwith

On leaving Gainsborough the river passes the jetty of the Trent wharfage and storage group on the left. This is the destination of the large coasters which ply the Trent above Gunness, where they discharge cargoes of ferro-metals, timber, fertilisers, bulk chemicals and animal feeds. They are able to carry loads of up to 1250 tonnes at a time, shipped from as far away as Sweden. Then the navigation bends sharply to the left, passing Gleadell's wharf with its Flemish gables, and winds its way past the hamlet of Walkerith towards West Stockwith. Immediately after the sharp right-hand bend in the river the entrance lock into the Chesterfield canal is visible on the left, giving access into the basin with its boatyard, moorings and friendly Yacht Club. Just downstream from the basin the River Idle, barricaded in by steel flood doors, joins the Trent beside West Stockwith's unusual 18thC Georgian church. This was once the main highway from the industrial areas of South Yorkshire, terminating at a large wharf in Bawtry. Goods travelled to and from the town by horse and cart and before the development of the River Don as a reliable navigation, were dependent upon the river for onward transport. In draining the Isle of Axholme in the 17thC Cornelius Vermuyden modified the course of the Idle and drastically reduced its effectiveness as a navigable waterway. From the river West Stockwith, now a conservation area, presents a closed-in, almost intimate, aspect with its many tall three-storey buildings. It is possible to catch the occasional tantalising glimpse into the village up tiny passages, or gunnels, running between the houses. Once a thriving boat building community – there were five boatyards only a hundred years ago – West Stockwith had a population of 5000 in the 1880s; it is now reduced to 240. The brick-built church looking more like a chapel capped with a squat bell tower, is one of only three of its kind and was completed in 1722. Inside the plasterwork is classic Adam. See page 44 for further details on the village. Leaving West Stockwith the Trent follows a comparatively straight course passing the isolated hamlets of Gunthorpe and Wildsworth, barely visible to the boater hidden as they are below the river's flood banks. All this area bordering the river was, in AD 886, part of Danelaw, and place names with 'by' and 'thorpe' endings are of Danish derivation. A sense of isolation and independence persists into the 20thC from a time when the Wash, the Trent and the Humber effectively cut this area off from the remainder of the country. In those times the inhabitants identified more with Denmark, Holland and the sea than with the rest of England.

Navigational notes
1 The lock at West Stockwith is keeper-operated. The operation of the lock is dependent on the height of the tide, but a passage can usually be made 2½ hours before to 4½ hours after high water which is on average 2 hours after the times published for Hull.
2 Keepers at both West Stockwith and Keadby locks can be contacted on marine band VHF radio channel 74 – channel 16 in emergencies – or by telephone using the numbers listed on page 159.
3 Deep draught commercial traffic, especially coasters, require the deepest channel on the navigation at all times. Be prepared to give way to allow for this.

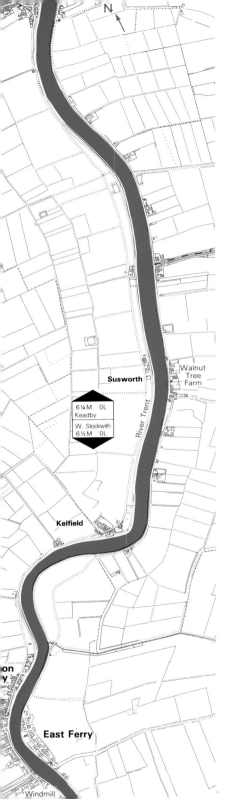

Owston Ferry

The conical tower of an old windmill on the left bank has been restored as part of a spacious new dwelling on a fairly grand scale – even to the point of having a helipad sited on an adjacent field. This feature, very much of the 20thC, contrasts strongly with the mellow buildings of Owston Ferry directly ahead. As the channel swings to the right the pleasing scale of the riverside houses becomes apparent. Skilfully constructed using local brick and tile, they are both solid and graceful in appearance. There is something reminiscent of a Dutch painting in the views over the river seen from the lower part of the village. The church, standing a little way from the waterway, is largely medieval, but with early 19thC Gothic additions, and inside there is an attractive rood screen dating from 1897. Although modern executive dwellings have crept into the village, generally by way of infill, it is the largely three-storey, Dutch-influenced buildings that still predominate. At Robin Hood's Well to the north west, Roman coins have been found, indicating that this is a settlement of some antiquity. Flowing northwards the river regains its isolation amidst the flat, fertile countryside behind the flood banks. Throughout history this area has been known as the Isle of Axholme – once a wetland prone to seasonal flooding and anciently a forest, heath and then marsh. It is a tract of low flat land less than 100 feet above sea level, some 5 miles wide and running for approximately 18 miles along the Trent's western bank. In 1625 a Dutchman, Cornelius Vermuyden, was brought over to oversee the draining of the area at a cost of £56,000. The land's natural fertility was soon realised under the Dutch and French Protestant settlers that followed him, much to the disgust of the ousted native inhabitants. After lengthy litigation the land was finally divided in 1691, the 'locals' receiving 10,532 acres and the settlers 2868 acres. The chief town in the area is Epworth, some 4 miles west of Kelfield and famous as the birthplace, in 1703, of John Wesley, founder of Methodism. His father was rector of the parish for 59 years. Over the years the pattern of agriculture in the area has varied, reflecting a changing society. At the time when the Wesley family lived at Epworth, flax and hemp, used in the manufacture of sacking and canvas, were amongst the principal crops. Walnut trees were plentiful along the east bank of the river, the nuts being gathered as a further source of income. Today intensive vegetable growing, cereals and root crops predominate.

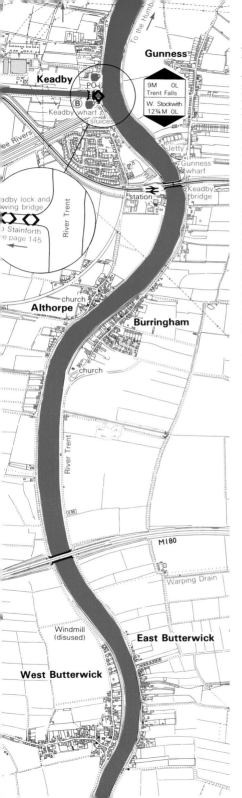

Keadby

The twin villages of East and West Butterwick now come into view, facing each other across the river. As seems so often to be the case on the lower part of the Trent, the village to the west is larger than its eastern counterpart. West Butterwick is another village with a strong Dutch influence evident in the local buildings. It has an attractive church built in 1841 from creamy white brick, deceptively stone-like from a distance. It follows the Gothic style, has a small octagonal spire together with period interior fittings. In contrast, East Butterwick is a plain place with a small church built in 1884 at a cost of £500. It was once described as being 'surrounded by root crops and often by fog'. Now the river begins to broaden out passing under the M180 viaduct, built in 1978, and rising out of the flat countryside to clear the navigation. The scale of the river is such that the boater can now begin to appreciate just how major a watercourse the Trent really is. 150 miles long, with a catchment area of over 4000 sq miles, it once flowed due east from Nottingham discharging into The Wash. At some point in pre-history this channel became blocked and the river turned north, picking a course through the soft keuper marls, still evident in the many shoals along the navigation, to its present junction with the Ouse. 3000 cubic feet of water a second discharge into the Humber, a volume greater than that from the Thames into the estuary. Throughout history the Trent has been exploited as both a trunk navigation and for its inherent fertility. For centuries farmers working the land beside the river have encouraged it to flood the fields during the winter months, by directing its water along warping drains cut at right angles to the waterway. North of the M180 two further villages sit opposite one another – behind flood embankments – before Keadby is reached. These are Burringham to the east, with its early Victorian brick and slate church squatting beside the river, and Althorpe to the west. Here the church nestles in with the houses. Dedicated to St Oswald, it owes its origins to Sir John Nevill, whose 1483 tower and chancel are incorporated into a larger structure. Both his Coat of Arms, together with that of the Mowbray family, appear in stone, carved on the ogee arch of the west door. Less than a mile downstream of these villages is the combined road and rail bridge, built in 1916, which was the only bridge into the Isle of Axholme before the construction of the motorway viaduct. Boaters should follow the channel between the right-hand pier and the bank under the lifting section of the bridge, and beware of large vessels at Gunness wharf immediately below. A further half mile below this bridge, on the left, is Keadby Lock (for further details of Keadby see entry on page 145) leading into the Stainforth & Keadby section of the Sheffield & South Yorkshire Navigation. The entrance is often totally obscured by coasters unloading at the wharf between the sluice at the Three Rivers' outfall and the lock itself.

Navigational notes
1 Three red lights are normally displayed at all times when the Keadby Lock is not available. A green light will be shown when there is sufficient depth of water over the cill to work the lock. This is theoretically up to 7 hours after high water, but despite constant dredging a sand bar builds up in front of the lock and 5 hours is often the maximum realistic time after high water that passage can be effected.
2 Shelter passes are available from the lock keeper for non-registered craft using BW navigations and/or moorings for a limited period.
3 Along the Stainforth & Keadby Canal there are two locks and numerous swing bridges that are not at present boater-operated. These are only manned *during normal working hours and not at all over weekends in the winter period Oct-Mar.* Contact the Waterway Manager for further details on 0636 704481.

TRENT & MERSEY

Maximum dimensions

Harding's Wood to Middlewich
Length: 72'
Beam: 7'
Headroom: 5' 9"
Middlewich to Anderton
Length: 72'
Beam: 14' 6"
Headroom: 7'
Anderton to Preston Brook
Length: 72'
Beam: 7'
Headroom: 7'

Manager

(0606) 40566

Mileage

HARDING'S WOOD, junction with
Macclesfield Canal to King's Lock,
Middlewich, junction with Middlewich
Branch: 10½
Anderton Lift, for River Weaver: 22¾
PRESTON BROOK, north end of tunnel and
Bridgewater Canal: 29¾

Locks: 36

This early canal was originally conceived partly as a roundabout link between the ports of Liverpool and Hull, while passing through the busy area of the Potteries and mid-Cheshire, and terminating either in the River Weaver or in the Mersey. One of its prime movers was the famous potter Josiah Wedgwood (1730-1795). Like the Duke of Bridgewater a few years previously he saw the obvious enormous advantages to his – and others' – industry of cheap, safe and rapid transport which a navigation would offer compared with packhorse carriage (the only alternative then available). Wedgwood was greatly assisted in the promotion of the canal by his friends, notably Thomas Bentley and Erasmus Darwin. Pamphlets were published, influential support was marshalled; and in 1766 the Trent & Mersey Canal Act was passed by Parliament, authorising the building of a navigation from the River Trent to Runcorn Gap, where it would join the proposed extension of the Bridgewater Canal from Manchester.

The ageing James Brindley was, of course, appointed engineer of the new canal. Construction began at once and much public interest was excited in this remarkable project, especially in the great 2900yd tunnel under Harecastle Hill.

Once opened in 1777 the Trent & Mersey Canal was a great success, attracting much trade in all kinds of commodities. Vast tonnages of china clay and flints for the pottery industry were brought by sea from Devon and Cornwall, then transhipped into canal boats on the Mersey and brought straight to the factories around Burslem, taking finished goods away again. Everyone near the canal benefited: much lower freight costs meant cheaper goods, healthier industries and more jobs. Agriculture gained greatly from the new supply of water, and of stable manure from the cities.

The Trent & Mersey soon earned its other name (suggested by Brindley) as the Grand Trunk Canal – in the 67 miles between Fradley Junction and Preston Brook Junction, the Trent & Mersey gained connection with no less than eight other canals or significant branches.

By the 1820s the Trent & Mersey was so busy that the narrow and slowly-sinking tunnel at Harecastle had become a serious bottleneck for traffic. Thomas Telford was called in; he recommended building a second tunnel beside Brindley's old one. His recommendation was eventually accepted by the company, and a tremendous burst of energy saw the whole tunnel completed in under three years, in 1827. A much-needed towpath was included in this tunnel although this has now been removed so that boats can use the headroom in the centre of the channel.

Although the Trent & Mersey was taken over in 1845 by the new North Staffordshire Railway Company, the canal flourished until the Great War as a most important trading route. The complete canal is covered in Book 2 – this section, Harding's Wood to Preston Brook, is included to complete the coverage of the 'Cheshire Ring' canal circuit within this volume.

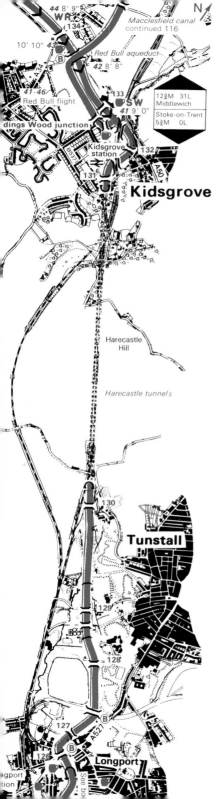

Harding's Wood Junction

The Trent & Mersey from Harding's Wood to
Preston Brook Tunnel is included in this book
to complete the coverage of the 'Cheshire
Ring'. Those on the ring with time to spare
may wish to have a look at the northern
entrance of the Harecastle Tunnel, only a
short walk from Harding's Wood Junction, or
even make a 'through and back' journey,
winding at Longport Wharf (bridge 126).
Those who make the passage will not regret it.
Coal and Calor gas are available at a yard by
bridge 132. The Trent & Mersey descends
from the summit level through a flight of
paired narrow locks, passing under the
Macclesfield Canal at Red Bull Aqueduct.

Navigational note
Harecastle Tunnel Do not enter in an
unpowered craft. With the complete removal
of the towpath, headroom is no longer the
great problem it used to be. A one-way system
operates, so follow the instructions of the
tunnel keepers. *Open: summer 08.00–last
passage 16.00; spring & autumn 08.00–last
passage 15.00; winter Sat only 08.00–13.00.*

Kidsgrove
Staffs. MD Tue. All services. Originally a big
iron and coal producing town. Kidsgrove was
much helped in its growing size and prosperity
by the completion of the Trent & Mersey
Canal, which gave the town an outlet for these
goods. James Brindley is buried in the town in
a churchyard at Newchapel.
St Saviour's Church Butt Lane. This
building is unusual in looking quite unlike a
church. Built in 1878, it was designed in
black-and-white Tudor style.

The Three Harecastle Tunnels
There are altogether three parallel tunnels
through Harecastle Hill. The first, built by
James Brindley, was completed in 1777, after
11 years' work. To build a 9ft wide tunnel 1¼
miles long represented engineering on a scale
quite unknown to the world at that time, and
the world was duly impressed. Since there was
no towpath in the tunnel the boats – which
were of course all towed from the bank by
horses in those days – had to be 'legged'
through by men lying on the boat's cabin roof
and propelling the boat by 'walking' along the
tunnel roof. (The towing horse would have to
be walked in the meantime over the top of the
hill.) This very slow means of propulsion,
combined with the great length of the narrow
tunnel and the large amount of traffic on the
navigation, made Harecastle a major
bottleneck for canal boats. So in 1822 the
Trent & Mersey Canal Company called in
Thomas Telford, who recommended that a
second tunnel be constructed alongside the
first one. This was done: the new tunnel was
completed in 1827, with a towpath (now
removed), after only three years' work. Each
tunnel then became one-way until in the
20thC Brindley's bore had sunk so much from
mining subsidence that it had to be
abandoned. An electric tug was introduced in
1914 to speed up traffic through Telford's
tunnel; this service was continued until 1954.
The third tunnel through Harecastle Hill was
built years after the other two, and carried the
Stoke–Kidsgrove railway line. It runs 40ft
above the canal tunnels and is slightly shorter.
This tunnel was closed in the 1960s: the
railway line now goes round the hill and
through a much shorter tunnel. Thus two out
of the three Harecastle tunnels are disused.

BOATYARDS

BW Red Bull Yard North of bridge 134. (0782 785703). R W

Ⓑ **David Piper** Red Bull Basin, Church Lawton, Kidsgrove (0782 784754). By Red Bull Aqueduct. W D Pump-out, gas, overnight mooring, long-term mooring, winter storage, slipway up to 60ft, chandlery, books and maps, boat building, boat sales, engine sales and repairs. Useful source of information regarding tunnel opening times.

Ⓑ **Stoke-on-Trent Boat Building** Longport Wharf, Longport, Stoke-on-Trent (0782 813831). R S W D E Pump-out, gas, overnight mooring, long-term mooring, winter storage, slipway, chandlery, books and maps, boat building and repairs, boat sales, engine sales and repairs, gift shop, toilet.

Ⓑ **Smithsons Solid Fuel** Near bridge 132. D Calor gas, solid fuel at competitive prices.

PUBS

🍺 **Red Bull** Canalside by the Red Bull flight. Popular pub close to the junction with the Macclesfield Canal serving Robinson's real ale. Food *lunchtime and evenings but not Mon, Tue, Wed, Fri evenings out of season.* Vegetarians catered for. Canalside garden seating area.

🍺 **Blue Bell** At the junction with the Macclesfield Canal. Friendly one bar local serving Boddingtons, Whitbread and Castle Eden real ale. Bar snacks *lunchtime only.*

🍺 **Tavern** Opposite the Blue Bell. Basic lockside pub offering Tetley's and Marston's real ale. Bar snacks *lunchtime and evenings (not Sun).* Garden area, disco *Thur & Sun.*

🍺 **Duke of Bridgewater** Near bridge 126. The bar is decorated with canal and narrowboat paintings and adorned with butty tillers. Bar snacks *lunchtime and evenings (not Sun).* Canalside garden. Quiz night is *Mon.*

🍺 **Pack Horse** Station Street, canalside at bridge 126. A lively pub dispensing Ansells, Tetley's and Ind Coope (Burton), together with further guest real ales. Bar snacks *lunchtime until 16.00. Weekend* jazz evenings. Garden.

🍺 **Railway** Near Longport Railway Station, west of bridge 126. Meals and snacks *lunchtime and evenings (not Sun evenings).* Garden.

Harecastle Tunnel, Trent & Mersey Canal. *Derek Pratt.*

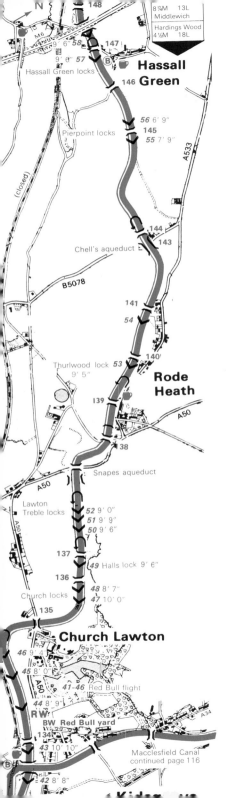

Rode Heath

Leaving behind the spire of Church Lawton, the canal continues to fall through a heavily locked stretch sometimes called 'heartbreak hill' but known to the old boatmen as the 'Cheshire Locks'. The countryside is entirely rural and pleasant, slightly hilly and wooded. Two minor aqueducts are encountered, but the locks are more interesting: they are all pairs of narrow locks, side by side. Some of the duplicate locks are unusable or even filled in, but many of them are in good condition, so navigators can choose whichever lock is set in their favour. The duplicate lock at Thurlwood, alongside the existing lock, used to be one of the strangest structures on the waterways network. Known as Thurlwood Steel Lock, it was built in 1957 to overcome subsidence caused by local brine pumping, and was a massive and complicated affair, with a huge steel superstructure. Unused for many years, it was dismantled in 1988. At Hassall Green a *PO, tel, and stores* incorporating a canal shop and boatyard services can be found just by the new concrete bridge. The M6 motorway crosses noisily nearby.

Rode Heath
PO, tel, stores. A useful shopping area right by bridge 140. There is a butchers shop at bridge 139.
Rode Heath Rise Once the site of a salt works, it has now been landscaped and restored as wildflower meadow as a community project, maintained by the local primary school. Ring 0477 34115 if you require further information

BOATYARDS
Ⓑ **Vistra Marina** Hassall Green, Crewe (0270 762266). Ⓢ Ⓦ Ⓓ Pump-out, gas, long-term mooring, winter storage, groceries, books and maps, engine repairs. Also post office, general store, off-licence, gifts, café, paraffin, coal. Emergency repairs and boat fitting, tea room.

BOAT TRIPS
Shearwater Takes up to 12 people to Church Lawton and back. Restaurant and bar. Ring 0270 762266.

PUBS
🍺 **Romping Donkey** Hassall Green. A pretty country pub, offering Tetley's real ale, and bar meals and snacks *lunchtime and evenings.* Cosy bars and outside seating. Children welcome.
🍺 **Broughton Arms** Canalside at Rode Heath. A friendly family pub recently refurbished, with comfortable bars and canalside seating. A range of Marston's real ales are served with an imaginative selection of food in the bar and dining area *lunchtime and evenings.* Vegetarians catered for.
🍺 **Lawton Arms** ½ mile from bridge 134 on Knutsford Road, Church Lawton. A locals' pub dispensing Robinson's real ale. Garden. Busy at *lunchtime.*

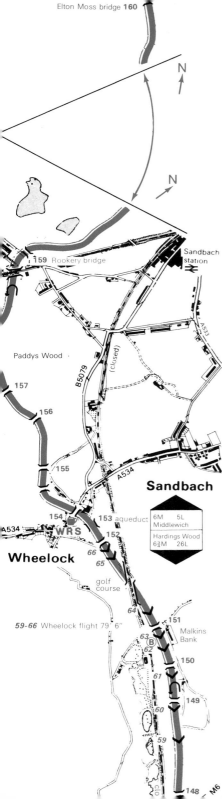

Elton Moss bridge **160**

N

N

159 Rookery bridge

Sandbach station

Paddys Wood

B5079

(closed)

A533

157

156

155

A534

Sandbach

6M	5L
Middlewich	
Hardings Wood	
6¾M	26L

154   **153** aqueduct

A534 **WRS**

152

Wheelock

66

65

golf course

64

59-66 Wheelock flight 79' 6"

151

Malkins Bank

B

62

150

61

149

60

59

148   M6

Wheelock

The canal now descends the Wheelock flight of eight locks, which are the last paired locks one sees when travelling northwards. The countryside continues to be quiet and unspoilt but unspectacular. The pair of locks halfway down the flight is situated in the little settlement of Malkin's Bank, overlooked by terraced houses. The boatman's co-op used to be here, in the small terrace of cottages. At the bottom of the flight is the village of Wheelock; west of here the navigation curls round the side of a hill before entering the very long-established salt-producing area that is based on Middlewich. The 'wild' brine pumping and rock-salt mining that has gone on hereabouts has resulted in severe local subsidence; the effect on the canal has been to necessitate the constant raising of the banks as lengths of the canal bed sink. This of course means that the affected lengths tend to be much deeper than ordinary canals. Non-swimmers beware of falling overboard.

Sandbach
Ches. EC Tue. MD Thur. PO, tel, stores, garage, bank, station. 1½ miles north of Wheelock. An old market town that has maintained its charm despite the steady growth of its salt and chemical industries. After walking from the canal you can refresh yourself with a pint of real ale from any of the seven pubs visible from the seat in the market place.
Ancient Crosses In the cobbled market place on a massive base stand two superb Saxon crosses, believed to commemorate the conversion of the area to Christianity in the 7thC. They suffered severely in the 17thC when the Puritans broke them up and scattered the fragments for miles. After years of searching for the parts, George Ormerod succeeded in re-erecting the crosses in 1816, with new stone replacing the missing fragments.
St Mary's Church High Street. A large, 16thC church with a handsome battlemented tower. The most interesting features of the interior are the 17thC carved roof and the fine chancel screen.
The Old Hall Hotel An outstanding example of Elizabethan half-timbered architecture, which was formerly the home of the lord of the manor, but is now used as an hotel.
Wheelock
Ches. EC Tue. PO, tel, stores, garage, fish and chips. Busy little main road village on the canal.

BOATYARDS

Ⓑ **Malkins Bank Canal Services** (0270 764595). Ⓦ Overnight mooring, long-term mooring, slipway, chandlery, boat building and restoration. Breakdown service.

PUBS

🍺 **Cheshire Cheese** Wheelock. Canalside pub serving Tetley's real ale and bar food *lunchtime and evenings.* Children's play area.
🍺 **Commercial** Near bridge 154, Wheelock. Set in a Georgian house with an old fashioned and spacious feel this pub serves Boddingtons and Marston's real ale. *Closed lunchtime Mon-Sat.*
🍺 **Nags Head** ¼ west of bridge 154, Wheelock. A small black and white pub serving Chester's real ale. Garden. Children welcome. Chinese take-away opposite.
🍺 **Market Tavern** The Square, Sandbach. Opposite the crosses. Lively town pub serving Robinson's real ale and bar food *lunchtime and evenings until 20.00 (not Sun).* One of the seven real ale pubs in, or close to, the square.

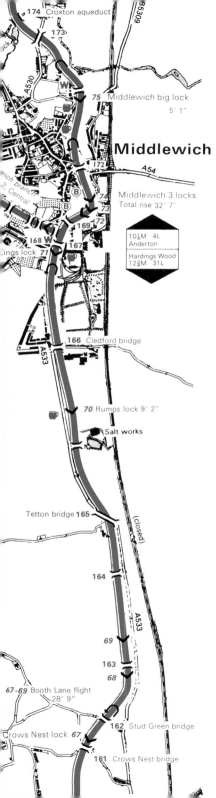

75 Middlewich big lock
5' 1"

Middlewich

Middlewich 3 locks
Total rise 32' 7"

10¼M 4L
Anderton

Hardings Wood
12¾M 31L

166 Cledford bridge

70 Rumps lock 9' 2"

Salt works

Tetton bridge 165

(closed)

164

69

163
68

67-69 Booth Lane flight
28' 9"

162 Stud Green bridge

Crows Nest lock 67

161 Crows Nest bridge

Middlewich

The navigation now begins to lose the rural character it has enjoyed since Kidsgrove. Falling through yet more locks, the canal is joined by a busy main road (useful for fish and chips, west of Kings Lock; and Chinese take-away, west of bridge 166) which accompanies it into an increasingly flat and industrialised landscape, past several salt works and into Middlewich, where a branch of the Shropshire Union leads off westwards towards that canal at Barbridge. There is a useful shop at bridge 166. The Trent & Mersey skirts the centre of the town, passing lots of moored narrowboats and through three consecutive narrow locks, arriving at a wide (14ft) lock (which has suffered from subsidence) with a pub beside it. This used to represent the beginning of a wide, almost lock-free navigation right through to Preston Brook, Manchester and Wigan (very convenient for the salt industry when it shipped most of its goods by boat), but Croxton Aqueduct had to be replaced many years ago, and is now a steel structure only 8ft 2in wide. The aqueduct crosses the River Dane, which flows alongside the navigation as both water courses leave industrial Middlewich and move out into fine open country.

Middlewich
Ches. EC Wed. PO, tel, stores, bank, garage. A town that since Roman times has been dedicated to salt extraction. Most of the salt produced here goes to various chemical industries. Subsidence from salt extraction has prevented redevelopment for many years, but a big renewal scheme is now in progress. The canalside area is a haven of peace below the busy streets. The Tourist Information Centre is by bridge 172.
St Michael's Church A handsome medieval church which was a place of refuge for the Royalists during the Civil War. It has a fine interior with richly carved woodwork.

BOATYARDS
Ⓑ **Andersen Boats** Wych House, St Anne's Road, Middlewich (0606 833668). Ⓦ Pump-out, gas, narrowboat hire, overnight mooring (*not weekends*), books and maps, toilets.
Ⓑ **Middlewich Narrowboats** Canal Terrace, Middlewich (0606 832460). ⓇⓈⓌⒹ Pump-out, gas, narrowboat hire, overnight mooring (*not Fri*), long-term mooring, dry dock, groceries, chandlery, books and maps, boat building, engine repairs, toilets, laundry service, breakdown service. *Closed Sun*. Useful tool hire shop next door.

PUBS AND RESTAURANTS
🍺 **Big Lock** Middlewich. Canalside. Basic canal pub with outside seating overlooking the lock. Bar food *lunchtime and evenings*.
🍺✕ **Boars Head** Kinderton Street, Middlewich (0606 833191). Large rambling pub offering Robinson's real ale and *lunchtime* meals. Children's room in hotel next door. Garden. Restaurant serving meals *lunchtime and evenings*.
🍺 **Newton Brewery Inn** ¼ mile south of Big Lock, Middlewich. Marston's real ale served in a small friendly pub with an attractive garden running down to the towpath. Excellent selection of meals and snacks *lunchtime and evenings*. Children welcome.
🍺 **Cheshire Cheese** Lewin Street, Middlewich. Basic but welcoming pub offering Boddingtons real ale and bar snacks *lunchtime and evenings*. Small patio area. Children welcome until *21.00*.
🍺 **Kings Lock** Middlewich. Overlooking the lock. Bar food and outside seating.
🍺 **Kinderton Arms** Close to canal 1 mile south of Middlewich, by lock 70. Ignore its dour appearance and walk in to enjoy Tetley's real ale, bar snacks, tea and coffee.

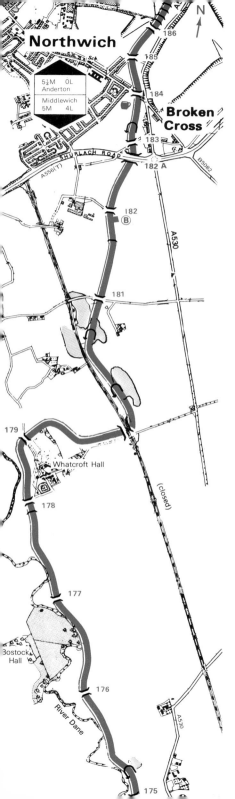

Dane Valley

Initially, this is a stretch of canal as beautiful as any in the country. Often overhung by trees, the navigation winds along the side of a hill as it follows the delightful valley of the River Dane. The parkland on the other side of the valley encompasses Bostock Hall, a school for children with learning difficulties. At Whatcroft Hall (privately owned), the canal circles around to the east, passing under a derelict railway before heading for the industrial outskirts of Northwich and shedding its beauty and solitude once again. The outlying canal settlement of Broken Cross acts as a buffer between these two very different lengths of canal.

Navigational note
There are several privately owned wide 'lagoons' caused by subsidence along this section of the Trent & Mersey, in some of which repose the hulks of abandoned barges and narrowboats, lately being salvaged. Navigators should be wary of straying off the main line, since the offside canal bank is often submerged and invisible just below the water level.

Northwich
Ches. EC Wed. MD Fri, Sat. All services.
Regular buses from Barnton. A rather attractive town at the junction of the Rivers Weaver and Dane. (The latter brings large quantities of sand down into the Weaver Navigation, necessitating a heavy expenditure on dredging.) As in every other town in this area, salt has for centuries been responsible for the continued prosperity of Northwich. The Weaver Navigation has of course been another very prominent factor in the town's history, and the building and repairing of barges, narrowboats, and small sea-going ships has been carried on here for over 200 years. Nowadays this industry has been almost forced out of business by foreign competition, and the last private shipyard on the river closed down in 1971. The wharves by Town Bridge are empty, and are an excellent temporary mooring site for anyone wishing to visit the place. The town centre is very close; much of it has been completely rebuilt recently. There is now an extensive shopping precinct. Although the large number of pubs has been whittled down in the rebuilding process, there are still some pleasant old streets. The Weaver and the big swing bridges across it remain a dominant part of the background.
Salt Museum Weaver Hall, London Road, Northwich (0606 41331). The history of the salt industry from Roman times to the present day, housed in the town's former workhouse. Look out for the remarkable model ship, made from salt of course. *Open all year Tue–Sun 14.00–17.00 (Jul & Aug & B. Hol Mon 10.00–17.00).* Audio visual introduction. Charge.

BOATYARDS

ⓑ **Orchard Marina** Beside bridge 182. (0606 42082). ⓡ ⓢ ⓦ ⓓ Pump-out, gas, moorings, slipway, dry dock, boat and engine repairs, boat building and sales, shop, chandlery, toilets, showers, launderette, picnic area.

BOAT TRIPS

Weaver Sovereign offering *daily trips in Aug* to various destinations along the River Weaver, with *less frequent departures Apr–Oct.* All trips leave from the Town Quay, Northwich and include a commentary and bar. Weston Docks, Runcorn is visited occasionally. Details from 0606 76204 or 0860 609636.

PUBS

🍺 **Old Broken Cross** Canalside, at bridge 184. A very attractive old pub serving well kept Greenall Whitley and Stones real ales. Food *Mon–Fri lunchtime only.* Vegetarians catered for. Small canalside garden. Shops and launderette are just a short way past the pub.

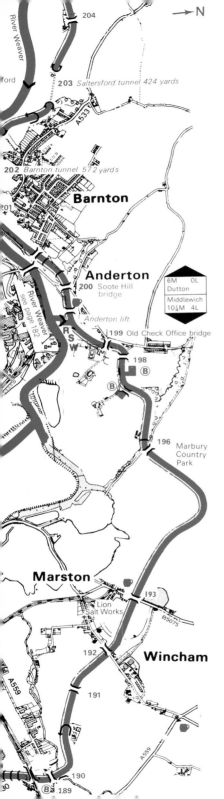

Anderton Lift

This is another length in which salt mining has
determined the nature of the scenery. Part of it
is heavily industrial, with enormous ICI works
dominating the scene; much of it is devastated
but rural (just), some of it is nondescript, and
some of it is superb countryside. Donkey
engines can still be seen in surrounding fields
pumping brine. Leaving the vicinity of
Lostock Gralam (licensed grocer 100 yds east
of bridge 189 *open every day until 22.00)* and
the outskirts of Northwich, one passes
Marston and Wincham (*PO, tel, stores*). Just
west of the village, one travels along a ½-mile
stretch of canal that was only cut in 1958, as
the old route was about to collapse into –
needless to say – underground salt workings.
Beyond the woods of Marbury Country Park
(attractive short stay moorings) is Anderton
(*PO, tel, stores*) – the short entrance canal to
the famous boat lift down into the Weaver
Navigation is on the left. The main line
continues westward, winding along what is
now a steep hill and into Barnton Tunnel. At
the west end one emerges onto a hillside
overlooking the River Weaver, with a
marvellous view straight down the huge
Saltersford Locks. Now Saltersford Tunnel is
entered: beyond it, one finds oneself in
completely open country again. There are
good moorings in the basins to the east of both
tunnels.

Navigational note
Saltersford Tunnel is crooked, affording only
a brief glimpse of the other end. Two boats
cannot pass in this or Barnton Tunnel, so take
care they are clear before proceeding.

Anderton Lift
An amazing and enormous piece of machinery
built in 1875 by Leader Williams (later
engineer of the Manchester Ship Canal) to
connect the Trent & Mersey to the flourishing
Weaver Navigation, 50ft below. As built, the
lift consisted of two water-filled tanks
counterbalancing each other in a vertical slide,
resting on massive hydraulic rams. It worked
on the very straightforward principle that
making the ascending tank slightly lighter – by
pumping a little water out – would assist the
hydraulic rams (which were operated by a
steam engine and pump) in moving both
tanks, with boats in them, up or down their
respective slide.
In 1908 the lift had to have major repairs, so it
was modernised at the same time. The
troublesome hydraulic rams were done away
with; from then on each tank – which
contained 250 tons of water had its own
counterweights and was independent of the
other tank. Electricity replaced steam as the
motive power. One of the most fascinating
individual features of the canal system, it
draws thousands of sightseers every year.
Currently being extensively rebuilt and
restored, ring 0606 40566 to check if it is
operational.
Marston
Ches. Tel. A salt-producing village, suffering
badly from its own industry. The numerous
gaps in this village are caused by the
demolition or collapse of houses affected by
subsidence. Waste ground abounds.
The Lion Salt Works Offershaw Lane,
Marston (0606 40555). Beside the canal at
bridge 193. The Thompson family established
an open pan salt works in Marston in 1842,
producing fishery salt, bay salt, crystal salt and
lump salt. The salt was pumped as wild brine
from 45 yds beneath the works and evaporated
in a large iron pan. The crystals thus formed
were raked into tubs to form blocks, and
subsequently dried in brick stove houses,
before being exported (with the first part of
the journey by canal) to India, Canada and
West Africa. The works closed in 1986 but is
currently being restored and is well worth
visiting. Excellent audio visual display and
many exhibits. *Open 14.00-17.00 Mar-Oct,
14.00-16.00 Nov-Dec.* Charge. Also
information on the attractive countryside of
Vale Royal and its rich industrial heritage.

Marbury Country Park A 200 acre park occupying the landscaped gardens of the former Marbury Hall and estate, once the home of the Barry and Smith-Barry families. Overlooking Budworth Mere, the house was demolished in 1968 and the much neglected gardens restored to their former glory by Cheshire County Heritage and Recreation service. The Information Centre (½ mile north of bridge 196) houses a display of Marbury's wildlife and history, including its use as a POW camp during World War II. Visitor's moorings and picnic area.

BOATYARDS

Ⓑ **IML Waterways Cruising** Anderton Marina, Uplands Road, Anderton (0606 79642). Services are on line – do not enter the marina unnecessarily. Ⓡ Ⓢ Ⓦ Ⓓ Pump-out, gas, narrowboat hire, overnight mooring, long-term mooring, slipway, books and maps, restaurant. *Closed Mon.*
Ⓑ **Clare Cruisers** Uplands Basin, Uplands Road, Northwich (0606 77199). Ⓡ Ⓢ Ⓦ Ⓓ Pump-out, gas, narrowboat hire, overnight mooring, long-term mooring, winter storage, books and maps, engine repairs, toilets.
Ⓑ **Colliery Narrowboat Co** Wincham Wharf (bridge 189). Lostock Gralam, Northwich (0606 44672). Ⓡ Ⓦ Ⓓ Pump-out, day hire craft, overnight mooring, long-term mooring, crane, dry dock, chandlery, books and maps, boat building, boat sales, engine sales and repairs.

BOAT TRIPS

Golborne is a 48-seater restaurant boat with a bar, operating charter trips from Wincham Wharf. Public service *bank holidays and some weekends*. Ring 0606 44672/43048 for details.

PUBS AND RESTAURANTS

🛥 **Red Lion** Barnton, just east of bridge 201. Inexpensive bar food, garden, children's room. Regular music nights.
🛥 **Stanley Arms** Canalside, right opposite the Anderton Lift (also PO, stores). A friendly real ale pub with a lovely family room, where children are welcome. Food *lunchtime and evenings*. Putting green and outside seating area.
🛥 **Salt Barge** Marston, opposite the Lion Salt Works, beside bridge 193. A deceptively large pub with a friendly atmosphere, neatly divided into cosy areas, and with an inviting family room. Stones real ale and good food *lunchtime and evenings*. Garden with play area.
🛥 **Black Greyhound** Wincham, ½ mile east of bridge 191 along footpath. A plush roadside pub serving Greenall Whitley real ale and bar food *lunchtime and evenings, together with Sunday roasts*. Vegetarians catered for, children welcome. Garden.
🛥✕ **Brindley's** Wincham Wharf, canalside by bridge 189 (0606 48354). A tastefully renovated warehouse building with waterside seating and regular jazz and folk evenings. Boddingtons real ale and bar food *lunchtime and evenings. Pub open 11.00–23.00.* Separate restaurant open *daily* where children are welcome.

The Anderton Lift, Trent & Mersey Canal. *Derek Pratt.*

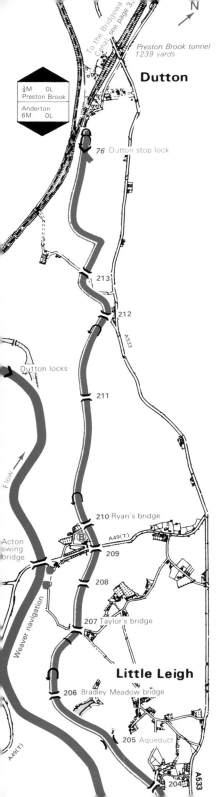

Dutton

This, the northernmost stretch of the Trent & Mersey, is a very pleasant one and delightfully rural. Most of the way the navigation follows the south side of the hills that overlook the River Weaver. From about 60ft up, one is often rewarded with excellent views of this splendid valley and the occasional large vessels that ply up and down it. At one point one can see the elegant Dutton railway viaduct in the distance; then the two waterways diverge as the Trent & Mersey enters the woods preceding Preston Brook Tunnel. There is a stop lock just south of the tunnel just beyond a pretty covered dry dock; there are often fine examples of restored working boats moored here. At the north end of the tunnel a notice announces that from here onwards one is on the Bridgewater Canal, see page 32. There are good moorings north of bridge 213, and to the south of Dutton stop lock.

Navigational notes
1 Access to Preston Brook Tunnel is restricted *on Sat, Sun & B. Hols May-Oct; Southbound 07.30-08.30, 10.30-11.30, 13.30-14.30, 16.30-17.30, 19.30-20.30; Northbound 09.00-10.00, 12.00-13.00, 15.00-16.00, 18.00-19.00, 21.00-22.00. At all other times* ensure the tunnel is clear before entering, as two boats cannot pass.
2 North of Preston Brook Tunnel you are on the Bridgewater Canal, which is owned by the Manchester Ship Canal Company, see page 32. A British Waterways licence is valid for three consecutive days on this canal.

Dutton
Ches. Tel, garage. Small settlement on top of Preston Brook Tunnel, at the end of the lane uphill from the south end of the tunnel.
Preston Brook Tunnel
1239yds long and forbidden to unpowered craft. It is crooked, like Barnton and Saltersford Tunnels, and there is no towpath.

BOATYARDS
Ⓑ **Black Prince Holidays** Bartington Wharf, Acton Bridge, Northwich (0606 852945). Ⓡ Ⓢ Ⓦ Ⓓ Pump-out, gas, narrowboat hire, day hire craft, overnight mooring (*not weekends*), groceries, chandlery, books and maps, boat sales, engine sales and repairs, toilets, gifts.

PUBS AND RESTAURANTS
▬✕ **Horns** (0606 852192). 200yds south of bridge 209 on the A49, by Acton Swing Bridge. Busy roadside pub serving Greenall Whitley and Stones real ale together with bar food *all day*. Cosy bars and restaurant for meals *lunchtime and evenings*. Garden and children's play area.
▬✕ **Leigh Arms** ¼ mile south of bridge 209, overlooking the Weaver and Acton Swing Bridge. Burtonwood real ale in an attractive old coaching inn with stained glass windows in the bar. Food *lunchtime and evenings*. Restaurant and outside seating area. Regular music nights.

WEAVER NAVIGATION

Maximum dimensions

Winsford to Winnington
Length: 150'
Beam: 30'
Headroom: 29'
Winnington to Weston Point
Length: 176'
Beam: 30'
Headroom: 56'

Manager

(0606) 40566

Mileage

WINSFORD BRIDGE to
Northwich: 5½
Anderton Lift (Trent & Mersey Canal): 7
Acton Bridge: 11
Sutton Bridge: 17
WESTON POINT DOCKS (Manchester
Ship Canal): 20

Locks: 5

The Weaver Navigation still carries a large amount of commercial traffic. In general terms, this must be due to its fortunate position in the centre of the salt and chemical industries, its endless supply of water, and the enterprising attitude of its past (and present) administrators.

The river itself, which rises in the Peckforton Hills and proceeds via Wrenbury, Audlem, Nantwich, Church Minshull and Winsford to Northwich and Frodsham, is just over 50 miles long. Originally a shallow and tidal stream, it was long used for carrying salt away from the Cheshire salt area. The mineral was carried down by men and horses to meet the incoming tide. The sailing barges would load at high water, then depart with the ebbing tide. It was a somewhat unsatisfactory means of transport.

In the 17thC the expansion of the salt industry around Northwich, Middlewich and Winsford gave rise to an increasing demand for a navigation right up to Winsford. In 1721, three gentlemen of Cheshire obtained an Act of Parliament to make and maintain the river as a navigation from Frodsham to Winsford, 20 miles upstream. Plans were drawn up, labourers were organised, and by 1732 the Weaver was fully navigable for 40-ton barges up to Winsford. It was naturally a great boost to the salt industry near Winsford, which now exported salt and imported coal via this splendid new navigation. Clay was also brought upstream to Winsford: it was then carted up to the Potteries by land.

When the Trent & Mersey was planned in 1765 to pass along the River Weaver the trustees of the Weaver were understandably alarmed; but in the event the new canal provided much traffic for the river, for although the two waterways did not join, they were so close at Anderton that in 1793 chutes were constructed on the Trent & Mersey directly above a specially built dock on the River Weaver, 50ft below. Thereafter salt was transhipped in ever increasing quantities by dropping it down the chutes from canal boats into 'Weaver flats' (barges) on the river. This system continued until 1871, when it was decided to construct the great iron boat lift beside the chutes at Anderton. This remarkable structure (which still operates) thus effected a proper junction between the two waterways. Trade improved accordingly.

The Weaver Navigation did well throughout the 19thC, mainly because continual and vigorous programmes of modernisation kept it thoroughly attractive to carriers, especially when compared to the rapidly dating narrow canals. The Weaver locks were constantly reduced in number and increased in size; the river was made deeper, and the channel wider; the docks at Weston Point (built in 1806 along with the canal from Frodsham Cut to the docks) were duplicated and enlarged. Eventually coasters were able to navigate the river right up to Winsford. Much of this progress was due to the efforts of Edward Leader Williams, who was the engineer of the Weaver Navigation from 1856 to 1872, when he left to become engineer of the new Manchester Ship Canal.

In spite of this constant improvement of the navigation, the Weaver's traditional salt trade was affected by 19thC competition from railways and the new pipelines. However, the chemical industry began to sprout around the Northwich area at the same time, so the salt and clay traffic was gradually replaced by chemicals. Today, ICI's chemical works at Winnington and British Waterways' Anderton Depot supply all the traffic on the river: coasters up to 1000 tonnes deadweight capacity ship cargoes through the Manchester Ship Canal and to various ports in the UK and Europe. Meanwhile Weston Point Docks profit from being beside the Manchester Ship Canal (opened in the 1890s) and continue to flourish.

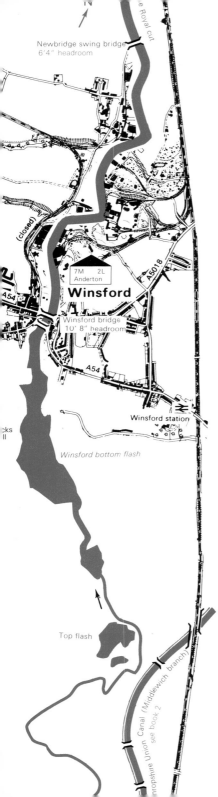

Winsford

Although Winsford Bridge (fixed at 10ft 8in) is the upper limit of navigation for shipping and the limit of British Waterways jurisdiction, canal boats can easily slip under the bridge and round the bend into the vast, wonderful and deceptively shallow Winsford Bottom Flash. Navigation upstream of the Bottom Flash is unreliable, for the channel is shallow and winding, but can apparently be done by adventurous persons with small craft. The Top Flash is situated just beside and below the Middlewich Branch of the Shropshire Union Canal, but there is no junction between them here. Downstream of Winsford Bridge, there are some disused wharves – a good place to tie up. Further down is a winding stretch of little interest: each bank is piled high with the industrial leftovers of chemical industries. But soon the horizon clears as one arrives at Newbridge, beyond which is the superb stretch known as Vale Royal Cut.

Navigational notes
1 Newbridge swing bridge no longer opens, imposing a height restriction on the river above here of 6ft 4in.
2 The operating times for locks and bridges are *08.00-16.00 Mon-Thur, 08.00-15.00 Fri. Closed weekends and B. Hols.* All are manned.
3 The Weaver is a river navigation that carries a substantial traffic – transported not in canal boats or barges, but in small sea-going ships displacing up to 1000 tonnes, which use the navigation at all times of day or night. The locks are correspondingly large and often paired. The bridges are either very high or are big swing bridges operated by British Waterways staff. With the exception of Town Bridge in Northwich and Newbridge below Winsford (6ft 8in) none of these bridges need to be swung for any boat with a height above water of less than 8ft. Those craft which do require the bridges to be opened should give prior notice to the British Waterways Area Office. Unless there has been heavy rain, the current is quite gentle – however, as on any river navigation, an anchor and rope should be carried, and the rules should be adhered to. There are few facilities for pleasure craft.

Winsford
Ches. MD Sat. All services. A busy salt-mining town astride the Weaver. The centre of town used to be very close to the river, but now a huge new shopping precinct has shifted the heart of the town well away from it.
Winsford Bottom Flash
This very large expanse of water, in an attractive setting among wooded slopes, was created by subsidence following salt extraction in the vicinity. It is a unique asset for the town, whose citizens obviously appreciate it to the full. Three caravan sites and a sailing club are based along its banks, anglers crouch in the waterside bushes, and at the northern end (nearest to Winsford) one may hire dinghies and runabouts by the hour. It is, however, quite shallow in places – those in canal craft beware!

PUBS
🍺 **Red Lion** Winsford. Riverside, at Winsford Bridge.
🍺 **The Ark** Winsford.
🍺 **Bees Knees** Winsford. Riverside, above Winsford Bridge.

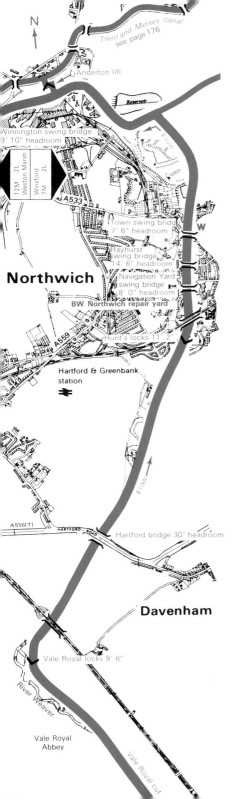

Northwich

The Vale Royal Cut typifies the Weaver at its most attractive. The river flows along a closely-defined flat green valley floor, flanked by mature woods climbing the steep hillsides that enclose the valley. No buildings or roads intrude upon this very pleasant scene. Vale Royal Locks are at the far end of the cut; the remains of the old Vale Royal Abbey (believed to have been founded by Edward I and dissolved by Henry VIII) is just up the hill nearby. It is now much changed, and is a summer school for an electronics firm. Beyond is a tall stone railway viaduct, then Hartford Road Bridge, a steel girder construction offering to ships a headroom of only 30ft – by far the lowest fixed bridge between Winsford and the Mersey. Another stretch of pleasant water meadows leads to Hunts Locks, another railway viaduct and the three swing bridges that are so much a feature of the town of Northwich. The trip through Northwich is pleasant enough, but north of the town the river twists and turns through a repetition of the industrial landscape that predominates outside Winsford. This stretch does not last long, and as the Anderton Lift (see page 176) comes into view one rounds the bend to be confronted by the shipping tied up at Winnington wharves.

Northwich
Ches. EC Wed. MD Fri, Sat. All services. A rather attractive town at the junction of the Rivers Weaver and Dane. (The latter brings large quantities of sand down into the Weaver Navigation, necessitating a heavy expenditure on dredging.) As in every town in this area, salt has for centuries been responsible for the continued prosperity of Northwich. The town's motto is *Sal est Vita*, Salt is Life, and there is a salt museum in London Road. The Brine Baths in Victoria Road are still open throughout the year for the benefit of salt-water enthusiasts. The Weaver Navigation has of course been another very prominent factor in the town's history, and the building and repairing of barges, narrowboats, and small seagoing ships has been carried on here for over 200 years. Nowadays this industry has been almost forced out of business by foreign competition, and the last private shipyard on the river closed down in 1971. The wharves by Town Bridge are empty, and are an excellent temporary mooring site for anyone wishing to visit the place. The town centre is very close; much of it has been completely rebuilt, with an extensive shopping precinct. Although the large number of pubs has been whittled down in the rebuilding process, there are still some pleasant old streets. The Weaver and the big swing bridges across it remain a dominant part of the background.
Salt Museum Weaver Hall, London Road, Northwich (0606 41331). The history of the salt industry from Roman times to the present day, housed in the town's former workhouse. Look out for the remarkable model ship, made from salt of course. *Open all year Tue-Sun 14.00-17.00 (Jul, Aug & B. Hol Mon 10.00-17.00).* Audio visual introduction. Charge.

BOATYARDS
British Waterways Northwich Area Offices and Repair Yard (0606 74321). Alongside the extensive workshops is the Area Engineer's office – formerly the Weaver Navigation Trustee's offices. As usual, this yard contains many mellow 18thC buildings. There is also an elegant clock tower on the office block.

PUBS AND RESTAURANTS
Northwich pubs include:
🍺 Beehive.
🍺✕ Crown Hotel.
🍺 Sportsman.

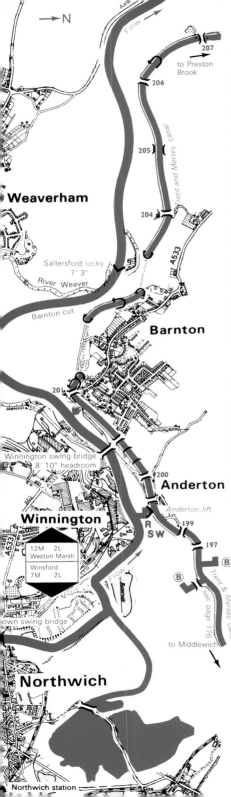

Barnton Cut

North of Northwich, the river begins to
meander extravagantly in a general westerly
direction. The amazing structure that is
Anderton Lift is on one side of the river: this is
on the way up to the Trent & Mersey Canal
(see page 176), which runs along the Weaver
Valley as far as Dutton Locks. Beside the lift is
the thriving Anderton Depot, which can
handle ships of up to 1000 tonnes deadweight
capacity. Opposite Anderton Lift is
Winnington. Here are a large ICI chemical
works and extensive wharves, where several
ships are usually to be seen. These ships take
their cargoes of potassium, caustic soda and
soda ash (used for making glass) to many
countries around Europe – and to Israel. With
these ships about, pleasure boats should keep
a good lookout from Winnington onwards to
Weston Point, especially on the bends. (The
rule of the road is of course 'keep to the right'
and out of the deep-water channel.) It is also
important to give correct sound signals. Below
Winnington, the river runs again along a
peaceful green valley, lined by hills on its north
side, and is inaccessible to motor cars. Part of
the route is canalised, leading to Saltersford
Locks. The town of Weaverham is on the hills
to the south.

Weaverham
Ches. PO, tel, stores, garage. The heart of this
town contains many old timbered houses and
thatched cottages – but these are now heavily
outnumbered by council housing estates. The
church of St Mary is an imposing Norman
building containing several items of interest.

BOATYARDS
These are both on the Trent & Mersey
ⓑ **IML Waterways Cruising** Anderton
Marina, Uplands Road, Anderton (0606
79642). Services are on line, do not enter the
marina unnecessarily. R S W D Pump-out,
gas, narrowboat hire, overnight mooring, long
term mooring, slipway, books and maps,
restaurant. *Closed Mon.*
ⓑ **Clare Cruisers** Uplands Basin, Uplands
Road, Northwich (0606 77199). R S W D
Pump-out, gas, narrowboat hire, overnight
mooring, long-term mooring, winter storage,
books and maps, engine repairs, toilets.

PUBS
🍺 **Red Lion** Barnton. Between the river and
canal. Food *lunchtime and evenings.* Children
welcome, garden.

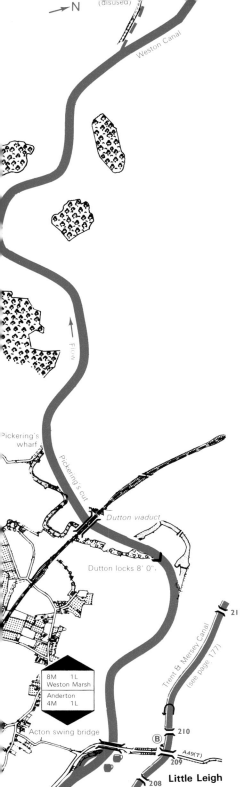

Acton Bridge

The A49 joins the river for a while, crossing at
Acton Bridge. A backwater here houses a boat
club; pubs and a riverside restaurant are
nearby. A mile further on, Dutton Locks lead
to the Dutton railway viaduct, whose elegant
stone arches carry the main electrified West
Coast line. Beyond the viaduct one comes to
Pickering's Wharf, the site of a swing bridge
long gone. From here down to Frodsham, the
Weaver Valley is a beautiful green, narrow
cutting reminiscent of Vale Royal. Woods are
ranged along the hills on either side. There are
no roads, and no houses except for one farm.
It is a delightfully secluded rural setting. As
the valley gradually widens out to reveal the
impending industrialism that stretches along
the river from Sutton Bridge, one may notice a
branch off to the left. This is where a cut from
the navigation leaves to fall through a shallow
lock before rejoining the river course. This was
the old line of navigation until 1827, when the
Weston Canal was constructed to take the
main line of the Weaver Navigation to Weston
Point. One may still venture down the old cut
to a swing bridge, now fixed, and the derelict
lock. (The size of the lock reveals how much
the navigation has been improved and
enlarged in the past 100 years.)

Acton Swing Bridge
An impressive structure weighing 650 tonnes,
which uses a very small amount of electricity
to open it; 560 tonnes of its weight is borne by
a floating pontoon. It was built in 1933.

BOATYARD
This is on the Trent & Mersey.
Ⓑ **Black Prince Holidays** Bartington
Wharf, Acton Bridge, Northwich (0606
852945). Ⓡ Ⓢ Ⓦ Ⓓ Pump-out, gas,
narrowboat hire, day hire craft, overnight
mooring (*not weekends*), groceries, chandlery,
books and maps, boat sales, engine sales and
repairs, toilets, gifts.

PUBS AND RESTAURANTS
🍺✕ **Horns** Acton Bridge (0606 852192).
Between the bridge and the Trent & Mersey
Canal. Busy roadside pub serving Greenall
Whitley and Stones real ale together with bar
food *all day*. Cosy bars and restaurant for
meals *lunchtime and evenings*. Garden and
children's play area.
🍺 **Leigh Arms** Acton Bridge. Riverside, at
the bridge. Burtonwood real ale in an
attractive old coaching inn with stained glass
windows in the bar. Food *lunchtime and
evenings*. Restaurant and outside seating area.
regular music nights.
✕ 🍷 **Rheingold Riverside Inn** Acton Bridge.
(0606 852310). Riverside, on south side of the
river. *Evenings.*

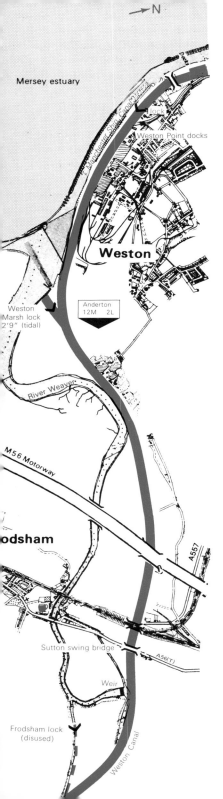

Weston Point

Passing the former Sutton Flood Lock, now completely disused, the Weston Canal section of the Weaver Navigation now runs along the side of the valley, while the river follows its own twisting course down towards the Mersey. By Sutton (Frodsham) swing bridge the charming pastures that flank the Weaver are left behind for good; chemical works line one side of the canal all the way from here to Weston Point. The wooded hills and grassy fields of the Weaver suddenly seem very distant. At Weston Marsh there is a lock down into the Manchester Ship Canal (see navigational note below). Beyond here the navigation goes right alongside the Ship Canal from which it is separated by a tall bank. Eventually, after passing the entrance lock up into the abandoned Runcorn & Weston Canal, one arrives at a low (about 5ft) swing bridge. Beyond it are the Weston Point Docks and another lock into the Ship Canal. There are *shops*, *fish & chips* and *pubs* at Weston Point, through the dock gates.

Navigational note
Those wishing to pass through Weston Marsh Lock should give British Waterways advance notice (0606 40566) and get clearance from the Manchester Ship Canal Company (061-872 2411).

Weston Point Docks
The docks, at the junction of the Weaver Navigation's Weston Canal and the Manchester Ship Canal, are an industrial centre. The docks have been modernised and their facilities expanded to handle ships up to 2500 tonnes.
Christ Church Situated between Weston Point Docks and the Manchester Ship Canal, this church was built by the Weaver Navigation Commissioners. Known as 'the island church', its tall spire is a distinctive landmark.

PUBS
☎ **Netherton Hall** Chester Road, Frodsham. Ind Coope and Tetley's real ales in a converted farmhouse. Food *lunchtime and evenings*. Garden.

A BRIEF HISTORY OF BRITISH CANALS

River navigations, that is rivers widened and deepened to take large boats, had existed in England since the Middle Ages: some can even be traced back to Roman times. In 1600 there were 700 miles of navigable river in England, and by 1760, the dawn of the canal age, this number had been increased to 1300 miles. This extensive network had prompted many developments later used by the canal engineers, for example, the lock system. But there were severe limitations: generally the routes were determined by the rivers and the features of the landscape and so were rarely direct. Also there were no east-west or north-south connections.

Thus the demand for a direct inland waterway system increased steadily through the first half of the 18thC with the expansion of internal trade. Road improvements could not cope with this expansion, and so engineers and merchants turned to canals, which were used extensively on the continent.

One of the earliest pure canals, cut independently of existing rivers, was opened in 1745, at Newry in Northern Ireland, although some authorities consider the Fossdyke, cut by the Romans to link the Rivers Trent and Witham, to be the first. However, the Newry is more important because it established the cardinal rule of all canals, the maintenance of an adequate water supply, a feature too often ignored by later engineers. The Newry Canal established the principle of a long summit level, fed by a reservoir to keep the locks at either end well supplied. Ten years later, in England, the Duke of Bridgewater decided to build a canal to provide an outlet for his coal mines at Worsley. He employed the self-taught James Brindley as his engineer, and John Gilbert as surveyor, and launched the canal age in England. The Bridgewater Canal was opened in 1761. Its route, all on one level, was independent of all rivers; its scale of operations reflected the new power of engineering, and the foresight of its creators. Although there were no locks, the engineering problems were huge; an aqueduct was built over the River Irwell at Barton, preceded by an embankment 900yds long; 15 miles of canal were built underground, so that boats could approach the coal face for loading (eventually there were 42 miles underground, including an inclined plane), and the puddled clay method was used by Brindley to make the canal bed watertight. Perhaps most important of all, the canal was a success financially. Bridgewater invested the equivalent of £3 million of his own money in the project, and still made a profit.

Having shown that canals were both practical and financially sound, the Bridgewater aroused great interest throughout Britain. Plans were drawn up for a trunk canal, to link the four major rivers of England, the Thames, Severn, Mersey and Trent. This plan was eventually brought to fruition, but many years later than its sponsors imagined. Brindley was employed as engineer for the scheme, his reputation ensuring that he would always have more work than he could handle. The Trent & Mersey, and the Staffordshire & Worcestershire Canals received the Royal Assent in 1766, and the canal age began in earnest.

Canals, like the railways which followed, were built entirely by hand. Gangs of itinerant workmen were gathered together, drawn by the comparatively high pay. Once formed, these armies of 'navigators' - hence 'navvies' - moved through the countryside as the canal was built, in many cases living off the land. All engineering problems had to be solved by manpower alone, aided by the horse and occasional steam pump. Embankments, tunnels, aqueducts, all were built by these labouring armies kept under control only by the power of the section engineers and contractors.

The Staffordshire & Worcestershire Canal opened in 1770. In its design Brindley determined the size of the standard Midlands canal, which of course had direct influence on the rest of the English system as it was built. He chose a narrow canal, with locks 72ft 7in by 7ft 6in, partly for reasons of economy, and partly because he understood that the problems of an adequate water supply were far greater than most canal sponsors realised. This standard, which was also adopted for the Trent & Mersey, prompted the development of a special vessel, the narrowboat, with its 30-ton payload. Ironically, this decision by Brindley in 1766 ensured the failure of the canals as a commercial venture 200 years later, for by the middle of the 20thC a 30-ton payload could no longer be worked economically.

The Trent & Mersey was opened in 1777; 93 miles long, the canal included five tunnels, the original one at Harecastle taking 11 years to build. In 1790 Oxford was finally reached and the junction with the Thames brought the four great rivers together. From the very start English canal companies were characterised by their intense rivalries; water supplies were jealously guarded, and constant wars were waged over toll prices. Many canals receiving the Royal Assent were never built, while others staggered towards conclusion, hampered by doubtful engineering, inaccurate estimates, and loans that they could never hope to pay off. Yet for a period canal mania gripped British speculators, as railway mania was to grip them 50 years later. The peak of British canal development came between 1791 and 1794, a period that gave rise to the opening of the major routes, the rise of the great canal engineers, Telford, Rennie and Jessop, and the greatest prosperity of those companies already operating. At this time the canal system had an effective monopoly over inland transport: the old trunk roads could not compete, coastal traffic was uncertain and hazardous, and the railways were still a future dream. This period also saw some of the greatest feats of engineering.

A contemporary view of canal promoters. *Eric de Maré.*

The turn of the century saw the opening of the last major cross-country routes; the Pennines were crossed by the Leeds & Liverpool Canal between 1770 and 1816, while the Kennet & Avon (opened in 1810) linked London and Bristol via the Thames. These two canals were built as broad navigations: already the realisation was dawning on canal operators that the limits imposed by the Brindley standard were too restrictive, a suspicion that was to be brutally confirmed by the coming of the railways. The Kennet & Avon, along with its rival the Thames & Severn, also marks the introduction of fine architecture to canals. Up until then canal architecture had been functional, often impressive, but clearly conceived by engineers. As a result the Kennet & Avon has an architectural unity lacking in earlier canals. The appearance of architectural quality was matched by another significant change: canals became straighter, their engineers choosing as direct a route as possible, arguing that greater construction costs could be outweighed by smoother, quicker operation, whereas the early canals had followed the landscape. The Oxford is the prime example of a contour canal, meandering across the Midlands as though there were all the time in the world. It looks beautiful, its close marriage with the landscape now makes it ideal as a pleasure waterway, but it was commercial folly.

The shortcomings of the early canals were exploited all too easily by the new railways. At first there was sharp competition by canals. Tolls were lowered, money was poured into route improvements; 14 miles of the Oxford's windings were cut out between 1829 and 1834; schemes were prepared to widen the narrow canals; the Harecastle Tunnel was doubled in 1827, the new tunnel taking three years to build (as opposed to 11 years for the old). But the race was lost from the start. The 19thC marks the rise of the railways and the decline of the canals. With the exception of the Manchester Ship Canal, the last major canal was the Birmingham & Liverpool Junction, opened in 1835. The system survived until this century, but the 1914-18 war brought the first closures, and through the 1930s the canal map adopted the shape it has today. Effective commercial carrying on narrow canals ceased in the early 1960s, although a few companies managed to survive until recently. However, with the end of commercial operation, a new role was seen for the waterways, as a pleasure amenity, a 'linear national park 2000 miles long'.

Water supply has always been the cardinal element in both the running and the survival of any canal system. Locks need a constant supply of water - every boat passing through a wide lock on the Grand Union uses 96,000

The rudimentary tools of the early 'navvies'. *Hugh McKnight.*

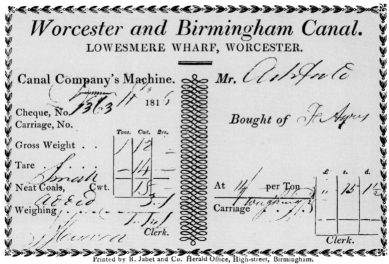

Worcester and Birmingham Canal Company toll ticket, dated 1816. *Hugh McKnight*.

gallons of water. Generally two methods of supply were used: direct feed by rivers and streams, and feed by reservoirs sited along the summit level. The first suffered greatly from silting, and meant that the canal was dependent on the level of water in the river; the regular floods from the River Soar that overtake the Grand Union's Leicester line show the dangers of this. The second was more reliable, but many engineers were short-sighted in their provision of an adequate summit level. The otherwise well-planned Kennet & Avon always suffered from water shortage. Where shortages occurred, steam pumping engines were used to pump water taken down locks back up to the summit level. The Kennet & Avon was dependent upon pumped supplies, while the Birmingham Canal Navigations were fed by six reservoirs and 17 pumping engines. Some companies adopted side ponds alongside locks to save water, but this put the onus on the boatman and so had limited success. Likewise the stop locks still to be seen at junctions are a good example of 18thC company rivalry; an established canal would ensure that any proposed canal wishing to join it would have to lock *down* into the older canal, which thus gained a lock of water each time a boat passed through.

Where long flights or staircase locks existed there was always great wastage of water, and so throughout canal history alternative mechanical means of raising boats have been tried out. The inclined plane or the vertical lift were the favoured forms. Both worked on the counterbalance principle, the weight of the descending boat helping to raise the ascending. The first inclined plane was built at Ketley in 1788, and they were a feature of the West Country Bude and Chard Canals. The most famous plane was built at Foxton, and operated from 1900-10. Mechanical failure and excessive running costs ended the application of the inclined plane in England, although modern examples work very efficiently on the continent. The vertical lift was more unusual, although there were eight on the Grand Western Canal. The most famous,

built at Anderton in 1875 (and currently being rebuilt), stands as a monument to the ingenuity shown in the attempts to overcome the problems of water shortage.

Engineering features are the greatest legacy of the canal age, and of these, tunnels are some of the most impressive. The longest is at Standedge, on the Huddersfield Narrow Canal (not navigable throughout, but restored in part). This tunnel runs for 5716yds through the Pennines, at times 638ft below the surface. It is also on the highest summit level, 644ft above sea level. The longest navigable tunnel is the Dudley Tunnel, at 3154yds long (but internal combustion engines must not be used, due to inadequate ventilation). Others of interest include: Blisworth, at 3056yds long; the twin Harecastle Tunnels on the Trent and Mersey Canal - the first 2897yds long and now disused, the second 2919yds and still in use; Sapperton, which carried the Thames & Severn Canal through the Cotswolds, and Netherton on the Birmingham Canal Navigations. This last, built 1855-58, was the last significant tunnel to be built in England, and was lit throughout by gas lights, and at a later date by electricity.

Netherton Tunnel was built wide enough to allow for a towing path on both sides. Most tunnels have no towing path at all, and so boats had to be 'legged', or walked through.

The slowness and relative danger of legging in tunnels led to various attempts at mechanical propulsion. An endless rope pulled by a stationary steam engine at the tunnel mouth was tried out at Blisworth and Braunston between 1869 and 1871. Steam tugs were employed, an early application of mechanical power to canal boats, but their performance was greatly limited by lack of ventilation, not to mention the danger of suffocating the crew.

An electric tug was used at Harecastle from 1914 to 1954. The diesel engine made tunnel tug services much more practical, but diesel-powered narrowboats soon put the tugs out of business: by the 1930s most tunnels had to be navigated by whatever means the

Islington Tunnel during construction. *Hugh McKnight.*

boatman chose to use. Legging continued at Crick, Husbands Bosworth and Saddington until 1939.

Aqueducts contribute significantly to the excitement of the canal system, with Telford's elegant structure at Pontcysyllte on the Llangollen Canal standing head and shoulders above all others. It crosses the River Dee at a height of 120 feet, using a cast iron trough mounted on slim stone pillars. Taking ten years to build, it opened in 1805. A couple of miles away, on the same canal, the sturdy stone built aqueduct at Chirk would seem impressive, werè it not for the magnificence of its close neighbour. Amongst many others, Sir Edward Leader Williams' swing aqueduct at Barton is particularly interesting, ás it crosses the Manchester Ship Canal with a 234-ft 800-ton section which swings at right angles to let ships through.

Until the coming of the diesel boats, the horse reigned supreme as a source of canal power. The first canals had used gangs of men to bow-haul the boats, a left-over from the river navigations where 50-80 men, or 12 horses, would pull a 200-ton barge. By 1800 the horse had taken over, and was used throughout the heyday of the canal system. In fact horse towage survived as long as large-scale commercial operation. Generally one horse or mule was used per boat, a system unmatched for cheapness and simplicity. The towing path was carried from one side of the canal to the other by turnover bridges, a common feature that reveals the total dominance of the horse. Attempts to introduce self-propelled canal boats date from 1793, although most early experiments concerned tugs towing dumb barges. Development was limited by the damage caused by wash, a problem that still applies today, and the first fleets of self-propelled steam narrowboats were not in service until the last quarter of the 19thC. Fellows, Morton & Clayton, and the Leeds & Liverpool Carrying Co. ran large fleets of steam boats between 1880 and 1931, by which time most had been converted to diesel operation. With the coming of mechanical power

the butty boat principle was developed: a powered narrowboat would tow a dumb 'butty' boat, thereby doubling the load without doubling the running costs. This system became standard until the virtual ending by the late 1960s of carrying on the narrow canals. Before the coming of railways, passenger services were run on the canals; packet boats, specially built narrowboats with passenger accommodation, ran express services, commanding the best horses and the unquestioned right of way over all other traffic. Although the railways killed this traffic, the last scheduled passenger service survived on the Gloucester and Berkeley Canal until 1935.

The traditional narrowboat with its colourful decoration and meticulous interior has become a symbol of English canals. However, this was in fact a late development. The shape of the narrowboat was determined by Brindley's original narrow canal specification, but until the late 19thC boats were unpainted, and carried all male crews. Wages were sufficient for the crews to maintain their families at home. The increase in railway competition brought a reduction in wages, and so bit by bit the crews were forced to take their families with them, becoming a kind of water gipsy. The confines of a narrowboat cabin presented the same problems as a gipsy caravan, and so the families found a similar answer. Their eternally wandering home achieved individuality by extravagant and colourful decoration, and the traditional narrowboat painting was born. The extensive symbolic vocabulary available to the painters produced a sign language that only these families could understand, and the canal world became far more enclosed, although outwardly it was more decorative.

As the canals have turned from commerce to pleasure, so the traditions of the families have died out, and the families themselves have faded away. But their language survives, although its meaning has mostly vanished with them. This survival gives the canals their characteristic decorative qualities, which make them so attractive to the pleasure boater and the casual visitor.

INDEX

192

Leeds & Liverpool Canal near Gargrave. *Derek Pratt.*